Roger Maynard is a former BBC reporter and correspondent for *The Times*, the *Independent* and CNBC. A
past president of the Foreign Correspondents' Association
of Australia, he has been a journalist for nearly five
decades. He is the author of six books of true crime and
military history.

For more information visit www.rogermaynard.com.au

ROGER MAYNARD

AMBON

THE TRUTH ABOUT ONE OF THE MOST BRUTAL POW CAMPS IN WORLD WAR II AND THE TRIUMPH OF THE AUSSIE SPIRIT

hachette AUSTRALIA

Published in Australia and New Zealand in 2014
by Hachette Australia
(an imprint of Hachette Australia Pty Limited)
Level 17, 207 Kent Street, Sydney NSW 2000
www.hachette.com.au

10 9 8 7 6 5 4 3 2 1

National Library of Australia
Cataloquinq-in-Publication data:

Maynard, Roger, author.
Ambon/Roger Maynard.

978 0 7336 3048 4 (pbk.)

World War, 1939–1945 – Prisoners and prisons, Japanese.
Prisoner of war camps – Indonesia – Ambon Island.
Prisoners of war – Australia.
Prisoners of war – Indonesia – Ambon Island.
Ambon (Indonesia)– History.

940.547252

Cover design by Luke Causby
Cover photos courtesy of Australian War Memorial, 124983 (front) 030368/02 (back)
Author photo courtesy of Corey Maynard
Text design by Bookhouse, Sydney
Typeset in 11.5/15 pt Sabon LT Pro by Bookhouse, Sydney
Printed and bound in Australia by Griffin Press, Adelaide, an accredited ISO AS/NZS 14001:2009 Environmental Management System printer

This book is dedicated to Max 'Eddie' Gilbert,
Ralph Godfrey, Walter Hicks, Tom Pledger, Jimmy
Morrison and Ed Weiss, whose vivid memories
of a terrible time made this book possible.

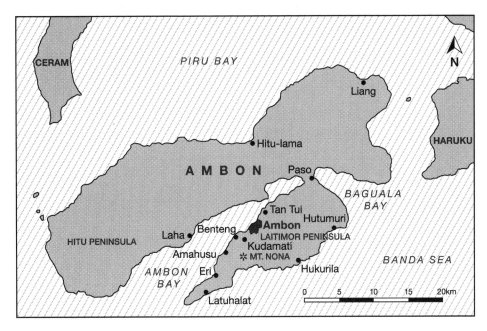

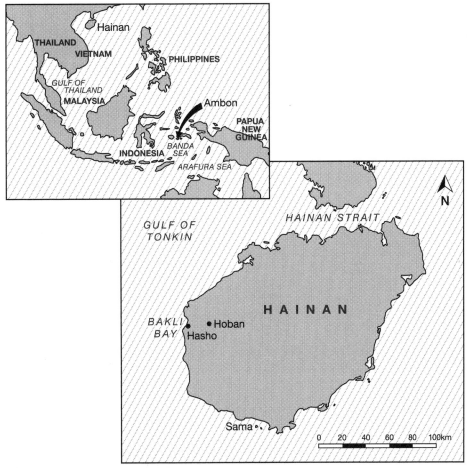

CONTENTS

PROLOGUE

How had it come to this? It was a question that would strike at the very core of Australian military tradition. Where was the mateship, the fairness, the spirit of egalitarianism? Where was the justice? If the cage was a penalty of last resort it said little for the state of army discipline or morale on Ambon in the final year of the Second World War. Yet here it was a reality of life for those men of the 2/21st Battalion who resorted to petty theft to relieve their hunger. It was a box within a barracks, within a jail, within an island prison. And what made it worse was that their jailors were fellow Australians.

The cage and all it represented would haunt the men who served on Ambon for decades and form part of a much greater tragedy which was none of their doing.

The 2/21st Battalion and several smaller units were brought together in the early days of the war to form Gull Force, which was committed to defend the strategically important island of Ambon in the Dutch East Indies should the Japanese invade south-east Asia.

It was an ill-fated plan hatched by Australian, Dutch and British military top brass in Singapore in late 1940 and early 1941. Under the agreement the Dutch pledged to provide air back-up in defence of Malaya should the Japanese enter the war, in return for a similar commitment by Australia to protect Timor and Ambon, which were part of the Dutch East Indies.

The 2/21st Battalion effectively drew the short straw which would see it sent to defend an island that was impossible to hold against the might of the Japanese military. After a few days of fighting the Australian troops were forced to capitulate and spend the next three-and-a-half years as prisoners of war.

Sick, starving and demoralised, the men found that camp discipline also became a problem, an issue that led to the erection of the cage, which was roughly 6 feet square and constructed from natural materials.

It was essentially a cell without a roof, but one from which it was impossible to escape. For the 'boob', as it was also known, was encased in barbed wire, its metal tentacles and sharp spikes capable of drawing blood at every turn. Each movement required an acute degree of delicacy and precision. One ill-judged stretch or repositioning of the body could leave a painful and potentially fatal gash in the flesh. Infected wounds were as much a threat to prisoners as beri-beri, cholera, malaria and dysentery.

Ostensibly the cage was the idea of Major George de Verdon Westley, who sought the permission of Japanese high command to impose a dose of home-grown discipline on his men. Other officers had supported the plan and, according to some reports, may even have instigated it, but Westley took responsibility. Previous attempts to keep the light-fingered and the malcontents in order, such as fines or loss of rank, had proved to be of little use as deterrents. Why would a man worry about his military or financial future when his very life was under threat?

That's why bandicooting had been so rife. The act of burrowing underground to steal another man's vegetables while leaving the leaves and stalks in place had become an art form among some of the less scrupulous, whose motivation had more to do with hunger than greed. Starving and emaciated, they'd also raid the vegetable garden tilled by the Australian officers, who deemed such behaviour a threat to their own survival.

Their officer status, which exempted them from the back-breaking manual labour the lower ranks were forced to carry out, allowed them plenty of time to nurture the vegetables which bolstered their health, arguably at the expense of the other prisoners. If this unequal arrangement had created resentment in the camp, the rest of the battalion didn't show it. What did incur their wrath was the punishment meted out to those offenders who were caught and held overnight in the cage.

Max Gilbert recalls three of his mates ending up there. 'The idea was that anyone caught pinching stuff during the night was locked in there when they came home from their work party and kept inside, irrespective of what the weather was like.'[1] They were fed, watered and given a blanket, but there was little protection from the elements and by daybreak those incarcerated were hardly fit for another day's labour.

The 'boob' came to symbolise the loss of respect and sense of injustice the men felt towards their superiors. It gouged a wound that even after 70 years has not yet healed, and epitomised what happens when officers and men turn against each other.

Discontent among the men of the 2/21st had been simmering long before the cage arrived. There was a perception that some of the senior officers had let them down. Rightly or wrongly, a few were accused of not complaining to the Japanese for fear of 'making them angry'. Only under 'the greatest pressure' would extra food and medical supplies be requested. And sometimes they'd threaten to hand some of their own men over to the Japanese for punishment. This was no idle warning. On one occasion it actually happened, much to the disgust of the offender's mates.

By war's end the allegations made against some of the Australian top brass who were in charge of the 2/21st were taken so seriously that an official inquiry was ordered. It followed a formal complaint from two American prisoners of war who took exception to the way the camp had been run for the past three-and-a-half years. They accused the Australian officers of operating a 'closed corporation, whose primary purpose was their own welfare and saving their own skin'.[2] Prisoners who were too weak or sick for manual labour were, they claimed, pulled from their beds and compelled to work. The camp staff did not give the men their fair share of rations. And on two occasions men who'd committed offences were 'severely beaten' by other POWs.

While the US servicemen might well have had their own agenda in demanding the inquiry, they reflected the sentiments expressed by many of the Australian POWs on Ambon at the time. The military did not waste time in launching their investigation.

At 1400 hours on Monday, 17 September 1945, a mere fifteen days after the official Japanese surrender, the Allied Land Forces, South West Pacific Area, held a Court of Inquiry on Administration and Control of the Tan Tui prisoner of war camp on Ambon, in what was then the Dutch East Indies.

How it had reached this stage was a vexed and uncomfortable question for the military establishment. In truth, the breakdown of trust between the leaders and the led was one of many aspects of a much bigger story which encompassed the soldiers of the 2/21st during the Second World War and which continued to unfold for years to come. Theirs was an unhappy and often brutal experience which would take them from the backblocks of Victoria to Alice Springs and on to Darwin in the Northern Territory before they eventually encountered enemy action. Along the way there would be fear and frustration, death and bloodshed, hope and courage, illness and starvation. And heroism of a scale few would have believed possible.

For some who refused to accept their loss of freedom there was the prospect of escape. Others who were sent to the Chinese island of Hainan disappeared into enemy territory, never to be seen again, engendering speculation over their likely fate. Where did they hide? How did they survive? Could they have been alive at war's end? And if so, what happened to them? It is a question that has never been satisfactorily answered and remains one of the battalion's great unsolved mysteries.

And what of the characters who comprised the cast of this epic drama? People like the popular Lieutenant Colonel Len Roach, who proudly led his men to Ambon only to be replaced by the ageing World War One veteran Lieutenant Colonel William Scott. Or the vicious interpreter Ikeuchi Masakiyo, who ran the Ambon prison camp in such a ruthless fashion and whose guards proved all too willing to emulate his vicious style. And the rank and file soldiers like Bill Doolan, who was stationed on the outskirts of Ambon town as the Japanese advanced and simply refused to leave his post. Armed with six hand grenades, a rifle and a revolver, Doolan is said to have killed or wounded 80 Japanese while perched in a tree, before he fell dead himself. His body was found and buried a few days later. The cross that marked his grave was eventually placed in the Australian War Memorial.

And so the Ambon legend evolved, reinforced by countless stories of suffering, not least the massacre of more than 300 Australians and Dutch who were held captive near the island airstrip at Laha. It was one of the most monstrous acts of cruelty to be recorded during the Japanese occupation of south-east Asia and the Pacific, and turned Ambon into an island synonymous with the bloodiest of war crimes. Yet it was only after liberation that the initial hints of what had happened during the first few weeks of Ambon's capitulation began to emerge.

At the beginning of the war, Gull Force and a number of support units which accompanied the 2/21st to Ambon consisted of 1150 men. In addition, there were some 2600 Dutch and indigenous troops stationed on the island. Of the total number of Australians, just over 300 lived to tell the tale. The death rate on Ambon was a staggering 77 per cent of all those held in captivity. Those who were sent on to Hainan – about a third of those Australians held prisoner on Ambon – fared slightly better, with about one in three losing their lives.

These were shocking statistics and represented some of the highest casualty rates in military history, including those of the Charge of the Light Brigade on 25 October 1854.

The battle of Ambon might have been a very different valley of death but manifested the same suicidal tendencies as the Battle of Balaclava nearly a century earlier. For this was an unwinnable conflict, given the might of the Japanese military and Australia's lack of firepower. Despite the courage of the men who took on the Japanese – and their heroism has never been properly acknowledged – Ambon was ripe for the taking.

It has since emerged that the officer in charge of the Australian Section of the Imperial General Staff, Major Vernon Sturdee, made the decision to send his men to Ambon while privately conceding that they didn't have a hope in hell of repelling the Japanese. That he persevered with his suicidal strategy while being advised by others that it was militarily unsound is one of the great scandals of the Ambon operation. All too aware that his men were ill-equipped to withstand even a moderate incursion, let alone a full invasion force of Japanese troops, Sturdee deliberately withheld arms and other military support to avoid them falling into the hands of the enemy.

Yet the man who effectively appointed himself as commander-in-chief of the area decided to ignore his own military instincts and the better judgement of others in pursuit of a strategy that was destined to fail. It was a decision he was later to regret, but by then it was too late to save the lives of hundreds of his soldiers, and the freedom of many more. For the next three-and-a-half years the men of the 2/21st Battalion and sundry other units endured a living hell at the hands of their captors in conditions so appalling that many died from starvation or disease. Some endeavoured to escape and, incredibly, made their way back to Australia. Others were gunned down by Chinese guerillas. But it was the cruelty of the Japanese that would be so hard to forgive.

In the war crimes trials that followed, fifteen Japanese officers and guards were jailed or executed for what happened on Ambon. Another fifteen were imprisoned or condemned to death for their treatment of Australians and other Allied servicemen on Hainan. But while the trials provided a degree of retribution for those who suffered and died at the hands of the enemy, there was no sense of closure for survivors. Their story was far from over as they battled depression, alcoholism and ill-health. And there was the memory too of the ugly rift between officers and men, a sore which continues to fester. At the time of writing only a few survivors are left, but the wound refuses to heal.

If the cage was a low point in Australian military history, the role of Ambon in the south-east Asian theatre of war will also be remembered as an ill-conceived and ill-fated exercise. The generous might agree that it held up the Japanese advance for a few weeks and thereby delayed plans to move further south towards Australia, but the cost of the strategy far exceeded the merits.

The debacle that was Ambon could have been avoided. Instead, it doomed hundreds of diggers to three-and-a-half years of hunger, sickness and brutality, which for many ended in death, as well as affecting the lives of thousands of men and women who lost their loved ones. It is also a tragedy which not only spanned a war, but effectively transcends more than a century of Australian history. Many of the characters who were to play a key role in the ill-judged Ambon operation were born in the latter part of the nineteenth century, when military strategy was based on horse-drawn armaments and scant regard for human life. Remarkably, the judgements made by officers who grew up then continue to echo into the 21st century, as the men they led ponder their contribution to the Second World War and recall those dark days as if they were yesterday.

1

PREPARING FOR WAR

'THE TRUTH IS the War does feel like yesterday,' Tom Pledger confides, as he draws on a menthol filter cigarette and places his frozen roast lamb dinner-for-one in the microwave. Tall, erect and an accomplished surfer in his time, Tom walks to the shops, enjoys a glass of wine or whisky and only recently stopped driving his much loved Morris Minor.

It is 19 November 2012, a few days after his 95th birthday.

A black and white photograph taken in 1940 of him and his late wife, Jessie, stands proudly on a table in the dining room. She didn't know whether he was dead or alive for nearly four years, but even so, she waited. They married on 1 December 1945, the day after he was discharged.

On a shelf opposite there's a framed certificate confirming he was mentioned in despatches for distinguished service. 'Must have been something I did,' he smiles.

There are a lot of memories in this bungalow, which sits on a gently rising slope in Sydney's south-western suburbs. It's where his twins, Paul and Nan, grew up; where the Pledger family celebrated life's triumphs and occasionally suffered the failures. He's lived here for nearly 65 years after spotting the footings being built and offering the owner a £10 deposit. It's so long ago he's forgotten the purchase price, but the property is as spick and span now as it was when he moved in. (He only recently finished painting and decorating the inside by himself.)

While his hearing is fading, his memory remains as sharp as a tack. His mum and dad, Harry and Katherine, 'were the best parents you could ever have'. They christened him Athol, but his dad thought the name too sissy and called him Tom. His eyes are welling now, as he recalls his childhood back in Byron Bay, where he landed a job as a railway porter after leaving school. He describes the lunchtime surf he'd take and the frantic race back to work with dripping towel and surfboard under his arm. Then promotion to stationmaster at Mullumbimby, before moving south to Gloucester and on to Maitland.

That's where he caught his first glimpse of army life. There was a military camp in Maitland and men in uniform were a familiar sight. 'You'd see all these chaps marching through and I suppose it just got to me, so I enlisted,' he explains. Of course he'd heard about the fighting in Europe and Australia's contribution to the war effort but the gently undulating terrain of the New South Wales Hunter Valley was far removed from Hitler's march of terror. If Tom was apprehensive about what to expect, he didn't show it. He's not a worrier now and certainly wasn't then. So he packed his bags and headed for Broadmeadow, in Newcastle, to sign up. The date was 27 August 1940; it was the beginning of an epic journey that would consume the next five years.[1]

Despite the war which had been declared almost a year earlier, there was still a certain innocence about Australia's involvement. After all, the hostilities were more than 19 000 kilometres away, a distance which psychologically inured Australians to the gathering storm. Newspaper advertisements of the day seemed blissfully unaware of international conflict, with luxury products such as radiograms retailing for 27 guineas and a three-piece lounge suite for £16.[2] In Melbourne's Como Park you could pick up a 'delightful, architect-built, three bedroom home with an exquisite bathroom' for £3300 or, at Disney Motors, an Austin Seven for £70. For the rich, there was a Standard Flying 14 Sedan for £235.

With so many blokes away at the war, jobs were also plentiful. In the situations vacant column of the Melbourne *Argus* there were rows of classified ads for manual and unskilled labour. A wholesale fruit store wanted a man with a good knowledge of wrapping and packing and was willing to pay him £5 a week. A qualified nurse could earn over £4, while her semi-trained equivalent could expect more than £2 a week.

Times were good for those in work and with a little spare cash. Cinemas and theatres were booming. The violinist Yehudi Menuhin was playing his farewell recital at Melbourne's Town Hall, David Niven was starring in the Hollywood movie *Raffles* and Walt Disney's *Pinocchio* was on at The Savoy. Unlike Britain there was no sign of rationing, with a slab of MacRobertson's chocolate offering four rows of different flavours including fruit sundae, strawberry cream and Turkish delight. But if life's little luxuries were still widely available, those who studied the newspapers carefully might have had cause for concern.

On the day Tom joined up, a report from New York quoted Rear Admiral Yates Stirling, former chief of the Naval Staff, as saying that war between the United States and Japan was inevitable, 'unless their ever mounting differences are composed'.[3] And in a clear warning of what such a confrontation would mean to its Allies in the Pacific, he predicted that a Japanese–American conflict would be a naval war fought mainly in the Orient.

If Australians were worried about the prospect of military action on their doorstep, they remained quietly confident about the outcome. Hadn't Arthur Fadden, the Minister for Air, only that day alluded to the nation's expanding aviation power? Australia's air defences had reached a level of strength and efficiency which could never have been contemplated a year ago, he had announced. Pilots, air gunners and wireless operators were being trained in ever-increasing numbers. Unfortunately, most of them were headed for Europe and there was even less detail about the number of aircraft coming off the production line.

In fairness, it wasn't only the war that Australians had to worry about. Rural areas were in the middle of a drought, with much of Victoria and New South Wales at a particularly 'critical' stage. In South Australia the cost of wheat was up to five shillings a bushel and in Queensland they were talking about roast beef soon becoming a luxury item, with cattle values being the highest for twenty years. 'Beef has become so dear in fact that a number of cafes have removed it from their menus,' one local paper reported.[4]

The weather, it seems, was as unpredictable then as now, with the elements playing unusual tricks in August – 'usually a month of cold winds . . . But already the birds in the trees are chirruping gaily and have been discarded. Spring is in the air and at the weekend hundreds of people had their first dip in the surf.'[5] It wasn't to last. The papers warned that a wintry blast was on its way.

The minutiae of Australian life as reported by the newspapers may have provided a comforting sense of normality for men like Tom Pledger as they made their way to Sydney, Melbourne and other state capitals for their initial training, taking their minds off the horrors that might lie around the corner and galvanising a sense of purpose. After all, wasn't this about protecting the free world from tyranny and ensuring the future of civilisation at home and abroad? Surely Australia was worth fighting for.

––––––––

Unlike the thousands of young men who were signing up all over Australia, the old guard had seen it all before. Many of the senior officers who were standing by to take command had known action in the First World War. Military tradition and a sense of duty were in their blood.

Sir Vernon Ashton Hobart Sturdee, who was to take command of Eighth Division, came from a family of soldiers and sailors. His father Alfred, who had trained as a doctor, used his medical experience in Gallipoli as a member of the 1st AIF 2nd Field

Ambulance. One of his uncles, Sir Donavan Sturdee, was an officer in Britain's Royal Navy and eventually rose to become Admiral of the Fleet. Charles, another uncle, became a lieutenant colonel with the Australian Light Horse. It was only natural that Vernon, who was born in 1890, should enter the services after leaving Melbourne Church of England Grammar School and taking an apprenticeship as an engineer.

Still in his mid-teens, he became a sapper in the Corps of Australian Engineers, Militia, and in 1908 was commissioned. Three years later the man who was to play such a decisive role in the fate of the 2/21st Battalion on Ambon was appointed lieutenant on probation, Royal Australian Engineers, Permanent Military Forces. By August 1914 he was on his way to Egypt as a member of the AIF. A few months afterwards he was promoted to captain and on 25 April 1915 landed at Gallipoli as adjutant, 1st Divisional Engineers.

A year later he was transferred to France, where he was praised for his 'skill and energy'. Captain Vernon Sturdee was gaining a reputation for getting things done under difficult circumstances. The way he prepared for major operations in the Cordonnerie sector near Armentières did not go unnoticed by his superiors. He was awarded the Distinguished Service Order and in 1917 was promoted to temporary lieutenant colonel, commanding the 4th Pioneer Battalion.

Sturdee's teenage experience as an engineer proved invaluable when it came to repairing and maintaining roads, laying underground cables and building army accommodation. To say he was in his element was an understatement. War was his calling and his commitment to King and country unwavering. With a DSO, an OBE and two mentions in despatches under his belt, Vernon Sturdee returned to Australia to work at Duntroon's Royal Military College and later as director of military operations at Army Headquarters in Melbourne.

By now a career soldier with a wealth of active service behind him, Sturdee was clearly being groomed for even greater responsibilities. As the news from overseas grew bleaker by the day and the spectre of international conflict loomed large, he was made the army's First Director of Staff Duties and in 1939 was appointed head of Eastern Command.[6]

Maric (Eddie) Gilbert grew up in a world far removed from army life. At 91 he peers out of the window of his suburban bungalow and looks back on his childhood and teenage years in Melbourne with a mixture of pride and nostalgia.

He was a pupil at Brighton Road State Primary School in St Kilda and was a choirboy at the local church. Mum and Dad had great plans for him and organised a part scholarship for their boy to Caulfield Grammar, but after two years and one term he had to leave. 'They were still recovering from the Great Depression and couldn't keep up the fees anymore,' he says, in a tone hinting at what might have been.

Instead Maric, or Eddie as he was to become known in the army, got a job with a wholesale jewellery company in Little Collins Street. The year was 1936. On the other side of the world Adolf Hitler was playing host at the Berlin Olympics, his Nazi empire poised to straddle most of Europe and engulf much of the rest of the world in flames. In faraway Melbourne Eddie's dad Ulric, who worked at the State Electricity Commission, was more concerned with getting his lad a job at the SEC. 'You'd have a better future there,' he'd say. Eddie took some persuading but eventually got the message and succeeded in securing a job as a storeman there.

He was still a teenager and while he'd enjoyed a loving childhood there was one part of his life that had always niggled him – that name. My, was he teased about it! Maric was 'Mar' from Marion, his mum's name, and 'ic' from Ulric. 'I hated it because sometimes I would be mistaken for a girl, for Marie. I was so sensitive about it.'

He needn't have worried. Soon Maric would change his name to Max, only for his army mates to nickname him Eddie.[7]

———————

William John Rendel Scott, like Vernon Sturdee, was a product of an earlier military era. Born in 1888 at Bingara in New South Wales, he went into the insurance business before enlisting in the AIF in May 1915 and serving with the 19th and 20th Battalions in France.[8]

The Battle of the Somme was one of the bloodiest campaigns in the First World War and Scott's work at Flers was to earn him the Distinguished Service Order. Twice mentioned in despatches, he was a fighter whose courage was without dispute. A colourful character with a devilish reactionary streak, he was wounded in France and in April 1917 was promoted to major.

Scott had no intention of pursuing an army career on his return to Australia and instead founded an insurance brokerage in Sydney. But the world of business could not compete with the draw of matters military. He was a strong supporter of veterans' organisations and occasionally found a role for himself in local militias. Perhaps bored with his professional responsibilities and secretly missing the thrill of battle, his right-wing tendencies grew ever more extreme. At one stage he formed a 'White Army' to counter Australia's increasingly militant socialist and trade union movements.

By 1931 he was chief of staff of a secret army known as the Old Guard. It had 30000 members and aimed to impose the rule of law in the event of the civilian government being overthrown. Increasingly powerful on the far right of politics, Scott used his influence to gather intelligence about Japanese activities in Australia while publicly calling for closer ties with Tokyo. He wrote letters to the newspapers defending Japanese foreign policy and spoke to meetings. 'Japan is an old and civilised country, demanding our respect and understanding,' he declared in a speech to a luncheon club in Sydney. 'It has been suggested that Japan is preparing to invade Australia. Such utterances are foolish and ignorant.'[9] Scott even paid an official visit to Japan in 1934 to look at sheep and wool production and explore the possibilities of staging cultural exchanges.

Intriguingly, while extolling Japanese virtues to anyone who would listen, he was also engaged in military and civilian intelligence. As a member of the Australian–Japanese Society he had a plausible cover for asking questions and gaining information. But Scott's success in the field of espionage annoyed the professionals, including the police, whose own intelligence officers labelled him arrogant and high-handed. Eventually he became so difficult that he was forbidden access to secret files.

Personal and professional relations with Scott were often strained. He was proud of his reputation as a soldier and a leader of men and expected others to recognise his status. Sadly, his ambition and his restless energy were to be his undoing. Scott's early military experience might have earned him a reputation as a fearsome soldier, but it proved of little benefit a quarter of a century later when his renewed lust for combat contributed to the disaster that was Ambon. Neither did it sit comfortably with another side of his character, which was to be so graphically exposed behind barbed wire.[10]

―――――――

As the storm clouds of international conflict continued to gather over Europe, Walter Hicks was reminded of his own family's involvement in the Great War. His father had been in the Royal Navy and his mother, who had three sisters and six brothers, had seen the results of the battlefield firsthand. One of her brothers was killed at Fromelles, another lost a leg in the same battle and a third died from a gas attack. Walter Dunstan Hicks, who was born on 24 January 1920 in Bordertown, South Australia, was all too familiar with the aftermath of conflict. He also had a nose for history and even as a young man he realised that if something wasn't done to stop Hitler, he would take over the world.

He'd grown up in the country and was a crack shot with a rifle so he knew he had the basic qualities of a good soldier. But Walter was also making his way in civilian life, securing a good job with a promising future at the State Savings Bank in Melbourne. He was nineteen, ambitious to succeed and his career was uppermost in his mind.

It was a Friday night in September 1939 when all that changed. Walter had been working as a clerk in the Centre Road branch at Bentleigh, in the Melbourne suburbs. In those days the banks would open for an hour in the early evening and as he served the customers he noticed a crowd gathering outside a radio shop some 100 yards down the road. Curious to know what the fuss was about he heard the faint sound of a gravelly voice coming from a wireless which people on the pavement were listening to.

It was Britain's Prime Minister Neville Chamberlain broadcasting from the Cabinet Room in Ten Downing Street.

> This morning the British Ambassador in Berlin handed the German Government a final note stating that, unless we hear from them by 11 o'clock that they were prepared at once to withdraw their troops from Poland, a state of war would exist between us. I have to tell you now that no such undertaking has been received and that consequently this country is at war with Germany.

In one of those impromptu exchanges which seem much more memorable in retrospect, an old man standing next to Walter asked, 'Are you going to war?' Before he had time to reply, Walter turned round to see George Nasen pull up his trouser leg and show him the scar from a bullet wound he'd suffered in the First World War. It made an indelible impression on Walter Hicks, who would soon be going to war himself.[11]

———

Of all the men who were to form part of Gull Force, Lieutenant Colonel Leonard Roach would be remembered as the officer who might have saved the 2/21st Battalion, had the authorities accepted his wise counsel or listened to his pleas.

As a private in the First World War, Roach saw service at Gallipoli and in France and rapidly made his way up the military ladder, first as a corporal and latterly as Camp Commandant, Headquarters, 2nd Brigade. By the war's end he had been awarded the Military Cross and in 1918 gained a commission in the Indian Army which took him to Persia and Afghanistan, before returning to Australia, where he was made a captain in the Reserve of Officers.

By all accounts Roach, who combined a part-time role in the militia with his work as a Melbourne businessman, was a quiet but popular officer, a man who enjoyed the respect and loyalty of all those who served under him. Ostensibly shy and modest, he had a reputation for enforcing discipline while maintaining a friendly and approachable manner. Throughout the twenties and the thirties he held posts at Branch Headquarters, 4th Division, the 3rd Division Artillery and as major in the 37th/39th Battalions. While he was not a career soldier as such, he maintained strong bonds with the army and by 1939 was made the 14th Battalion's temporary lieutenant colonel.

By July 1940 he had enlisted in the 2nd AIF and was back as a full-time military man, commanding the 2/21st Infantry Battalion of the 23rd Brigade, 8th Division, soon to be better known as Gull Force. Lieutenant Colonel Len Roach, the man who would eventually be known as the 'father' of the battalion, was assembling his men and facing up to the responsibilities of war. Perhaps because he began his military life as a private, he forged a stronger bond with other ranks, though the respect he enjoyed from most of his men did not always extend to the officer class. As the leader of the 2/21st prepared his men for action, there would be serious disagreements with his superiors over the wisdom of Australia's decision to defend the island of Ambon,

933 kilometres north of Darwin. There would also be criticism of his troops' behaviour before they embarked for the Dutch East Indies, after reports of indiscipline among lower ranks.

Controversy over Roach's role as CO and his disapproval of the 8th Division's military strategy in the Banda Sea would ultimately be his undoing, but for now Gull Force was still in its infancy and its members largely ignorant of the grave threat they were facing.[12]

————

Jimmy Morrison, who enlisted at the end of 1939 before joining Gull Force, would go on to share his then commanding officer's sentiments. He was only twenty at the time and, like all young men, keen to do his bit for King and country. Yet more than 70 years later, and with the benefit of hindsight, he ponders the folly of his masters. 'We were put there to be slaughtered,' he declares. 'We had nothing when we got there and the Japs walked all over us.'

Jimmy's brutal judgement is delivered in his ninety-third year, his memory slightly clouded but his opinions based on the harsh reality of war. He is one of the few who are still alive to offer a firsthand account of life as a POW on Ambon and Hainan.

He'd found himself in the Dutch East Indies after joining the 2/12th Field Ambulance Unit. Jimmy didn't have any medical experience, not even first aid, but they were looking for volunteers when he enlisted at the Gladesville drill hall in Sydney and soon he was on his way to Cowra and then on to Darwin.

Until then he'd been working in a paint factory at Rhodes and helping in his dad's tomato garden in Ryde. They were a big and loving family. His parents Monty and Alice had five daughters and three sons. 'They were very good people,' Jimmy recalls, and he would miss them dearly over the next four years as hunger, illness and the brutality of Japanese prison life consumed his every waking hour and much of his sleep. It was to become a living nightmare.[13]

———

And so Jimmy Morrison, Tom Pledger, Walter Hicks, Eddie Gilbert and the rest of Gull Force made ready for Ambon under the command of Lieutenant Colonel Len Roach and his second in command, Major Ian Macrae.

It was a long wait as the War Cabinet and Army HQ in Melbourne developed their strategy for the Dutch East Indies and kept a wary eye on Japan.

Few realised then that it was a disaster waiting to happen.

2

THE DOOMED GRAND STRATEGY

W<small>HAT A CHEERY</small> throng they were that morning. It was July 1940 and the men who would go on to form Gull Force were being drawn from across Victoria and beyond.

Eddie Gilbert had started out a few weeks earlier in Melbourne's Royal Park, where hundreds of men had arrived to volunteer. Within a few days of enlisting he was given a uniform and was on his way to Shepparton in country Victoria, where he dossed down in the fat sheep pen at the local showground.

Training was rudimentary. Handed a broomstick for a rifle, Eddie and his mates paraded around the showground and pretended to be soldiers – not to make light of their commitment, but this was their level of inexperience and innocence. Many had never handled a gun and while some might have had a taste of the militia, the majority were country boys drawn from Mildura, Geelong, Colac and the Riverina, over the border in New South Wales.

By mid-1940 the call to arms had attracted almost 50 000 recruits across Australia, and the army was running out of space. Shepparton Showground was bursting at the seams, forcing the military authorities to set up a new camp at Trawool, on the banks of the Goulburn River near Seymour. Nearly 100 kilometres from Melbourne, Trawool had been a popular spot for army manoeuvres since before the First World War. It had even received a visit from British Field Marshal Lord Kitchener in 1910, when he was on a visit to Australia. It also had the advantage of a railway line, which aided troop transportation and communications. Trouble was the weather. With little in the way of solidly built accommodation, the men were mostly forced to shelter under canvas from the mid-winter rain and freezing winds which swept through the Trawool Valley.

It was not a comfortable stay and there was much relief when they were transferred to Bonegilla, close to Albury on the Victoria–New South Wales border. By now they were officially part of the 2/21st Battalion of the 23rd Brigade of the 8th Division of the Australian Imperial Force.

Major General Sturdee had taken command of 8th Division on 1 August 1940, though he was succeeded by Major General Gordon Bennett on 24 September after several senior officers and politicians were killed in a plane crash near Canberra. In the subsequent reorganisation Sturdee became the Chief of the General Staff.[1]

Lieutenant Colonel Leonard Roach was made the 21st's commanding officer. He was a popular choice among the men, some of whom had known him in the peacetime militia and were keen to continue to serve under a man they admired and respected. They were not to know that within eighteen months he would have left the battalion under a cloud.

Bonegilla was nearly 250 kilometres away and in an effort to boost morale and improve physical fitness it was decided the men would march all the way. It took them eleven days – it has been described as the longest military manoeuvre ever undertaken in the history of Australia[2] – and proved to be a rare example of inspired military wisdom. Despite initial reservations about the long, north-easterly trek, it gave the men their first real opportunity to act as one, to demonstrate they were more than an ill-disciplined bunch of boys drawn from the city and the bush, and to show pride in their appearance as they made their way through country towns and settlements.

Even the locals were impressed as the 2/21st strode purpose-fully along the highways and byways of rural Victoria. Mothers and babies waved from their verandahs. Shopkeepers emerged from their stores to catch a glimpse of the fighting force which offered so much promise in these uncertain times. Farmhands in the fields whistled and shrieked messages of support in the distance. These were heady times for the likes of Eddie Gilbert and his new-found comrades. To the public they were heroes in the making. For the first time since becoming part of Len Roach's battalion they were able to share a genuine sense of pride and purpose.

But maintaining the sudden surge in morale would not be easy. Though they were physically fit after their eleven-day hike, training conditions at Bonegilla left much to be desired. For men who were supposedly being taught the art of modern warfare, there was a singular lack of appropriate weaponry. Many of the guns were from the First World War era. Initially, there was no rifle range to practise on. The lack of facilities meant a trip to the Albury and Wodonga ranges for those on small arms courses. But the overall standard of shooting was poor, with few of the men reaching an acceptable level of proficiency during their Bonegilla stay.[3]

Such negative assessments were not universal. While the specialist training could have been more effective, the new recruits enjoyed the relative comfort and newly built facilities of the camp. Eddie Gilbert revelled in the daily round of running, marching, jumping and wading to improve his physical fitness. 'It was a great camp and I was happy there,' he remembers. 'The training was pretty intensive, but it was relieved by the fact we were fairly close to Albury and the people there were very hospitable.'

If Bonegilla appeared more like a holiday camp than a training facility for serious killing, the future would make up for it. At the back of everyone's mind was the question, Where next? Most assumed they were destined for the Middle East, to where the

6th Division had already been posted; the 7th Division would soon follow. In fact, the 2/21st would kick their heels for about sixteen months before being deployed overseas and it would be even longer before they saw enemy action. The first hint that their military career was to take an unexpected course came in early 1941, when they were herded aboard a train to Alice Springs. Nobody knew their ultimate destination but even those with the slightest geographical knowledge realised they were heading north. As the Northern Territory emerged from the wet season, the battalion found itself on the Stuart Highway en route to Darwin. It was the beginning of a downward spiral that would embrace boredom, ill-discipline, hunger, disease, despair, defeat and for many, death.

––––––––

By now Brigadier Edmund Lind, who was in charge of the 23rd Brigade, had organised the formation of three separate troop deployments who would be known as Lark Force, Sparrow Force and Gull Force. Lark, which was made up of men from the 22nd Battalion, would be sent to Rabaul; Sparrow, most of whom were from the 2/40th, was earmarked for Timor; and Gull was destined for Ambon, though few of the men from the 2/21st were aware of it at the time.

In addition to the 21st, Gull Force was also made up of several specialist units who joined the battalion at a later stage. These included the Army Catering Corps, the 104th Light Aid Detachment, the Australian Anti-Tank Battery, a signals section from the 23rd Brigade, a dental unit, members of the Intelligence Corps, the 2/11th Field Engineers and the 2/12th Field Ambulance. All would come under the Gull Force umbrella and work alongside the 2/21st Battalion, whose fate, as it turned out, was sealed long before it left Australia.

The strategy that saw Gull Force's undoing was largely the result of decisions made during a series of Allied meetings which stretched from October 1940 to February 1941 in the tropical heat of Singapore.

The first conference, instigated by the British chiefs of staff and supported by the Australian War Cabinet, was also attended by staff officers from India, New Zealand and Burma. The defence of East Asia was the initial brief, but before the meeting got underway on 22 October it was agreed to extend the area under consideration to most of the Pacific. The line of defence forces posted at Ambon (Gull Force), Timor (Sparrow Force) and New Britain (Lark Force) became known as the Malay Barrier. The aim was to devise a strategy to combat Japanese forces should they enter the war on the side of the Axis powers, which seemed increasingly likely. Barely a month earlier, in September, Japan had signed a ten-year pact with Germany and Italy 'to assist one another with all political, economic and military means if one of the high contracting parties should be attacked by a Power not at present involved in the European war, or in the Sino-Japanese conflict.'

The western powers got the message. The United States Ambassador to France, William Bullitt, told the Council on Foreign Relations in Chicago that the pact was a 'contingent declaration of enmity'. 'If ever a clear warning was given to a nation that the three aggressors contemplated a future assault upon it, that warning was given to the American people,' he declared.[4]

Keen to push the United States into a more aggressive stance, the British Prime Minister Winston Churchill asked President Roosevelt if it might be possible to send an American squadron on a friendly visit to Singapore. 'If desired, occasion might be taken of such a visit for a technical discussion of naval and military problems . . . and the Dutch might be invited to join.'[5] Roosevelt declined the invitation, concluding that sending a squadron to Singapore might precipitate Japanese action against the United States.

Even so, it wasn't long before representatives of the Dutch East Indies joined the British and Australians at the conference table in Singapore to thrash out a joint Allied response to protect their interests in the Far East. Over the following months they examined their military options in minute detail, negotiating mutual support agreements should Japan attack one or more of their territories.

By now it was increasingly apparent that the region was in desperate need of a modern air force, in the absence of British air and naval support to protect Singapore and Malaya.

A key decision came in the final week of February 1941, when the Dutch pledged to provide air back-up in defence of Malaya should the Japanese enter the war, in return for a similar commitment by Australia to protect Timor and Ambon, which were part of the Dutch East Indies. The Dutch sold the idea to Canberra on the grounds that Ambon was an important link between Java and Australia and might aid its defence in the event of a Japanese invasion of Australia's northern coastline. The deal was that the Netherlands would transfer a total of 24 aircraft to Singapore, while Australia would supply three squadrons to operate over Ambon and Timor.[6] Australia agreed to provide army units to both islands after Sir Charles Burnett, who was Australia's Air Chief Marshal, demanded that if he sent his planes there, Australian ground troops must be provided to protect them.[7]

According to the man who devised the Singapore agreement, Britain's Air Chief Marshal Sir Robert Brooke-Popham, Australia also agreed to provide army units to both islands. Australian troops would protect Australian and Dutch planes on Timor and Ambon while offering futher aerial support out of Darwin.[8]

The Australian chiefs of staff were left to sort out the details and report back at a later date. It was here that understandings started to unravel.

Back in Darwin, Gull Force was still kicking its heels. While unaware of the grand strategy hammered out in Singapore, the rank and file were becoming increasingly restless.

The battalion had arrived in April 1941 to discover a camp site devoid of the sort of accommodation provided at Bonegilla in Victoria. It was scrubland with tents. To make the living conditions more acceptable, the men set about building tin huts to live and sleep in. What they had overlooked was that this was the start of the dry season, when the Northern Territory became unbearably hot and metal structures heated up like ovens.

To make matters worse, they were a long way out of town, at Winnellie, several kilometres from Darwin's drinking holes and other modest social attractions. The food was nothing to write home about, and because of the distance from Victoria, opportunities for leave were virtually non-existent. There was also the as yet unanswered question of what they were doing there. Desperate for action and bored with day-to-day life in the Top End, they became known as 'the lost legion'. Morale plummeted and discipline followed suit.

There were almost riots, according to Walter Hicks, who recalls it as a far from happy time. 'We were bored stiff, in the main,' adds Eddie Gilbert. 'It was like living in a wild west town, and to pass the time fellas either boozed or gambled or did both.' Fortunately for Eddie he had other distractions. Soon after arriving in Winnellie he was chosen to join B Company's mortar team, which meant going away for weeks of training. 'It was great because it eased the boredom.'

The men of the 2/12th Field Ambulance, including Tom Pledger, set up camp about a quarter of a mile away from the 2/21st and kept themselves to themselves.

Jimmy Morrison, who until now had never been out of Sydney, was shocked by the Northern Territory's simmering racial tensions. Relations between the predominantly white diggers and the Indigenous locals occasionally boiled over. One night he witnessed an ugly clash between a soldier and a young Aboriginal woman who ended up being 'ripped right across the face' and left in the gutter. 'It was shocking,' he says, 'but those sort of things went on in Darwin. There were fights every night.'

Perhaps the most damning description of military life in Darwin came from William Scott, who would later command Gull Force. While much of his report was based on hearsay, his findings, if true, cast doubt on the quality of training the men were receiving and the level of discipline imposed on them by Lieutenant Colonel Roach. There was talk of drunkenness, gambling, fighting and insubordination. He painted a picture of a battalion who were out of control. Though it would emerge that Scott, whose own actions would later bring him into disrepute, had a vested interest in badmouthing his predecessor and thereby tarnishing the image of the men.

Even taken with a pinch of salt, however, Scott's claims make for uncomfortable reading. 'Discipline was becoming bad, gambling was carried on openly in defiance of orders, troops drank heavily at night time and there was much disorderly noise and cat-calling after lights out,' he reported. It got worse. Officers were heckled, threatened and assaulted. Bottles were thrown at them. An officer suffered bruising and abrasions to the face during a particularly unpleasant altercation.

Another night there was a near riot by D Company after one of their number was placed in the detention compound. Angered by their mate's incarceration, the rest of the party marched to the compound and demanded his release. On another occasion an officer was called a bastard for ordering a stop to drinking and gambling at lights out. When the revellers refused to co-operate, more officers intervened and fighting broke out. A private who tried to restore peace was so badly hurt that he needed urgent medical attention.

Significantly, nobody was charged, and in other cases the trouble was often covered up so that the authorities didn't hear of it.

There were some incidents which nobody could ignore and which struck at the very heart of the problem facing Gull Force – rebellion in the ranks. On several occasions the men openly booed their senior officers. During a boxing tournament there were cat-calls as the officers took their seats. 'The uproar reached its climax on the appearance of the CO and Brigadier,' observed Scott.

While this might be excused in retrospect as a mere outburst of Aussie larrikinism, there was worse to come. One evening Air Vice Marshal Brooke-Popham, who was on an official visit, suffered the same fate. Again there were boos and cat-calls. We can only speculate what the British defence chief made of the raucous reception but it clearly didn't enhance the battalion's image. Perhaps even more tellingly, no disciplinary action was taken over these incidents and nobody was charged.

Scott later insisted that the ill-discipline at Darwin reflected a lack of backbone among those in charge, whom he claimed were 'powerless and out of control'.[9]

Was Scott being unfair to Gull Force? Certainly there were rough elements in Darwin, but such qualities were not unique to the 2/21st. These men were straining at the leash for action, to prove their worth in combat and to defend Australia – no wonder they were frustrated. And if Scott needed a scapegoat to justify his own shortcomings, Gull Force was a convenient whipping boy.

Yes, much of Scott's Darwin assessment was based on gossip and on stories provided second-hand. And, conveniently, since many of the incidents were never subject to disciplinary action or courts martial, there was little documented record of the cases on which the allegations were based. Yet as Joan Beaumont writes in her history of Gull Force:

> Even if Scott did overstate his case, few of the officers of the 2/21st would deny that discipline became increasingly difficult to maintain as the frustrations of being in Darwin grew. Certainly the morale of the unit suffered and Macrae's [Major Ian Macrae, second in command] conclusion, looking back on the period years later, was that the 'general tone and esprit de corps of the battalion was never as high as it had been at Bonegilla'.[10]

Even official historian Lionel Wigmore conceded there were serious problems in the Top End as some of the troops 'became restive and resentful'. He wrote that 'the period of waiting proved a severe test for soldiers who were reading daily of the exploits of their comrades in North Africa, Greece, Crete and Syria. The number of breaches of discipline in some units increased disturbingly as the months went on.'[11]

And their behaviour and general depression didn't improve when on two occasions ten per cent of the battalion were posted to the Middle East as reinforcements. Those who were left behind felt useless and forgotten.

For Brigadier Edmund Lind, Commander of 23rd Brigade, keeping a lid on the men's frustrations in Darwin was one of several challenges he needed to address. His principal task was to defend the Northern Territory against possible Japanese attack, a challenge not to be underestimated given the length of the coastline. But there was another order which worried him still more and which remained top secret at that stage.

In May 1941 Lind was instructed to send two of his battalions north should the Japanese attack southward. Based on what had been discussed earlier at the Singapore meetings – which had been approved by the Australian War Cabinet as well as Britain's Air Chief Marshal Sir Robert Brooke-Popham, who was in overall charge of the plan – Sparrow Force would be despatched to Timor at the far eastern end of the Javanese archipelago, and Gull Force to Ambon, more than 900 kilometres away in the Moluccas.

Lind and his two infantry commanders, Lieutenant Colonel Geoffrey Youl of the 2/40th and Lieutenant Colonel Roach of the 2/21st, decided to reconnoitre both islands. What they discovered produced a sense of unease that would haunt all three men for the next eight months. Lind made it clear on his return that an isolated and inadequately armed battalion per island would be no match for the enemy. Further trips were made which only served to reinforce his concern.

His reservations were backed by Lieutenant Colonel Eric Scriven, officer commanding, the Royal Australian Engineers, who concluded that Ambon would be a difficult place to defend, given its steep, dense jungles. In a detailed report on the island he also pointed out the shortage of open space in which to manoeuvre troops and the limited local food production, which meant that supplies would have to be imported from Australia. Sadly, Scriven died in an accident in June at the age of 44 but his report contained some sound advice which, had it been taken seriously by the decision makers, might have changed their attitude towards Gull Force.

While on the face of it Sturdee stood doggedly determined to abide by the Singapore pledge to support the Dutch, he later admitted that he had also harboured genuine concerns about the wisdom of sending men there.[12] So why didn't he express his reservations to the War Cabinet at the time? Why did he continue to prepare for an ill-fated mission without the Cabinet knowing the chances of success were minimal? And this at a time when events gave him the perfect get-out clause.

As David A. Evans observes in his post-war examination of the Ambon debacle, the Japanese had rendered the Singapore strategy void after attacking south-east Asia and Pearl Harbor on a front that was broader than expected – a fact that should have prompted the War Cabinet to review its approach to strategy along the Malay Barrier before embarking any troops to Ambon and Timor. As it stood:

> Under the Singapore conference policy the Australian
> War Cabinet retained the right to unilaterally form high
> strategic policy in its theatre of operations, which included
> Ambon, and could withdraw or withhold forces from
> that commitment at any time subject to only informing
> Far East Command before taking such action . . . [It
> transpired that there] was no longer a logical strategic
> or political object in sending Gull Force to Ambon other
> than to occupy and hold.[13]

Given that Sturdee privately accepted that Gull Force stood little chance of defending Ambon for more than a few days in the face of an overwhelming Japanese onslaught, now was possibly the perfect time to advise the Australian government accordingly. But it appeared the Cabinet remained blissfully unaware of the very real danger facing Gull Force until after it had embarked for Ambon.

It was only a report of the mobilisation of Japanese forces in the Far East that started to concentrate Cabinet minds. By November Tokyo's plans were gathering pace for an attack on American, Dutch and British interests in south-east Asia and the Pacific. But it wasn't until January that Sturdee made mention of his growing doubts, suggesting that scattering troops too thinly around the islands north of Australia was a waste of men. By then it was almost too late. Evans claims Sturdee's withholding of information from the Australian War Cabinet about Gull Force's chances of survival had rendered it 'dysfunctional in properly performing its responsibilities to grand strategy and Gull Force'.

> It was within Sturdee's area of responsibility to inform
> the government of the strategic weakness in the scheme
> but he chose not to do that until the last moment. [Prime
> Minister] Curtin and the War Cabinet thus agreed to
> Sturdee's terms that Rabaul, and effectively Timor and
> Ambon, were to be left to their fate against overwhelming
> Japanese forces without the hope of reinforcement,
> withdrawal or rescue and all for the sake of a desperate,
> ill-considered and ill-prepared air observation policy
> that could have been carried out successfully by the
> RAAF alone.[14]

'This was a serious predicament that could have been addressed responsibly in the days leading up to December 16 and before Gull Force went to Ambon,' says Evans. 'Sturdee had failed to re-examine the strategic options responsibly and chose to ignore

Roach's protestations that Gull Force was inadequate to its allocated task' until it was too late.

It might have helped if the 2/21st had been allowed to sail to Ambon earlier to build their defences and work alongside 2500 Royal Netherlands East Indies Army troops already based on the island, but this idea was rejected by the Dutch on the grounds that it might be seen as a war-like gesture and provoke the Japanese. It was a telling response. The Dutch East Indies appeared to lack a certain fighting spirit – a view that would gain ground in the weeks and months ahead.

———

Back in Darwin the mood among the men had hardened. On 7 December, the Japanese bombed Pearl Harbor, sending the Allied powers into a frenzy of activity, not least in Australia. Gull Force was given just seven days to prepare for embarkation to the island of Ambon, but even as the men polished their boots and readied their weapons for war, Commander Roach continued to press Army HQ for more troops and better back-up. If he couldn't prevent them going to Ambon, he would damn well make sure they got the support they deserved.

Roach did not hold back. In a letter to Scott sent on 13 December he condemned his military superiors for doing nothing to address his and Lind's concerns: 'If any of my excellent fellows do not arrive at their destination it will not be a case of gallant sacrifice but of murder due to sheer slackness and maladministration,' he warned.[15]

Len Roach must have known there was little chance of a change of heart at this late stage. It was by now impossible to extricate the 2/21st from the defence strategy devised in Singapore and too late to send more arms and reinforcements to aid them when they reached Ambon. They were on their own, cast adrift and destined to suffer defeat at the hands of a brutal and unforgiving enemy.

3

DESTINATION AMBON

T HE THREE DUTCH vessels assigned to take Gull Force to
Ambon were slow but functional, with little or no firepower
to protect passengers from the Japanese menace. But who cared
about shipboard safety when submarines or enemy aircraft posed
a much more serious threat? Tom Pledger and his mates boarded
the *Patras*. Others sailed on the *Bhot* and *Valentine*. Though
normally used as inter-island ferries, their cargo was not restricted
to passengers. Often the ships were packed with livestock including
cattle, sheep and chickens. There were no cabins for the men;
some were forced to sleep in the cattle pen. Not that it mattered.
Wasn't it exhilarating just to be at sea?

'We were on our way to war,' says Eddie Gilbert. 'That's why
we enlisted, not to spend eight demoralising months at Darwin
digging slit trenches and learning how to be defensive.'

It was a three-day voyage and if there was apprehension
among the men, they didn't show it. Yet. Only the zigzagging
of their tiny fleet – an accepted anti-submarine tactic ordered by
the captain just to be on the safe side – provided a hint of the
underlying concerns. Two Australian navy vessels, the cruiser
Adelaide and the *Ballarat*, a corvette, also offered protection,
and several RAAF planes gave aerial cover.

Eddie's brain was ticking over. What if they were torpedoed and his ship sank? How would they survive? Where were the lifebelts? Nobody had raised such obvious questions, so Private Gilbert went straight to the point. The response from a passing Dutch crewman gave little cause for comfort. He said that it wasn't worth worrying about lifebelts as the ship's hold was full of 10-pound mortar bombs. 'He didn't have to spell out the likely consequences should we be hit by a torpedo – imagination did that,' Eddie records in his diary. 'This incident really was a sobering reminder that there really was a war on and that we were participants.'

Few of the nearly 1200 Australians who made their way across the Arafura Sea on the first leg of their 950-kilometre voyage north to the Moluccas had ever heard of Ambon. Until now, most had shown little interest in Australia's northerly neighbours. And why should they have? Historical ties to the mother country meant that most Australians still saw their homeland as an extension of the British empire, a distant colonial outpost which had little in common with Asia.

Suddenly, however, Australia was uncomfortably exposed. With the Japanese moving south there was a new sense of vulnerability. Nobody knew for sure if the Japanese had their eyes on Australia, but Canberra wasn't taking any chances.

The men of the 2/21st and the smaller units who accompanied them would soon find themselves in the front line of Australia's northern defences but like any armed force poised for battle it was the unknown that nagged at their subconscious. How would they cope under fire? These men were not hardened combatants and had no experience of war. What of the blood, the bombings and the mayhem of enemy contact? Would their courage crack under the frightening intensity of attack? Or would human instinct and self-preservation kick in to help protect them?

Such lonely thoughts were not openly discussed aboard the *Patras*, *Bhot* and *Valentine* as they steamed across the turquoise waters under a monsoonal sky. You kept your fears to yourself.

Any public admission of concern might be seen as weakness by your mates, so best to keep the imagination under wraps.

Every now and then a distant puff of black on the horizon reminded those on deck they still had friendly company. 'Just on dusk you'd see the old *Adelaide*. She'd blow off a lot of smoke ... and suddenly off she'd go. She'd disappear and we used to think, "Gawd, where's she gone ... we've got no protection",' Don Findlay recalled. 'But what she was doing [was] she was going in a big sweep all night around us and the next morning she'd be out there bang right in front of us again.'[1]

It was 17 December when three boatloads of Australian soldiers sailed into Ambon harbour, one of the most well-protected deepwater ports in the region. No wonder the Japanese were keen to occupy it. For centuries it had been a prized possession of the Portuguese, the English and eventually the Dutch. Portugal had established a garrison there in the early sixteenth century and Britain had also shown interest.

In 1579 the great British explorer Sir Francis Drake called into the Moluccas on his round-the-world voyage. He dropped anchor at Ternate, not far to the north of Ambon, and was soon to recognise the islands' potential as a source of spices. Elizabethan England and the rest of Europe had become partial to spices, which they regarded as essential to their less-than-flavoursome food. Cargoes of cloves, cinnamon, nutmegs and the like made big money overseas. Whoever controlled the so-called Spice Islands would hold sway over the tastebuds of Europe.

When Drake returned home on his galleon the *Golden Hind*, which was packed not only with jewels and precious metals sacked from other vessels but also a stock of tasty spices from the Moluccas, the English were determined to win a slice of the territory for themselves. The Dutch were also vying to conquer the islands and in 1605 wrested control, overpowering the Portuguese fortress of Victoria on what was then known as Amboyna.

The spice trade was a brutal business, with those in charge endeavouring to clamp down on competition from other nations, by force of arms if necessary. The English East India Company, a behemoth of far eastern merchant trading between the seventeenth and nineteenth centuries, was far from pleased by the victory of its Dutch rival. Relations deteriorated until they reached an understanding by which they would share the spice market and individual trading posts. But there was a disagreement over who had legal jurisdiction – a difference of opinion which was to have tragic consequences. And in a curious twist of history, which would be duplicated some three centuries hence, the crisis would be triggered by Japanese elements on Ambon.

In 1623 the Dutch became suspicious of British intentions when a Japanese mercenary in the employ of the Dutch East India Company was allegedly caught in the act of spying on Fort Victoria's defences. Interrogated under torture he not only confessed to conspiring with other Japanese mercenaries on the island, he also implicated several Englishmen, including Gabriel Towerson, captain and agent for the Dutch East India Company's British counterpart. The men were also subjected to torture, including an early form of waterboarding, and forced to admit their complicity.

On 27 February, Towerson, nine other Englishmen, nine Japanese and one Portuguese were all beheaded, with Towerson's head impaled on a pole in a public place for all to see.[2] The trial and punishment handed out to the alleged spies became a cause célèbre in London and triggered a diplomatic stand-off with Holland. The Dutch later accused the judges of misconduct, but eventually released them.

Stung by the execution of its employees, the British East India Company put its own corporate spin on the men's fate by producing a gruesome brochure reporting the various tortures inflicted on them in every grisly detail. It would go down in history as the Great Massacre of Amboyna, an atrocity that would not be forgotten by the English. In 1654, Oliver Cromwell, who had a long memory in these matters, exacted revenge and won compensation from the Dutch, but privately the British conceded defeat in Ambon, which finally became part of the Dutch East Indies. Holland's domination of the East Indies would continue until 1942, when the Japanese would return to Ambon and Australian troops would be called in to defend it.

If there was a certain symmetry to the events which would unfold 300 years later, it was reinforced by a further coincidence which sent a shudder down the spine of Private Walter Hicks. As he stepped ashore in the Moluccas, there on a memorial to those who were victims of the seventeenth-century Amboyna massacre was another Hicks. John Hicks was among the Englishmen beheaded on the island in 1623. Would the Australians be treated any differently? Was history about to repeat itself?

Walter and his mates quickly pulled themselves together. No point in mawkishness or melodrama. This was their new home and, to be honest, it looked surprisingly inviting. The deepwater harbour, which effectively separated Ambon's two peninsulas – Hitu to the north and Laitimor to the south – allowed them to sail right up to the wharves. And what a tropical paradise they found when they disembarked.

The two peninsulas, connected by a narrow isthmus at the far end of the bay, combine to form an unusual shape. On a map the island looks like a crocodile's head with its jaws half-opened, eager to gobble up those who stray into its greedy mouth. The lure of Ambon Bay had been obvious to sailors, explorers and traders for centuries. Apart from the nutmeg and cloves which were native to the area, the water, which had a depth of nearly 300 metres in parts, and the towering peaks on either side of the 17-kilometre long waterway provided guaranteed shelter and a welcome sanctuary for travellers.

The island was almost 52 kilometres from end to end and sitting, as it does, almost four degrees below the equator, it was blessed with a hot and humid climate and high rainfall.

When the 2/21st Battalion arrived at Ambon the men found a land of plenty. Local people, who numbered about 50 000, were friendly and keen to trade with the newcomers in the shops and markets. The lush, tropical terrain soon sucked the Australians into its exotic embrace. 'The very first impression was one of joy and the welcome we got from the children as they cried out, "Allo, Australie! Allo, Australie!" was a delight,' remembers Eddie Gilbert. 'We were so happy to be there, probably more so because we knew at last we were going to war.'[3]

Along the narrow coastline, where jungle-clad mountains towered more than 1000 metres over the scattered bayside settlements, life had barely changed in hundreds of years. The land provided adequate food and fresh water supplies were also plentiful.

The people, with their mix of Christian and Muslim religions, were welcoming and hospitable, though like their Dutch rulers they had a keen eye for business when it came to bartering. The spice route between Europe and the Far East had brought them into regular contact with other cultures and inhabitants from far distant lands. They knew of other worlds and civilisations, even if they had no personal experience of them.

Most of the population was centred on the main town, also called Ambon or Amboyna, about halfway along the southern peninsula, though there were countless smaller communities such as Paso, Eri, Hukurila, Hutumuri and Hitu-lama to the north. These names were largely ignored by Gull Force during the first few weeks, but would become frighteningly familiar in the weeks ahead.

Some of the men were sent to the northern peninsula, which boasted Ambon's most important defence facility: a runway. Laha airfield could only be accessed by boat or via a poorly maintained footpath, but it was the Dutch military's greatest asset. It was a pity the hardware lined up on the tarmac didn't inspire the same level of confidence. A couple of Brewster F2A Buffaloes, American fighter planes bought by the Dutch to supplement their own lack of aircraft, stood ready for action. They would prove to be a poor match for the Zeros and other enemy planes which would soon appear over the Moluccas. But that was still a few weeks away and the Australians had other things on their minds, not least their accommodation.

Tan Tui Barracks, just north-east of the main town, had been specially built for the diggers by the Dutch. While the water and power supplies had not yet been connected, the long wooden huts with their palm-thatched roofs were well furnished and positively five star compared with what they'd left behind in the Northern Territory. Some of the officers even had four-poster beds and a marble washstand in their room. They couldn't complain about the location, either. The barracks offered a staggeringly beautiful vista towards the bay. No wonder some of the men likened it to a holiday camp.

Only Lieutenant Colonel Roach and a few of his fellow officers fully appreciated the danger they faced. While the barracks were undoubtedly in a prime location, the Dutch had overlooked their vulnerability. Tan Tui was a sitting duck for enemy aircraft. But this was the least of Roach's worries. Still trying to convince Army HQ that Gull Force shouldn't be on Ambon in the first place, his fiery outbursts grow more defiant by the day. In one particularly stinging rebuke to Scott back in Melbourne, he wrote:

> I find it difficult to overcome a feeling of disgust and more than a little concern at the way in which we have seemingly been 'dumped' at this outpost position, in the first place without any instructions whatever . . . and in the second place with (so far) a flat refusal to consider any increase in fire power.
>
> Is the intention to continue the policy of allowing small forces inadequately equipped for their task, to be spread over a vast area, so that they can be defeated in detail?
>
> I submit that it would be far preferable, if the striking power does not actually exist for offensive action whilst these outposts are held, to 'cut the loss' and concentrate all available forces (including the American and the Dutch) further south for a decisive engagement.[4]

Roach, who was not enjoying the best of health at this stage, was clearly reaching the end of his tether. But he was not a lone voice.

The army sent out an intelligence officer to Ambon to see what all the fuss was about. Lieutenant Edgar Tanner's verdict was swift and forthright. If Gull Force was not evacuated smartish, there'd be a 'disaster', which would entail the 'futile sacrifice of valuable men'.[5]

At this point there were about 4500 troops on Ambon, including the 1150 Australians. The rest comprised Dutch officers and native soldiers, who were mainly of mixed European and Ambonese descent. Among them was a depot battalion of 300 Ambonese militia and another unit from the village of Bulam on the nearby island of Ceram (now known as Seram).

Although the Ambonese had the benefit of local knowledge there was doubt about their fighting fitness. Whether or not the indigenous army was ready for war was a matter of conjecture and only added to Roach's reservations about the defence of the island. If he'd known what the Japanese had up their sleeve he'd have been even more pessimistic.

––––––––––

To the north-west, Japanese forces were already well established on the Malay peninsula after landing just over the border in southern Thailand and further south at Khota Bharu, which fell to the Japanese on 9 December. Soon enemy aircraft were dropping bombs over 'impregnable' Singapore, the city being well within range of the bombers departing from their base in Saigon. Since their attack on Pearl Harbor the Japanese had moved with great speed through a large swathe of the Far East. In the Philippines, American naval forces had been destroyed and those that survived had withdrawn south to the Dutch East Indies. It seemed a safe haven, but the Japanese had other plans.

Major General Takeo Ito was a commander in the Japanese 38th Infantry Division and later assumed command of the 114th

Infantry Division. In December 1941 he was adding the final touches to Operation Ambon and Timor. He drew his troops from the 38th Infantry Division, who had proved themselves in the fight for Hong Kong, and the battle-tested 228th Infantry Regiment, with their artillery, engineer, transport and other supporting units. The Eastern Detachment, as it was now known, constituted a formidable strike force comprising 5300 men, 110 vehicles and 400 horses.

As a staff officer, Lieutenant Colonel Susumu Tozuka was privy to his government's grand strategy for the Moluccas and the surrounding region and was in no doubt about the ultimate goal, writing:

> The immediate purpose of the Ambon and Timor oper-
> ations was to cut the lines of communications between
> Australia and Java, isolate the latter and facilitate the
> invasion of Java. The ultimate purpose was to seize
> air and naval bases there and to form a defence line
> against an anticipated enemy counter-offensive from the
> Darwin area.[6]

The Eastern Detachment left Hong Kong for the voyage south on 12 January 1942. The initial destination of the five-vessel fleet was Davao, at the southern end of the Philippines. This was to be their assembly point. There they formulated their plan for the invasion of Ambon and on 27 January set sail for Menado on the island of Celebes (now known as Sulawesi), to the east of Borneo. Here the invasion force was augmented by two more ships carrying 579 officers and men who made up the 1st Kure Special Naval Landing Force.

The Kure unit, named after its base near Hiroshima, was a highly trained force renowned for its reluctance to surrender. When out of ammunition, troops resorted to fighting with their swords and often experienced heavy casualties. These men did not take prisoners. The Japanese clearly meant business.[7] Ultimately the total tonnage of the Japanese convoy would be sufficient to hold 30 000 men.

The idea was to mount two simultaneous landings on Ambon, one in the south and the other in the north, in the early hours of 31 January. The biggest operation would be at the end of the southern peninsula, where there was a neck of land about 1.5 kilometres wide and the Allies were believed to have comparatively light defences. This would be carried out by major assault elements of the Eastern Detachment, less one company. Their mission would be to head north as quickly as possible and seize the city of Ambon.

The northern landing was allotted to the 1st Kure Special Naval Landing Force, assisted by the 10th Company of the 3rd Battalion, 228th Infantry Regiment. Most of these men were experienced at landing in difficult conditions and the northern end of the island would certainly test their skills. They were to come ashore east of Wakal from an anchorage near the isolated community of Hitu-lama. As an invasion force these men were highly trained killers. There was no ambiguity in the assault troops' orders: contact and destroy the enemy.[8]

While the Japanese invasion strategy was being put together, the Australian officers on Ambon continued to wonder what they were doing there. Fundamental to Roach's concern was the apparent lack of any formal instructions. Brigadier Lind, who commanded 23rd Brigade and had earlier expressed his reservations about the Ambon mission, confirmed that they'd received no orders for the 2/21st and 2/40th Battalions.[9]

Without a clear brief from Army HQ, Gull Force was in a muddle. And that didn't help relations with the Dutch, who were officially in control of the island. Publicly Roach and Lieutenant Colonel J. R. L. Kapitz, Commander of the Royal Netherlands East Indies Army, presented a united front, but behind the scenes there were differences over defence measures. Eventually the two sides made their own plans, the Dutch citing language difficulties between the Australians and local soldiers.

While Kapitz could boast of an impressive armoury dotted about the island, his air and naval infrastructure was hopelessly inadequate. In addition to the two Brewster Buffalo fighters in service, there were several Catalina flying boats based in Binnen Bay, at the northerly end of the harbour. They represented easy pickings for the might of the Japanese air force. As for the Dutch navy, Kapitz had two armed motorboats at his disposal – hardly a match for the enemy's fleet.

For some time the RAAF had been providing a vital air link between Ambon and Australia, with two flights of Lockheed Hudsons, the American-built light bomber and reconnaissance aircraft which operated out of Darwin. But ground support for these planes in Ambon had dwindled, prompting one Australian air force officer to complain that stocks of ammunition and fuel were quite inadequate, maintenance facilities were negligible and dispersal for aircraft at Laha was very poor.

Roach's decision to go his own way when it came to defending the island was not helped by the fact that Kapitz was less than forthcoming about his own resources and deployment of men. In one glaring example of unnecessary secrecy, Roach was completely unaware of two 6-inch coastal guns the Dutch had hidden away in bunkers behind the town of Paso, overlooking Baguala Bay, near the isthmus connecting the peninsulas. Language problems were one thing, but obfuscation at such a crucial stage of war preparation was unpardonable. Kapitz and his counterparts were not endearing themselves to the diggers.[10]

Over and above these irritations there was the question of numbers. Roach had grave doubts about the Dutch being able to man all the posts and defences allotted to them. The basic strategy involved the Dutch protecting Ambon town and Paso at the northerly end of the Laitimor Peninsula, while the Australians were positioned in both the east and the west of the island, with a scattering of Dutch units in between. Ambon is a mountainous, rugged and jungle-clad island, which posed problems for both would-be invaders and those who were committed to repel them.

But how could it be properly defended when they didn't have sufficient men, tools or supplies?

Roach continued to pester Army HQ for reinforcements, more arms and extra food. 'Present combined army forces inadequate hold vital localities more than one day or two against determined attack from more than one direction simultaneously,' he warned. His demands included two troops of field and two of anti-tank artillery, six mortars, four medium machine guns, bush nets and medical equipment, as well as anti-tank guns.

The following day's reply from Deputy Chief of Staff Major General Sydney Rowell did not inspire confidence. 'Additional units you ask for not, repeat not, available. Your task in co-operation with local Dutch forces is to put up the best defence possible with resources you have at your disposal.'

Throughout this period of rising tension, the Japanese added to the psychological stress by launching their first air raids on the night of 6/7 January. Seven Japanese flying boats dropped 33 bombs over the island, damaging two Hudsons and a Buffalo in the process. Three native civilians were killed, but there were no military casualties. The pressure was on.[11]

Over the next few weeks Tom Pledger recorded thirteen air raids and 127 alarms. They worked from dawn until dusk, filling sandbags, digging holes and building sleeping huts. 'We dug our shell slits under our beds so we could be into them at the first warning,' he recalls. Despite the mounting Japanese threat, Tom and his mates remained upbeat, saving their daily ration of one bottle of beer to celebrate their survival after an air raid and dining on exotic fruits and suckling pig. 'We lived like lords,' he confides.

In the second week of January as the air raids intensified, Roach stepped up the pressure on Army HQ by claiming that a Japanese invasion of the island was imminent and that 'prospects are gloomy'. He suggested he fly to Darwin to discuss what they should do.

At the same time Area Combined Headquarters, stationed at Halong, the seaplane base in Ambon's Binnen Bay, radioed an urgent message to Melbourne, pointing out that Japanese air bases were now established some 580 kilometres away. 'Immediate reinforcements by fighters and dive bombers' were required. 'Only token resistance possible with present unsuitable aircraft against carrier-borne force,' it added.[12]

Relations between those on the ground in Ambon and their superiors safely cosseted away in army bunkers on mainland Australia were approaching crisis point. Something had to give.

On 13 January Lieutenant Colonel Roach sent a desperate signal to Army HQ in Melbourne alerting them to the fact that because of the overwhelming presence of enemy forces now gathered at Menado in north Celebes, Gull Force wouldn't be able to hold out for more than a day in the event of a Japanese attack. Given that his request for more manpower and arms had been ignored, he urged the immediate evacuation of the combined force.

It was the first time the E word had been mentioned and it clearly didn't please the powers that be. There would be no evacuation and Roach's messages should 'cease at once', he was warned by headquarters. The reason? 'Your staunch defence will have important effect . . . in regard future Australian Dutch cooperation,' he was advised.

Roach had shown his true colours, the top brass concluded. Where was the man's courage, his spunk, his sense of duty, they blustered? There was only one option. He had to be replaced.

Even the British Commander-in-Chief, Field Marshal Archibald Wavell, who was effectively in control of operations in the Dutch East Indies, was consulted on the matter. His response was not unexpected.

So far as I can judge position at Ambon not critical and
in any case I am opposed to handing out important
objectives to enemy without making them fight for it.
Quite appreciate feelings of lonely garrison but I am sure

Australians will put up stout fight whatever happens. No doubt it is wise to change commander.[13]

It amounted to a death sentence for Gull Force and to Roach's military career. The next day he received a signal informing him that Lieutenant Colonel William Scott would take over command. Scott arrived on the night of 16 January and Roach took the return flight back to Darwin.

Despite his age, and with little or no knowledge of Ambon or the men of the 2/21st, 53-year-old Scott had successfully volunteered himself as the new commander of Gull Force. It would prove to be one of the most foolish and ill-advised appointments ever rubberstamped by the Australian military.

Scott, who had carefully undermined Roach by leaking some of his desperate messages to Rowell, was no fool but was clearly unfit for the job, both physically and emotionally. In later years some would even question his sanity, but in January 1942 he provided a convenient foil. By supporting Sturdee and the rest of Army HQ, he could be relied upon to divert attention away from their ill-fated strategy. Privately, they must have been relieved that someone was prepared to volunteer for such a suicidal mission. The fact that he was obviously the wrong man for the job didn't enter into it.

When Scott took over on Ambon in the middle of January 1942, the impact on morale was devastating. 'Aloof and with-drawn', he impressed few of the 2/21st's officers and none of the men, who had respected Roach as one of their own and were angered to hear of his recall.[14]

Not surprisingly, the atmosphere between the two men during the handover was cool and unproductive. Scott acknowledged that there was little opportunity for discussion during the seven hours before Roach's 5 a.m. flight back to Australia. 'I found myself in command of a force of officers and men who were all entirely unknown to me,' he admitted. The same applied to his knowledge of the island. Unlike Roach, who had made several reconnaissance visits to Ambon before taking up command there, Lieutenant Colonel Scott knew zilch about the geography and had no personal experience of the challenges posed.

However, he didn't have to wait long to see the results of enemy action. In the first 24 hours of his arrival a number of Hudsons were destroyed on the ground in a daylight raid by 36 Japanese aircraft, and four members of the 2/21st, two riflemen and two signallers, were killed.[15] Both the Dutch and the Australians appeared to have been taken by surprise. Two Dutch Bofors, the only anti-aircraft guns on the island, achieved disappointing results. And Australian attempts to defend planes on the tarmac at Laha hadn't fared much better.

One issue Scott was quick to identify was the wide distribution of troops, who were scattered across the island in relatively small numbers. An Australian rifle section had been sent to an outpost position at Latuhalat, near the tip of the southern peninsula, in the hope of hampering any Japanese attempt to land there.

Lieutenant Ralph Godfrey, who was in charge of a machine gun platoon, had been told to keep a watch on the entrance to Ambon Bay. 'The Dutch expected the Japanese to attack through the harbour mouth, but they didn't. They came through the back door instead.' Ralph's machine gun platoon was in the wrong place. There would be no exchange of gunfire here.[16]

Eddie Gilbert's A Company, under the command of Major Westley, was placed at Eri on the bayside of the southern peninsula. 'We were allocated a position on a hill-top and were quickly befriended by an Ambonese family who kept us supplied with fresh fruit in exchange for our empty biscuit tins.' The family showed them how to erect a bamboo shelter with a roof made out of sago palm leaves to keep out the rain. The locals' friendly nature impressed Eddie and his mates, but how long would it last? Could the indigenous population be relied on if events turned nasty?

Further north at Cape Batuanjut, a platoon from Lieutenant William Chaplin's B Company stood ready for an offensive from land or water.

Captain Clive Newnham's D Company occupied a 1000-metre line which fell away sharply from Mount Nona to the beach at Amahusu on the western side of the Laitimor Peninsula. Down on the coast road overlooking Ambon Bay, loaded transport trucks stood by to move south or north depending on the direction taken by invading forces. Newnham also gained permission to place a pioneer platoon led by Lieutenant William Jinkins up on the Nona plateau, to ward off enemy troops who tried to occupy the high point and thereby gain a military advantage over the Australians based further down the hill.

It was C Company, under Major Mark Newbury, that drew the short straw, though nobody could foresee the outcome at the time. Together with units from B Company under the command of Captain Douglas Perry, they would defend Laha airfield on the Hitu Peninsula, on the other side of the bay. And as well as the Aussies there were Dutch troops.

Everyone knew this was a prime target with little opportunity for escape in the event of sustained bombardment. Behind the aerodrome was dense jungle and mountainous terrain. There were no roads and only a narrow footpath back to Paso, the nearest town, some 20 kilometres away. They could forget about a waterborne escape too. With the harbourmaster's two launches the only Allied maritime presence on the island, they were hardly a match for the might of the Japanese Imperial Navy.

Assuming that the main enemy attack would come from the east through Baguala Bay, the Dutch decided to station their principal forces around Paso, on the isthmus. Another Dutch company and a mortar unit were deployed at Hitu-lama on the far north coast of the Hitu Peninsula, to delay any thrust towards Paso from that direction.

A second company joined the Australians at Eri, although the Laitimor Peninsula was so steep and inhospitable that the Dutch believed the Japanese would be mad to attempt a landing there. The same thinking applied to the southern side of the peninsula, where, according to Kapitz, it would be so difficult to land that there was no point in engaging troops to defend it.

How wrong he was.

The gravity of the situation facing Gull Force and the Dutch would emerge on Australia Day, 1942. An RAAF reconnaissance plane from 13 Squadron sighted a fleet of Japanese warships off the north-east coast of Celebes, to the north-west of Ambon. The convoy included thirteen transport vessels, a heavy cruiser, three light cruisers and five destroyers. There were 22 ships in all, and they were heading in a south-easterly direction. There could be only one conclusion.

Alarmed at the implications for the base at Laha, the RAAF ordered the evacuation of their crews on Ambon, as well as the few remaining Hudsons.

A couple of days later Lieutenant Jinkins was able to provide incontrovertible proof of Japanese intentions. High up on the plateau of Mount Nona he witnessed the approaching Japanese fleet – only now it was even bigger than previously reported, with no fewer than seventeen warships and eleven transports.

Jinkins, not a man to panic, calmly picked up the phone to Area Command HQ and told them what he had seen for himself. The fleet was sitting about 16 kilometres offshore but from his position, nearly 1000 metres above sea level, the convoy's size and position was unmistakable.

The official response from HQ is not known but once word got out, there must have been more than a collective swallow. Kapitz and his cronies had got it wrong. Far from avoiding the southern peninsula's coast, that was precisely where the Japanese were preparing to come ashore.

Confirmation of their intentions came at dawn on 1 February when Lieutenant Jinkins and his platoon observed enemy troops in motorised landing craft at Hukurila. It was a similar story several kilometres up the coast at Hutumuri. But it was Private Walter Hicks who got the shock of his life while out mapping the same morning near Eri. He walked down to the beach to wash his face in a pool of water which he'd dug out of the sand. 'When I looked up, I couldn't believe my eyes. There were about ten Japanese transport ships sailing backwards and forwards across the heads and, beyond them, cruisers. I thought, Where the hell did they come from?'

Walter ran up the hill to raise the alarm. He would never forget the look on his mates' faces as they focused their eyes on the horizon. Among the cries of exclamation, Hicks insists he heard an officer shout, 'Oh my God, we're dead!'

'I replied, "We're not dead yet, but we soon will be."'[17]

The game was up. Let the battle commence.

4

SURRENDER

AМВОN WAS UNDER siege. Len Roach's warnings to Army HQ during the latter months of 1941 were about to assume a grim reality. Gull Force didn't have a hope in hell of repelling such a determined Japanese onslaught, and the Dutch, whose officer class was plagued by internal friction, couldn't rely on its local troops for support either. It wasn't long before many of the indigenous soldiers cast off their uniforms and returned to their villages to disappear into the native population.

The 2/21st could only wait. If there was trepidation among the men in their lonely outpost, no one was admitting it. Not publicly, anyway. In truth, there was little time to worry. Within hours of landing on the southern coast of the Laitimor Peninsula thousands of Japanese soldiers were pouring ashore and making their way across overland trails towards Ambon city and Paso, which had become the Dutch command centre.

In a hint at how the enemy's arrival would influence native loyalties, some locals guided the Japanese along the steep and winding paths to the coast road overlooking Ambon Bay.

The invasion was recorded in breathless detail by the *Nippon Times*. 'The Special Naval Landing party's human bullet battle on the Island of Amboyna is a record of blasting through forbidding mountains, thickly-woven jungles and impassable roads, of literally going over the bodies of dead comrades and hacking with blood and death into the midst of the enemy,' reported Genichi Yamamoto of the Navy Press Corp. It made for powerful reading back home and while the prose was colourful, it wasn't altogether untrue.

The initial attack, as outlined by Lieutenant Colonel Susumu Tozuka, involved four ships: the *Yamaura*, the *Africa*, the *Zenyo* and *Miike*. They entered the anchorage at the south-eastern tip of the Laitimor Peninsula at precisely 0100 on 31 January and by 0250 all landings were complete.

On stepping ashore, the 1st, 2nd and 3rd Battalions fanned out. The 1st moved to the southern sector, where the Australians were entrenched; the 3rd cut through the centre of the peninsula in a bid to split the Dutch and Australian forces; and the 2nd Battalion advanced north-west towards the Dutch-defended neck, or isthmus, between the peninsulas.

The Japanese rate of advance was extraordinary, given the distance and the rugged terrain. It was as though they glided through the dense jungle and over mountain slopes like winged beasts. By dusk an assault unit converged on Ambon city, driving a wedge between the Australian army, now trapped in the south of the peninsula, and most of the Dutch, who were sealed off to the north.

Meanwhile, on the other side of the island at Hitu-lama, the northern invasion was underway. It was, as Yamamoto testifies, 'A battle which took such heroism as to make the gods weep.' Not one to ignore the potential for sensation, he told how the moon was 'suddenly blotted out by thick curtains of heavy clouds and the unit pointing at the direction of the island of Amboyna was enveloped in the indigo dark covering the sea. The sudden darkness could only be called aid from heaven.'

It was 1.20 a.m. Craft from the 1st Kure Special Naval Landing Force containing some 850 men shot across the Bay of Hitu and onto the beach at Hitu-lama. 'Suddenly realizing that it was a surprise raid the enemy made up of about 300 began to fire blindly and hysterically with machine guns and trench mortars, but our landing party quickly cut away barbed wire entanglements made in the water and secured part of the beach,' said the *Nippon Times*.

There was no stopping the Japanese, or Genichi Yamamoto. He continued:

> Crawling across the beach and into the enemy's pill box positions, the first charge scattered the enemy. The village of Hitu-lama was taken without much effort. But the fighting had only just begun.
>
> Immediately plunging into the jungle and smashing the pill boxes holding the enemy at every point, the Japanese forces covered more than 30 kilometres of extremely difficult territory and at 4.30 p.m. engaged the enemy's main strength holding the Laha airfield.

To get there, reported Yamamoto, they'd 'crawled up steep cliffs, pounded through dark jungles and whirled like the wind through the village of Hasale'.[1]

How had the marines achieved so much in such a comparatively short time? The fault, it seemed, lay with Kapitz, whose decision to withdraw most of his men from Hitu-lama to reinforce Paso left the north coast hideously exposed. Only a few Dutch platoons remained to delay the Japanese, but the defending infantry and machine gunners were no match for the enemy as they swarmed ashore. As the Dutch retreated they had no time – or forgot – to blow up road bridges while hurrying back to Paso. This allowed the enemy landing force to make a quick and decisive thrust across the Hitu Peninsula towards Laha and Baguala Bay.

Back on the top of Mount Nona, Ambon's highest point, a new drama was unfolding. As Captain Newnham had anticipated, Japanese troops had identified the lofty plateau as a key observation point, offering them uninterrupted views towards Eri in the south and Ambon town to the north. Bill Jinkins's platoon now found itself defending this prized location from a horde of advancing Japanese. Backed by another platoon under the command of Lieutenant Sam Anderson, the two units opened fire on the enemy, who numbered about 300.

Anderson was among the first casualties. He was hit by a hand grenade, which badly injured his leg. As blood poured from his wounds, he turned to his senior NCO and admitted he was buggered. 'Go back and do your best for the platoon,' he ordered the corporal, who returned to the men and led them back down the line.

In the fear and confusion of battle, Jinkins's platoon wasn't sure where the next attack would come from. Somehow the enemy had got within 30 metres of them without being challenged, but their advantage was not to last. Foolishly, they tried to deceive the Australians by loudly proclaiming that they were Ambonese, but the ruse failed. Having blown their cover with a burst of gunfire which killed Sergeant Bruce Kay, the Japanese found themselves under attack from Jinkins's men, who replied with grenades and rapid fire sub-machine guns.[2]

Soon the Japanese were driven back, yelling loudly under the hail of bullets and mortar fire, but not before Lance Corporal Bill Tibbett was hit in the backside. 'They obviously got a great fright. They were yelling out like stuck pigs as we drove them down to the bottom of the hill,' he recalls.

Evidence of their speedy retreat was littered across the grassy slope. Jinkins couldn't resist picking up a full kit and rifle which had been abandoned halfway down. It was a small but significant trophy.

Pleased he had the enemy on the run, Jinkins turned to the fallen comrades who'd been wounded in the surprise attack. His immediate thoughts were for his fellow officer Lieutenant Anderson. Assuming that most of the Japanese would not understand English, he shouted his name. 'Anderson. Are you there?'

'Yes,' came the faint but reassuring reply. Anderson was alive, but he was in a critical condition.

'We'll come and get you,' Jinkins promised.

'No, leave me. Don't bother about me. I'm done for,' Anderson uttered in a stage whisper from about 30 metres away.

Jinkins was having none of it. He turned to the man on his right – Archie Buchanan was his name – and asked him if he would help to bring the injured officer back. The soldier didn't need asking twice. Within seconds the two had moved imperceptibly through the vegetation to reach Anderson's side.

'He was badly wounded behind the left knee and so weak from loss of blood that he fainted,' says Jinkins. Getting him out without being noticed was the challenge. The rest of Anderson's platoon had left the area and he needed medical attention urgently.

Suddenly a third man appeared, one Kenny Lawson, and helped Jinkins and Buchanan carry the gravely wounded officer back to their original position. It was an act of supreme courage, at great personal risk. Throughout Anderson's evacuation the rescue party came under heavy machine gun fire but miraculously survived unscathed.

As dawn approached the prospects looked even bleaker. Communications with headquarters were down and the enemy was attacking on two flanks. Even so, Jinkins's platoon was far from the point of surrender. They still had nearly 50 boxes of rifle grenades, although the platoon lacked manpower. With Bruce Kay dead from a bullet through the head and at least three other casualties, as well as six soldiers suffering from malaria, it was impossible to defend their position.

If they stayed there they'd be wiped out. Jinkins and his walking wounded needed to get out fast and a narrow cliff-top track seemed to be their only exit. Staggering single file along the lonely ledge there was momentary panic as a single blast rang out. Had they been spotted by a sniper? If so, they were sitting ducks. The truth was even harder to accept. Corporal Lindsay Mummery lay wounded from a grenade he'd thrown himself. The last thing the beleaguered platoon needed right now was an own goal.

Eventually they found an alternative position, about 100 feet below their previous outpost. It offered a temporary haven but Jinkins was acutely aware that time was running out. From his vantage point he saw a fleet of Japanese naval vessels in the bay, including two destroyers and a couple of cruisers. They occasionally shelled Eri at the southern end of the peninsula and across the harbour towards the aerodrome at Laha. To make matters worse, enemy aircraft were flying low on reconnaissance missions, identifying Australian and Dutch installations.

Jinkins was facing an undeniable truth. To have any hope of escape they needed to climb down the cliff face. But how could they manoeuvre Anderson's stretcher down such a steep incline? Lapsing in and out of consciousness, the injured officer again urged them to leave him behind. Jinkins asked for volunteers to carry him, but everyone agreed it was an impossible task.

It was Private Bill Wakeling and his mate Archie Buchanan who offered the solution. What about carrying Anderson through Japanese lines and asking permission to take him to hospital? It was a daring idea, but might be audacious enough to work, they reasoned.

The stretcher party made its way back to the platoon's old position – now occupied by some 500 Japanese troops – where much to Anderson's, Wakeling's and Buchanan's relief, they were allowed to pass through enemy lines. In a rare gesture of compassion two Japanese soldiers carried the stretcher on the final stage of its journey to Ambon hospital.

According to Jinkins's detailed account of the Mount Nona operation, nearly 24 hours had elapsed since the invasion began. It was 11.30 p.m. on 1 February and while he was pleased to have helped Anderson gain the medical attention he so desperately required, his platoon was still at war. Jinkins gathered together his dwindling patrol and set out for Amahusu, down on the coast overlooking the bay. Seeking shelter in a village along the way, he found it deserted apart from a lone native. The old man said the Japanese had reached Eri and most of the 2/21st Battalion were congregated at the tip of the southern peninsula. The news, if correct, did not bode well for Gull Force, but he was not convinced the fight was over. Lieutenant William Thomas Jinkins was determined to battle on.[3]

Back in the Dutch-held north of the island, Kapitz and his men were coming under severe pressure from the invading forces. Most of his own troops, who had retreated south from Hitu-lama, found themselves in unfamiliar territory. Paso, because of its position on the narrow neck of land linking the peninsulas, was seen as the cornerstone of the island's defences. Now the Dutch were faced with the previously unthinkable: evacuating Paso and moving their headquarters a few kilometres to the south-west at Nontetu, overlooking the old seaplane base in Binnen Bay.

This was military policy on the run and did little to instil confidence in Dutch strategy. To add to Kapitz's problems his native troops were rapidly losing their appetite for war. There was disillusion and even panic among the ranks. One senior Dutch officer branded them an 'indolent herd'.[4]

By now the Japanese who had landed at Hutumuri on the south-eastern coast of the Laitimor Peninsula were advancing steadily to the north via a track alongside Baguala Bay. This meant that Paso was under threat from both the north and south.

Kapitz didn't hang around. He chose the Nontetu option, where he hoped to bring a little order to his forces, which, quite frankly, were in a state of disarray. Here, details of Dutch intentions are shrouded in a fog of claim and counterclaim. There was talk of Kapitz ordering the flying of a white flag and other officers attempting to surrender to the Japanese. The enemy, however, was reluctant to accept the offer and the fighting continued. Dutch troops in the Paso area decided to adopt a 'wait-and-see' attitude but were soon overtaken by events. Dutch officers who returned to Paso found that resting troops had already been taken prisoner by the Japanese and the game was almost over.

Meanwhile Kapitz, now ensconced in the Lateri Battery, just outside Nontetu, was desperate for some shut-eye. After having got by on a few hours a day for the past week, he slumped into a corner and slept. When Lieutenant B. J. Huizing, Commander of the Dutch Reserve Corps, arrived at the battery later that night to enquire about his commander's whereabouts, a man raised his arm and muttered, 'Yes, that's me. What's the matter?'

'I said, "There's a Japanese officer who wants to talk to you, sir."

'Lieutenant Colonel Kapitz answered, "Well, let him come over here."'[5]

And so the end of Dutch rule on Ambon came not so much with a bang as a whimper, or in this case a yawn. Just a day after the Japanese launched their invasion of the island, the army of the Dutch East Indies had been beaten into submission.

In his official history of the battle, *The Japanese Thrust*, Lionel Wigmore reports that Kapitz was under the impression that the situation was worse than it was and that's why he put up the white flag. 'He considered that they had been intimidated by the bold action of small numbers of Japanese who had penetrated the lines and was ashamed that fighting had been given up so soon.'[6]

———

Private Eddie Gilbert and his five mates in B Company's mortar detachment were sitting on top of a ridge above the village of Eri towards the end of the southern peninsula when they spotted a low-flying enemy aircraft. They tried to hide but the vegetation was so sparse that their position was obvious. 'The Japs had complete control of the skies above and around Ambon but they showed little interest in us because their main thrust was towards the seaplane base and the township,' he recorded.[7]

At the other end of the army chain of command, Lieutenant Colonel William Scott was now three weeks into his new posting and must have been wondering whether Roach, his predecessor, had been right in his pessimistic assessment of Gull Force's chances. He knew they were in trouble, but remained unaware of the Dutch surrender.

Where was Kapitz? Scott tried to phone him without success and in an act of desperation sent a despatch rider to Paso. 'I don't know your HQ location. I have no information as to the position. I have no instructions,' he wrote. The reply, when it came, revealed nothing of consequence.

Thank God for Lieutenant George Russell. The 25-year-old Toorak boy, who was liaison officer at Dutch Headquarters, saw Kapitz disappearing down the road around the same time some Japanese soldiers appeared. 'I only had my batman with me and we were now quite alone,' said Russell. The quick-thinking young officer thought he'd better destroy all the maps and papers which, in the rush to save their arses, the Dutch had left intact. Lieutenant Russell and his batman then got into a truck and drove to Amahusu, where he informed Scott that Ambon town had been abandoned by the Dutch. It was final confirmation of what the CO had feared.

Immediately the decision was made to move the Australian HQ further south to Eri, while Captain Turner, second in command of Major Westley's B Company, would endeavour to hold the fort at Kudamati, just south of Ambon town. Scott telephoned Captain Newnham, whose men had been forced to beat a hasty retreat from Mount Nona. He suggested they also fall back to Eri, 'where the unit could make a stand for two or three days'. Newnham and his fellow officers did not need convincing and started moving south within the hour.

For all his faults, nobody could accuse Scott of being a pessimist. Unwavering in his faith, he was convinced air or naval support would arrive from Australia by the next day. Optimist? Or just plain stupid? His men would be left in little doubt by war's end.

What was becoming clear was the sheer hopelessness of their situation. As most of the 2/21st Battalion congregated south of the Amahusu line, the Japanese knew it was only a matter of days before the Australians capitulated. After all, they had nowhere to go. With the southern tip of the Laitimor Peninsula continually pounded by air and naval forces, the Japanese could afford to bide their time. Why would they risk their own men's lives by pushing further south to Eri?

The Japanese were already causing enough damage, as Walter Hicks could testify. He was taking a message to an officer when caught in the open by an enemy seaplane. 'The plane was flying down the harbour and he must have spotted me.' Instinctively Walter remembered the advice of his old uncle, who used to tell him, 'If you're ever caught in the open by an enemy aircraft, never run away from it.' 'He said if you ran towards the plane you're diminishing the time they can fire at you. You can see where the bullets are landing, kicking up the dirt or the mud, and you can jump to one side or the other to avoid them.'

His uncle's tip was to save Walter's life, though he didn't escape uninjured. The aircraft's bullets hit some coral and the casing from the cartridge chipped his leg. In fact, he hardly noticed the wound at first, until someone said to him, 'Yer leg's bleeding, Hicksy.'[8]

If Walter was playing the plucky digger, others were showing genuine fear. According to Major Ian Macrae, the battalion's second in command, there were several cases of hysteria and desertion as morale began to crumble. But this did not reflect the mood of most of the men. In Joan Beaumont's history of Gull Force, she writes, 'In his [Macrae's] opinion, the majority of the battalion was still willing to fight and felt there had been "too much sitting down and taking it".'

Was this a more accurate picture of the Gull Force character than the battalion condemned for lack of discipline in Darwin? Or, as Beaumont noted, did this confirm the Anzac legend, which suggested that the Australian digger might be undisciplined in camp but was courageous in battle? She cites Lieutenant Ron Green, in command of 17 Platoon, who offered his men the opportunity to take part in a last, almost certainly suicidal raid on Ambon. Perhaps surprisingly, they agreed to the idea without exception. Certainly all the evidence and eyewitness accounts of the fighting over the next few days reinforce the view that Gull Force didn't give up without a struggle.

One man who saw it with his own eyes was Philip Miskin, then a 23-year-old captain in charge of E Echelon at Battalion HQ. He was born in Wales but emigrated to Australia in 1936. Miskin was in charge of transport drivers, signallers and others unkindly dismissed as the odds and sods of the battalion. They were gathered in a coconut grove at Kudamati in the foothills of Mount Nona, just outside Ambon town.

Just below them was a cemetery, which would come in handy for hiding ammunition. Whitewashing the ammunition cases, Miskin planted them among the Christian, Muslim and Chinese graves so they wouldn't be noticed. The Welshman's cunning worked a treat. From the air, the caches of weapons looked like tombstones.

From its vantage point overlooking the bay, B Echelon had a grandstand view of the Japanese navy, which was now steaming through the heads. Soon enemy vessels began pounding Australian defences at point blank range. Miskin and his men, who were usually at the rear of the battalion, now found themselves in the front line, barely 500 metres from the billowing smoke of Japanese naval guns. A colourful post-war account of the clash that followed appeared in *People Magazine*.

The odds and ends of B Echelon fought back magnificently under the terrible pounding of the naval barrage. They swept the decks of the warships with rifle, machine gun and mortar fire. But the exchange was unequal. In return for .303 and .5 inch bullets and three inch mortar bombs they got 4 and 6 inch shells.

Even so, one of the unit's Brownings made life so uncomfortable for a Japanese minesweeper that it was forced to manoeuvre its way crab-like out of the machine gun's range. In doing so the vessel hit a mine and exploded, hurling a column of smoke and debris 400 metres into the air. Most of the hundred-strong crew died in the blast, much to the delight of Alex Hawkins, who'd fired the fatal round and claimed it as a 'kill'. Miskin promised to give him the Browning after the war as a prize but the gunner didn't live to collect his trophy.

The sinking of the Japanese warship would have other, even more dreadful consequences, which would resonate long after the war. They didn't know it then, but Hawkins' 'kill' would result in many more deaths in the weeks to come.

Come dusk, the entire sky was illuminated by the glow from oil storage tanks, deliberately blown up by Dutch and Australian engineers. By now the enemy was within a stone's throw of its objective. A Japanese column penetrated the town from the coast, convinced that the shelling had wiped out all opposition. Soon an entire battalion was swarming ashore.

People Magazine's prose might err on the sensational but it captured the scene in every gruesome detail.

> The Japs loosed a few rounds in the direction of the
> Australian positions and, drawing no reply, slung their
> arms and began to march up the hill in column of route.
> Miskin let them get within point-blank range then gave
> the order to fire.
>   The sudden hail of bullets and mortar bombs caught
> the Japs by surprise. They ran like rabbits back to the
> boats.

B Echelon's advantage did not continue for long. Later they found themselves being attacked from the east, this time by a Japanese contingent which had scaled a hill overlooking Miskin's unit. From there they were able to fire down into the Australian slit trenches.

There was a small Dutch hospital nearby and as the shooting continued an ambulance with a large red cross on the side drove up. Observing the articles of war, Miskin called a ceasefire.

Unfortunately, the Japanese didn't share his concern and seconds later fired off their mortar bombs in B Echelon's direction. Incensed by the Japanese lack of honour in such matters, Miskin organised a fighting patrol to take the mortar and silence those responsible. A young engineer named Campbell led the party who set off after nightfall to kill the Japanese and destroy the mortar. It was a brave act carried out with military precision and, thankfully, without the loss of Australian blood.

There were countless stories of valour that day but few eclipse the legendary example of Bill Doolan, whose determination to fight on regardless would become part of battalion and Ambonese folklore.

Along with some of his mates, Doolan, a transport driver, was a member of a reconnaissance patrol which was sent towards enemy lines under Sergeant Jack O'Brien. The volunteers had devised a daring plan to motor into town with such boldness that their sheer effrontery would make the enemy assume they were not a threat. Amazingly, their cheek worked.

Assuming the truck was one of their own, the Japanese waved the vehicle through to the enemy's newly established HQ. At which point the Australians tossed some grenades out of the truck and sprayed the enemy with a volley of gunfire, before jumping out and shooting their way back to base. It was an extraordinarily courageous and near-suicidal act of bravery, but it didn't end there.

Doolan, whose Irish ancestry had instilled in him the love of a good fight, offered to stay behind to guarantee the party's successful withdrawal. It didn't surprise those who knew him well. The Werribee lad's favourite phrase was: 'Give me a yard of bike chain and I'll do the ****ers over.'

While the exact details of what happened next may have been embellished over time, Doolan's heroic last stand was witnessed by his Ambonese wash boy, who told how the lone gunman turned on his pursuers and kept them at bay for several minutes with his machine gun, bayonet and grenades. Some said that 80 Japanese infantry were killed or badly injured as Doolan, perched in a tree, opened fire on them. By the time he fell dead there were reportedly two rings of Japanese bodies at his feet.

Doolan's remains lay under the tree until after the surrender. It was Lieutenant Denis Smith, leader of the transport unit at Kudamati, who found him a few days later. 'His body was riddled with bullets and his head practically severed by what appears to be bursts of machine gun fire at short range,' Smith reported.

The Japanese agreed that he could be buried beneath the tree where he had fallen, his grave marked by a simple wooden cross which was inscribed by those whose lives he had helped to save. In the years that followed, Doolan's grave became something of a shrine among Australian POWs, who sang a ballad in his memory whenever they passed it. Hardly a day went by when the native population did not deliver fresh flowers to the site.[9]

In the fierce fighting enveloping Ambon town and neighbouring Kudamati there was no time to dwell on another battle going on over the other side of the bay at Laha. Japanese warships were pounding the aerodrome on the Hitu Peninsula, backed up by fighter planes which had been strafing the airfield and the immediate hinterland.

This was where nearly 300 men from B and C Companies, as well as some Dutch, were trying to defend what had become Ambon's only link with the outside world. The runway was badly damaged but psychologically the airfield played a critical role. Once the runway was captured, the Allies could forget about escaping by air. They'd be prisoners of war and it was that prospect that fuelled B and C Companies' resolve. They were determined to resist the Japanese advance, which by now was making steady progress across the Hitu Peninsula.

It took the marines who landed at Hitu-lama in the north in the early hours of the morning barely fifteen hours to cover the 30 kilometres to Hoenot, overlooking Ambon Bay and ear-splittingly close to the artillery positions at Laha. Then came the rain. A torrential tropical downpour put a temporary halt to the advancing Japanese, who were not accustomed to such weather.

Genichi Yamamoto described overflowing rivers and rivulets, and tracks which were impassable. 'The way beyond was absolutely roadless and blocked by jungles and swamps,' he reported.

Tired and hungry, the marines pushed on through 'thigh deep mud and swirling rivers', but they were obliged to leave behind their armoured cars and cannon. Instead they relied on rifles and machine guns as they closed in on their target.

Most of the Australians had abandoned the airfield and were seeking refuge in the hinterland, waiting for the enemy beneath the jungle canopy or hidden amid the mangroves. Others took up position in pill boxes which were lined in rows four and five deep along the Laha riverbank and the hill overlooking the airfield. Large-calibre cannon and trench mortars were also aimed in the enemy's direction. They had the firepower but did they have the manpower?

Already bombarded from the air and from the sea, the men charged with defending Laha were about to face a land-based assault and were determined to give it their best shot.

Even Yamamoto conceded that the Japanese were under pressure and suffering heavy casualties.

At the slightest rustle of grass or the click of metal, enemy machine gun bullets would come flying like hail. Men hit by some of these bullets did not dare groan or cry, 'Long live his Imperial Majesty', lest the attacker should be located by the enemy, in which case the whole death band would perish in sight of their goal.

Inch by inch the members of the death band wormed forward, their bodies immersed in mud. At 2 a.m. they succeeded in cutting the barbed wire entanglements and clearing the way for the attack.

At once they rushed forward and captured the pill boxes . . . As morning dawned they dashed into the midst of the enemy situated in the concavity before the aerodrome. Slashing and bayoneting, they pursued the scattered enemy and piled dead on dead.

The 1st Kure Special Naval Landing Force, now almost certainly supplemented by other Japanese troops who had made the journey along the coastal track from Paso, were clearly meeting intense resistance. A plan was hatched to find another way through the Australian defences by infiltrating the jungle hinterland and attacking the airfield from the north.

At the same time – and seemingly out of thin air – a dozen tanks and armoured cars appeared which Gull Force had held in reserve. Now they were to be mobilised against the first wave of Japanese troops who attempted to take Laha. Even allowing for Yamamoto's deeply patriotic turn of phrase, the last-ditch stand by the Australians did not appear to delay the Japanese for long. 'Nothing daunted, they skipped through the ring of steel and thrust deep into the enemy encampment,' he writes.

But it was Chief Warrant Officer Shuzo Nagato and his men who were to achieve hero status in the *Nippon Times* as they rushed the tank group, firing their revolvers and 'causing them to swerve and topple over'. However, Gull Force replied with trench mortar shells, which hit their target. By the close of CWO Nagato's daring attack, the officer and all his men lay dead.[10]

The Japanese were struggling in the face of the intense response from B and C Companies. One of the Kure marines, Takada Haruo, was attached to a party which reconnoitred the hills behind Laha and later assisted some of his wounded comrades back to the nearby village of Soewakodo. In the early hours of 2 February, Japanese forces launched another attack on the Allied position at Laha. 'Strong resistance was encountered and Jap losses were heavy,' Takada admitted.

Around the same time, Major Ian McBride and his platoon were sent to guard the north-east approach to the airfield. Aware of a likely penetration by enemy soldiers from the north, McBride's hunch paid off. The Japanese gave themselves away by talking too loudly and soon found themselves engaged in a fierce confrontation with the Australians. Armed with bayonets, mortars and automatic weapons, the two sides even resorted to hand-to-hand fighting before the day was done.

Until now, many members of Gull Force had encountered little or no action and had certainly not experienced man-to-man combat. Now they faced the harsh reality of war, where physical strength could be as important as the thrust of steel into human flesh or a bullet in the guts. As they struggled to defend themselves, McBride called for reinforcements. More men were sent over from C Company to help close the gap which had been created and the wounded withdrew to have their injuries treated.

It was a bitterly fought engagement which might have ended far worse for the Australians were it not for the enemy's perceived shortcomings. As McBride observed afterwards, the Japanese 'failed to make use of the natural cover afforded them and seemed to be poorly trained in night fighting'. Also, put bluntly, they had no staying power. 'In individual fighting the enemy troops were no match for our men and did not display any fortitude when wounded,' McBride added.[11]

It wasn't until the following day that the sound of battle was replaced by an eerie silence. At precisely 2.30 p.m. all gunfire in the Laha area ceased. What happened next relies heavily on the Japanese interpretation of events, because the Australians involved did not survive to tell the story.

Major Newbury, who was effectively in overall charge of C Company and the other units from B Company, reportedly approached the Japanese, carrying a white flag. According to Takada Haruo, he met the major and about ten other men as they made their way to the nearby village of Soewakodo. They said they were on a surrender mission but did not have the power to negotiate on behalf of the Dutch or native troops.

The next day Takada and some of his men, now also holding a white flag, made their way down to the Laha battlefield and called out to the Australians to send a representative if they were prepared to surrender.

There was no reply, but nobody took a shot at them either.

The Japanese negotiating party returned to their base for further instructions and decided to approach the airstrip again, this time from the direction of the mountains. 'Finding that the Australians had vacated the air strip defensive positions we proceeded towards the jetty where we saw signs of enemy movement,' Takada added.

The atmosphere was tense. Who would make the first move? Then, at a building near the jetty, a party of Australian officers appeared, together with one Dutchman. 'After a discussion they agreed to surrender their troops who amounted to about 150 Australians, two or three Dutchmen and two or three natives.'[12]

The Allied troops were lined up on the airstrip and after a roll-call were billeted in a nearby barracks under a Japanese guard. The mood among the men relaxed a little. The enemy was behaving in a civilised manner, but how long would it last?

Major McBride, who was still free, had his doubts. Concealed in a dressing station with his injured platoon at the far west of the aerodrome, he made what turned out to be a life-saving decision. Gathering his men around him, the young officer invited those who were well enough to get out while the going was good. Those who were too badly injured and the medical staff from 2/12th Field Ambulance Unit could stay behind and take their chances. But the walking wounded who didn't want to spend the rest of the war behind barbed wire, or risk an even worse fate, were welcome to join him in an escape bid. They might perish along the way, but who knew, they might even make it back to Australia.

Hadn't they suffered enough already? They were lucky to be alive after the events of the past 24 hours and against all odds they still had their liberty. McBride was right. Escape was the only acceptable option.

One by one some twenty men in varying physical states rose to their feet and followed a creek that led them to the north of the island. As they gazed across the bay to the smouldering remains of bombed buildings on the Laitimor Peninsula they knew it was the right decision.

————

On the opposite side of Ambon Bay, A and D Companies and a smattering of Dutchmen were still holding out near Eri, at the southern end of the Laitimor Peninsula. They'd seen the Japanese flag flying across the water at Laha and assumed the worst. Enemy warships continued to shell the area and the men of the 2/21st did their best to retaliate with mortars and close-range fighting.

Their brief was to hold the position as long as possible and the Japanese attacks were successfully repulsed. But, truth be told, Gull Force was facing impossible odds. With the collective might of the Japanese air force, army and navy mounted against them, the Australians were almost spent. Food was in short supply and the diggers were exhausted.

On 2 February Scott called a conference with Macrae, Westley and Newnham to discuss the latest position and how to handle it. There was talk of capitulation but Major Macrae was having none of it. After all, they'd suffered only negligible casualties and some troops hadn't even seen action. Yet it was clear the invasion had taken its toll. As Newnham reported, 'It was apparent that all commanders and officers present were nearing exhaustion and on two occasions a senior officer dropped off to sleep through sheer fatigue.'[13]

Newnham admitted that the meeting 'lacked a definite spirit', making it difficult to think along defensive lines. Scott reasoned they'd be ill-advised to make a decision when they were all so tired, but he did agree to send a 23-strong fighting patrol that night to Latuhalat, led by Major Macrae. There had been reports of a Japanese landing at the far end of the Laitimor Peninsula. If that was the case the Australians would end up being sandwiched between enemy troops on both sides of Eri.

By dawn Macrae and his men had reached a gorge near Latuhalat and hid in a banana plantation in the hope of ambushing enemy soldiers in the area. They occupied a position near a wrecked bridge over the Patiroe River and grabbed a few hours of much-needed sleep while they waited. However, it wasn't the Japanese they had to worry about, but the local fruit. While looking for something to feed his patrol the officer ate some wild berries and became violently sick. Macrae was so incapacitated that a stretcher had to be summoned from Eri to evacuate him. When the bearers arrived they revealed that the battalion was about to surrender.

How could fate be so cruel? Events were going from bad to worse. Macrae, who had been so keen to continue fighting the night before, was now too ill to be of any use. Yet he was determined that his own bad luck would not spell doom for his men.

As a warrant officer and a sergeant loaded him onto the stretcher for the journey back to Eri, Macrae turned to the rest of the party and urged them to escape. They were near the beach and not too far from other islands. If they gained the assistance of locals, they just might make it to freedom. With the top brass at Eri close to surrender escape was the only option.

As the stretcher party turned to leave, Macrae gestured to his men to get on with it. They didn't need persuading. Captain Wilf Chapman assumed command and the party prepared for a perilous and physically challenging journey into the unknown.

———

Back at Gull Force's new base at Eri, Scott and his fellow officers contemplated the inevitable. Four incontrovertible factors influenced their final decision.

If they continued fighting, the bombing and shelling would continue, with further loss of life.

Food and water supplies were almost non-existent because of the influx of troops from Amahusu.

Morale was extremely low 'due to the influence of panic-stricken Dutch native troops in the area' and the fact that the Australians could see no possibility of extricating themselves from their predicament.

Tellingly, some members of Gull Force had already made up their minds and had been spotted walking towards Amahusu bearing white flags. Private Laurence Ryan, for example, saw the position as hopeless and quickly organised his own surrender party. He was barely 21 and over the past few months had earned himself a reputation as a troublemaker. Later, he'd be found guilty of desertion.[14]

With such mutiny in the ranks, what was the point of carrying on?

Eddie Gilbert, who was still up on the ridge overlooking Eri with his mortar platoon, had spent the previous night considering his likely fate. 'I was sure I'd never see another day, believing that we would be over-run during the night and that none of us would survive,' he recalls. 'So it was something of an anti-climax when, at daybreak on February 3rd, we were ordered by our officers to destroy our weapons and assemble on the road which linked Eri village to the town of Ambon.'

So far Eddie hadn't even set eyes on a Japanese soldier but as A Company moved out that morning he came face to face with his captors. They were not as he had anticipated. 'I was struck by how short they were compared with us ... and surprised that their footwear consisted of black sand shoes with a cleft for a big toe – just the thing, no doubt, for quiet and fast movement in jungle warfare.'

First impressions count when your enemy's reputation has achieved myth-like status and Eddie wasn't impressed. The enemy's appearance was in sharp contrast to the Dutch and Australian soldiers he was used to.

Eddie's column was allowed to proceed but just around the corner there was another shock. 'I saw and smelt something which brought home to me the horror and obscenity of the war – the bodies of two dead Ambonese soldiers lay beside the road. They must have been there for two or three days for their bodies had become distended, their uniforms drum-tight, their faces covered with flies.'

They were the first war victims he'd seen since the invasion of Ambon four days earlier. The grotesque memory would stay with Eddie for the rest of his life. More than half a century later he observed that 'the image is as sharp and as clear as though it were yesterday. My revulsion of war and all kinds of violence was born that day.'[15]

––––––––

The fast-moving events of 2/3 February had largely passed Bill Jinkins by. He and his platoon were completely out of the loop. After descending from Mount Nona, they'd remained in hiding for much of the day, unable to communicate with Scott or his fellow officers.

One of Jinkins's men, Private John Lewis, was sick and decided to walk to Eri in search of medical aid. On the way he caught up with a Dutch officer who told him he was taking a note to Scott to inform him that Kapitz had already surrendered and the Japanese had called a ceasefire until noon the next day. Lewis decided to return to his platoon with the latest news, but Jinkins wasn't convinced. He wanted to see the Japanese surrender terms for himself. Disregarding his own safety, he wrapped a white handkerchief around his arm, grabbed a bicycle and pedalled down towards Amahusu until he reached an enemy roadblock with two forward guns manned by an NCO and six men.

Undaunted, he rode up to them and demanded to see a 'shogun', someone in charge. Shortly a Japanese officer appeared and, speaking fluent English, asked what he wanted.

'I said I wanted the surrender note, so he sent me to Benteng barracks.'

There one of the more senior officers, Major Harakawa, agreed to the request and asked if he'd like to see his injured comrade, Lieutenant Sam Anderson, who had been injured on Mount Nona earlier. Sam was making good progress and the two men were fed and watered. It was all very civilised – more a friendly hospital visit than a confrontation with the enemy. It wouldn't last, of course. Soon Jinkins was on his way to the former Dutch headquarters, where he was introduced to Kapitz and an interpreter. Six Japanese with bayonets suddenly appeared and told him to sit.

They wanted to know who he was, what he was doing, where he had been, who was in charge. The questions came thick and fast, but the Australian officer replied merely with his name and number.

Who is Roach? Who is Scott? What does Kapitz do? the Japanese demanded. The rapid volley of questions grew louder as their countenances became more threatening. Each time Jinkins counted to ten before replying, 'I don't know.'

Relations were getting tense.

'The officer pulled out his sword and shouted, "Why do you answer so slowly?" "Because you don't speak good English."' The interrogator looked insulted but slid his sword back into its sheath and walked away.

Kapitz, who had been listening to the conversation with growing concern, relaxed and turned to Jinkins to confirm that the Dutch had surrendered the day before. He hoped Scott would follow his lead. A written note confirming the surrender was handed to Jinkins, who was then driven back to Japanese lines. Major Harakawa shook his hand and said, 'If you don't come back I hope we will meet in the field.'

Jinkins continued the rest of his journey by motorcycle and eventually made it back to Eri, where he informed Scott of the Japanese position. By then the CO had already agreed to negotiate.

On the morning of Tuesday, 3 February Scott sent Captain Bill Aitken, the battalion's medical officer, up to the Japanese lines to determine the surrender terms in detail. He drove to Amahusu in an ambulance and returned later. The official surrender was set for noon and the Australian officers would march as one to an area forward of the Amahusu line.

Ever the rebel, Jinkins at first refused to join them. 'I didn't want to march in with them but the CO said all the officers had to do it and we had to obey him. Scott realised he had put the men in a hopeless position and was now responsible for trying to save their lives,' he added. Jinkins knew it would never have happened under Roach. 'He would not have talked of surrender – we would have been wiped out.'

As the 2/21st marched up to enemy lines with fixed bayonets, the capitulation was filmed by Japanese cinematographers. It was the final humiliation for a once-proud battalion.[16]

Ostensibly fifteen members of Gull Force lost their lives in the defence of Ambon but the final death toll would turn out to be much higher. What no one knew at the time was that the bulk of Australian casualties would be at Laha, on the Hitu Peninsula. Another 309 officers and men, including some Dutch, either died in action or were executed over the next fortnight. Their sacrifice, which would not emerge until late 1945, would go down in military history as one of the bloodiest massacres of the Second World War.

5

THE MASSACRE

Death came swiftly for the men who were captured at Laha. One by one they were led out of the barracks with their hands tied and seconds later a sword or bayonet ripped their body asunder.

The executions were carried out between 5 and 20 February, largely in reprisal for the loss of men aboard the minesweeper which had been sunk in Ambon Bay in the opening days of the invasion. About a hundred crew died in the blast and as vengeance the survivors demanded three Allied soldiers for every Japanese who'd been killed. The Australians and several Dutchmen who'd been held after the fall of Laha would provide the perfect ratio.

At least, that's the theory. But like so much in subsequent accounts of the Ambon massacre, the evidence relies heavily on post-war Japanese reports of the executions and what led up to them. Several graphic statements about the events on Ambon would be made at war crimes inquiries after the end of the war in the Pacific and while some of the details were subsequently disputed, the barbarous intent of those involved and the level of savagery employed were not open to question.

Preparations for the executions, starting with the graves, reflected the sense of Japanese order in all things military. Thirty Japanese troops were sent to dig holes in a coconut plantation about 200 metres from Soewakodo, where between 40 and 50 of the POWs were being held, including Major Newbury. Lieutenant Nakagawa divided his men into three groups: the first to move the prisoners out of the house where they were confined, the second to prevent disorder on the way to the execution site and the third to bayonet or behead them.

The sheer mortal terror that consumed the captured men can only be imagined. They knew what was happening but were spared the sight as one by one they were led to a spot and made to kneel, with their eyes bandaged. A member of the third group of Japanese then appeared with a sword or bayonet and with one deadly stroke or stabbing motion calmly beheaded the POW or thrust his sharpened blade through the prisoner's chest.[1]

Takada Haruo, one of the marines who was with the 1st Kure Special Naval Landing Force which landed at Hitu-lama in the early hours of 31 January, estimated there were about 40 Allied prisoners under guard in the native school at Soewakodo near Laha on 5 February. About midday Lieutenant Nakagawa, acting on orders from Rear Admiral Koichiro Hatakeyama, said the POWs had to be disposed of. Takada tried to distance himself from what happened next, if his later testimony to the War Crimes Tribunal is to be believed: 'When I heard of the order to execute the prisoners I protested to Lieutenant Nakagawa, saying that as fighting had ceased there was no reason for the execution. There was no shortage of food and there were enough men to act as guards.'

Nakagawa agreed with him but it was an order and had to be obeyed. The lieutenant had a party of about 40 Japanese troops who were known as the Yoshihara Shotai and come from the 1st Sasebo Special Naval Landing Force. It was their job to assist in the executions. Warrant Officer Shiego Hamanishi, also from the Kure landing unit, helped to oversee the first batch of doomed men, who were led out of the school after lunch and taken to a patch of native bush about 350 metres away.

Before the killings, they were searched for valuables. At least two senior Japanese NCOs confiscated part of the prisoners' personal belongings, including money purses, pocketbooks, wristwatches and small quantities of tobacco and cigarettes. No doubt the condemned men's property would end up in Japanese pockets, because the mass executions would remain a closely guarded secret until after the war. Perhaps they intended to smuggle their western souvenirs back home, for they certainly had no wish to leave behind any evidence which might point to their involvement in the death of their captives.

Over the next few hours, guards from the Yoshihara Shotai escorted the POWs one by one to the place of execution. Ikeuchi Masakiyo, an interpreter who would become a familiar name in the chronicles of Ambon over the coming years, appeared to be Nakagawa's chief assistant and followed him around like a pet dog. At the execution site he talked to each prisoner before making the condemned man kneel on the rough earth, hands tied behind his back.

The execution of the prisoners was so swift and efficient, with swords only occasionally missing their exact target, that the despatch of the Australians became a macabre production line. Hamanishi's matter-of-fact description of the gruesome spectacle conjures up a vision of a cruelly efficient killing machine. 'Whilst they knelt on the ground Japanese executioners cut their heads with Japanese swords. Many heads fell off the bodies but there were also some partly cut off. However, death was almost instantaneous. As soon as one execution was over, another followed.'

But even the young warrant officer eventually wearied of the sight of so much slaughter, deciding to leave the site after witnessing the first 28 executions.[2]

The next day another 62 prisoners were executed, including Wing Commander Ernest Scott, who had been captured after making a valiant attempt to escape the island by boat a few days earlier. Like the other victims they'd been accused of disobedient and restive behaviour and ordered to be put to death. The method of despatch followed the same orderly routine, with the men, sensing the dreadful prospect that lay ahead, transported to a coconut plantation close by the Laha airfield and held temporarily in a nearby house. Possessed by the abject fear of condemned men, their names were called and one by one they were led out to meet their fate. Seconds later their corpse was buried in a round hole.[3]

Even more men were executed in the coming days as the survivors of the minesweeper demanded further retribution. Under their own military code they saw nothing wrong in their request. As Hamanishi said, 'The survivors had sought revenge [and] twice approached Rear Admiral Hatakeyama, the commander. It was said that the Rear Admiral turned down the request at first, but later acceded to it.'[4]

The last of the mass executions was the biggest and bloodiest, with an estimated 220 POWs dying by sword or bayonet in an operation which, by necessity, was carried out with military precision. This time Lieutenant Nakagawa arrived at Laha accompanied by 60 of his own men and another 30 from Minesweeper No. 9, reflecting the scale of the extermination they'd been ordered to carry out. As before, he divided the men into three parties, some to transport the condemned men, others to control them and the rest to kill them. Nakagawa's factual account of the executions was made all the more chilling by its simplicity but other descriptions of what happened between 5 and 20 February 1942 near Laha aerodrome provide a deeply disturbing glimpse of the unfolding horror.

On one occasion, as marines lined up 'keenly awaiting their turn' to decapitate their victim, the evening light began to fade, making it difficult to aim the deadly blow. Someone asked for a battery torch to help them see the backs of the necks. After the seventh or eighth Australian had been beheaded a marine who had borrowed a sword from Saburo Yoshizaki complained that the blade had been bent and blunted through dealing with one particularly large victim.

The sense of bloodlust that night made the Japanese immune to the desperate pleas of Dutch and Australian soldiers as they were led to the side of one of two large pits, which were dug about 5 metres apart. Forced to kneel and bow their heads, their last terrifying moments created a hideous final scene for the men who now waited their turn in line behind them. Their arms and hands securely bound, some had to stand for hours listening to the anguished cries of their mates. For Warrant Officer Kanamoto there was one sight even he would never forget – the beheading of a young prisoner who shouted 'desperately' before being decapitated on the nearest side of grave A. Seconds later another prisoner on the opposite side of the hole was similarly dealt with and toppled over into the pit.

After about twenty decapitations, curiosity drew Kanamoto to the graveside. He reported that 'Some corpses were headless but several bodies with heads half-attached were jerking feebly and making faint gurgling moans.'[5] Kanamoto's testimony, as reported in James MacKay's account of the war crimes trials in his book, *Betrayal in High Places*, leaves little to the imagination but also suggests his conscience had got the better of him. While maintaining he felt revulsion mixed with pity at the sight of the mass executions, he insisted he couldn't interfere in the punishments because they'd been ordered by the Japanese High Command. Doubtless designed to save his own skin, Kanamoto's post-war excuses did not impress his interrogators, who viewed his comments as deceitful.

Nor did his professed concern prevent the rest of the men from being executed that night. Every blow of the sword was greeted with shouts of jubilation by the Japanese marines mixed with ribald scorn as prisoners begged for their lives. Such was the impact of the sharpened steel on human flesh that some of the sword strokes produced 'a strange sound' and even sparks, MacKay reports.

Eventually it all became too much for Kanamoto, forcing him to retire to the garrison office about 10.30 p.m. as the executions continued. The final man was beheaded at 1.30 a.m., bringing the total number of Australians and Dutch massacred by the Japanese in and around Laha over those fateful few weeks to more than 300.

While some of the details of this horrific episode were subsequently disputed, the scale of the atrocity was without question. History would record it as one of the worst massacres of the Second World War.

————

On the other side of Ambon Bay the fate of the Laha units would remain a mystery until after the war. Efforts by Lieutenant Colonel Scott, commander of Gull Force, to find out more were invariably brushed aside, with the Japanese offering various explanations, the most frequent excuse being that the missing men had been taken by ship to Japan. With no evidence to the contrary Scott had to accept their word.

In sharp contrast to the barbarity suffered by the Allied forces on the Hitu Peninsula, the early weeks of incarceration at Tan Tui Barracks were relatively free of violence. Indeed, such was the relative freedom and easy availability of food that the men of Gull Force would come to reflect on this time as a halcyon period.

Tom Pledger was handed a bowl of rice, a couple of tins of meat and powdered milk and even some lollies immediately after he and his mates surrendered. He didn't realise it then, but the tinned meat turned out to be horse flesh. It wasn't exactly fine dining but the tucker was tasty and welcome. 'Very edible and quite acceptable,' was his verdict.[6]

Back in Tan Tui the men discovered that a lot of the Australian provisions they'd stored away had been pinched by the locals. Walter Hicks was 'horrified that there was virtually nothing left in the camp'.[7] This didn't improve relations with the Ambonese but the Japanese sympathised with the Australians and allowed them to retrieve the stolen food. They searched for the illicit stockpiles under armed escort and brought back tons of flour and tinned foodstuffs, including large quantities of bully beef.

At first Tan Tui prison camp was surrounded by fairly rudimentary barbed wire fencing punctuated by sentry posts and although the enclosure did not pose a serious challenge to would-be escapers, its psychological effect was significant. Said Eddie Gilbert:

> Our morale was low at this stage with much apprehension about what our captors intended to do with us. One way to combat the effects of low morale was to busy ourselves in whatever activities presented themselves. During the first six months of captivity we were left very much to our own devices.[8]

There were lectures, art classes, sporting events and concerts. The camp medical officer, Dr Peter Davidson, ran a first-aid course and for the more academically inclined there were political studies.

With plenty of flour available, Eddie Gilbert learned how to bake bread from his close mate Eric Stagg, who showed him how to produce buns and loaves from a wood-fired oven. If the diet ever got boring there was always the Ambonese market to supplement provisions. Once a week the Australians and the Dutch were able to buy sugar, eggs, fruit, tobacco and much more from the locals. Prices weren't cheap because the Dutch had more money than the Aussies, forcing up the cost of goods, but the market, held in a road which ran straight through the camp, provided another useful food source, at least for the time being.

The Japanese had agreed that the Australians and the Dutch should be housed in separate quarters. Because of the absence of the Laha 300 there was plenty of extra room for everybody and although the camp lacked electricity and a regular supply of running water (the pipe ended just inside the perimeter and was often turned off), life was bearable.

On some nights there was a party atmosphere, with the battalion band, which had managed to salvage its instruments after the surrender, providing the music and other POWs offering a song or a monologue. Eddie Gilbert's rendition of 'The Lion and Albert', made famous by the British entertainer Stanley Holloway before the war, was always popular.[9]

On the surface it appeared an easy-going lifestyle with a few armed guards posted at various intervals along the barbed wire fence and some patrolling the road down to the beach where the latrines were erected. According to Benjamin Amor, 'That was the extent of the Japanese guarding and they weren't too bad to us, although one or two of them got a bit nasty. But on the whole the treatment for the first short while was reasonable.'[10] Church services were held on Sundays and some of the men learned the local language during the week, while others preferred to be taught motor mechanics.

But beneath the semblance of normality, tensions continue to simmer between the Dutch and the Australians. A lot of the diggers believed the Dutch had let them down, while the men of the Royal Netherlands East Indies Army were none too impressed with the Australian government, which they considered had not done enough to defend Ambon.

There was also the largely unspoken criticism of Scott, who had replaced the much loved Len Roach at the eleventh hour and surrendered to the enemy a mere three days after their arrival. The role of the new commanding officer and his attitude to discipline would rankle the Australians in the coming months, particularly as the Japanese hardened their attitude towards the POWs and showed signs of a new brutality.

Privately many of the Australians also felt cheated because they had not been allowed to prove themselves as soldiers. Rightly or wrongly, there was a sense of shame at not having been able to put up a good fight against the enemy, and genuine bitterness that they'd apparently been sacrificed by the powers that be, for no great military advantage.

Lieutenant Ralph Godfrey believes that if Len Roach had remained commander they would never have surrendered. 'He would have just fought and fought, virtually to the last man. He would have broken us up into guerilla units and wouldn't have surrendered.'[11]

Some military strategists would later argue that the Ambon campaign at least held up the Japanese for a few weeks, delaying their invasion of Timor and air attacks on Darwin. But did this justify the cost? As they languished behind barbed wire over the next three-and-a-half years, many members of Gull Force would question the Australian government's decision to take on the Japanese at Ambon, and many families would mourn the loss of loved ones who died in captivity.

––––––––

The Japanese air force was seemingly unstoppable. The POWs on Ambon didn't know it at the time, but 183 attack aircraft would bomb Darwin a mere fortnight after their surrender. Most of the Japanese planes flew from aircraft carriers but some took off from Laha airfield on Ambon, now under Japanese control. Two hundred and forty-three people were killed and many more injured during that very first raid on Australia's Top End, which might have happened earlier had the Japanese not been tied up in the Moluccas. Or did the deployment of Gull Force just delay the inevitable?

It was an issue which would occupy those in the corridors of power in Canberra and Melbourne in the months to come as politicians and the military struggled to halt the advancing enemy wave in Java, the Banda Sea and the Pacific. And while those incarcerated on Ambon had little or no knowledge of the big picture, many were propelled by an overwhelming drive to do something to help themselves. For some that came down to one word – *escape*.

A few of the men were already on their way. Major McBride, who had seen the writing on the wall at Laha and wisely rounded up an escape party, had made it to the northern coast of the Hitu Peninsula. Most of his twenty-man party were walking wounded and, given the rough and hilly terrain, took several days to make the journey. Among them was Private Leslie Hopkins, from Ringwood in Victoria, who had conned his way into the battalion at the age of fifteen years eleven months and celebrated his sixteenth birthday on the voyage to Ambon. Originally employed as a runner in C Company, he'd already had some narrow escapes. 'One of the worst things about it was trying to pronounce the passwords to the native troops. Their orders were to shoot if it didn't sound right,' he recalled in a post-war memoir. Luckily he survived.

With Japanese in the area, the fleeing Australians also had to worry about being spotted by the enemy and there were additional concerns about who they could trust in the native population. It was common knowledge that some of the Muslim villagers, or Mohammadans as they were known, were in the pay of the Japanese and information about the whereabouts of escaped Allied soldiers commanded a handsome reward. Only the Christian Ambonese could be relied upon for help but locating and identifying them was often a matter of chance.

Thankfully, nine days after leaving Laha, McBride and his men were able to negotiate the purchase of a *prahu*, a native boat in which they set sail for the nearby island of Ceram. From there they made their way further along the coast to Amahai where they met up with several Dutch soldiers who were also trying to get away. The escape party was growing by the day and was soon making its way in a south-easterly direction across the Banda Sea to Dobo in the Aru Islands, where it picked up another 72 Dutch native troops.

Clearly the native *prahu* was not big enough to accommodate them all so two motorboats were acquired for the next stage of the voyage to Merauke, more than 300 kilometres away on the west coast of Dutch New Guinea. On the way they caught up with a *prahu* containing a Dutch family and sixteen Australian soldiers. What had started out as a one-vessel escape party led by McBride was now a flotilla of tiny boats making its way back to Australia.

By now they were in the Torres Strait, sailing towards the Gulf of Carpentaria. Four days after setting off from Merauke they landed at Karumba, at the bottom of the west coast of the Cape York Peninsula. What a feat! Against all odds, they'd defied the Japanese military and taken on the unpredictable waters of the Arafura Sea to make it safely back to Australia. But their reception was hardly encouraging. As Leslie Hopkins described it: 'When we tried to land we were fired on by our own troops. There were no casualties but if we'd have been Japanese we could have captured Australia.'[12]

Fortuitously, the Catalina flying boat service was still operating. Les and his party were able to hitch a lift to Bowen later that day, providing a colourful spectacle as they stepped off their flight wearing much the same clothing they'd had on for the past several weeks – muddy boots, torn shorts and the occasional sarong. When they turned up at the local cinema that evening they caused quite a stir.

At the same time Captain Chapman and his men were making promising headway after escaping from Latuhalat in the far south of Ambon's Laitimor Peninsula. Having been ordered by the battalion's second in command, the indisposed Major Macrae, to flee the Japanese advance, Chapman and twenty men from his patrol had made their way to Seri Bay, found themselves a *prahu* and sailed to Nusalaut Island, several kilometres to the east of Ambon.

From there they island-hopped to Saparua and Amahai, enjoying the support of friendly natives along the way. Considering most of the escape party had little or no sailing experience, they met the challenge of life on the ocean with surprising success, but their easy progress was not to last. At the village of Tehoru,

halfway along the southern coast of Ceram, they were informed
by locals that the enemy was just ahead. A motor launch carrying
50 Japanese was apparently patrolling the area.

The news sent a shudder down the spines of the Australians,
who now had to decide whether to press ahead and pretend to be
native fishermen or lie low for a while on land. Ten of Chapman's
party decided to hide in the bush until the threat passed while
the rest summoned the courage to continue and made their way
to Geser, a small island off the south-eastern tip of Ceram. From
there they sailed further south to Tual in the Kai Islands.

It had taken them roughly three weeks to reach this point, a
voyage of a few hundred kilometres. On 26 February they were
surprised to meet the men they had left behind at Tehoru, who had
caught up with them by walking along the Ceram coastline and
sailing on to Kai by native boat. The two groups were overjoyed
to be reunited, and it buoyed their resolve to complete the next
stage of their voyage home.

Meanwhile, Melbourne-born Wilf Chapman, a captain and still
only 21, showed his leadership qualities by somehow acquiring a
radio transmitter and sending a message to Bandung. 'One officer,
20 O.R.s [other ranks], escaped Ambon. Request instructions
and transport,' it read. Two days later came the reply, ordering
them to proceed to Dobo in the Aru Islands, to the east, where
a ship would meet them and transfer the party to Australia. The
rendezvous was set for eight days hence but when Chapman's
party reached Dobo there was no ship, only a Dutch infantry
company. Once again the diggers had been let down.

Undeterred, they set off in a few small fishing boats for
Merauke, in Dutch New Guinea. It was more than 200 kilometres
away but by hugging the coast for much of the voyage they could
shelter from bad weather and heavy seas. Merauke offered a
temporary sanctuary but the wait was far from over. Weeks passed
before a naval vessel arrived to ferry them to Thursday Island at
the top of the Cape York Peninsula. Along with Chapman and
the other Australians, sixteen Dutch troops, two Dutch women

and four children made their way across the Torres Strait on 12 April.[13]

The second party of Ambon diggers had made it back to freedom but the biggest and most daring escape was yet to come. Bill Jinkins, whose bravery and determination in the face of enemy attack had already been demonstrated atop Mount Nona, was not a soldier to accept defeat easily. He was a man of action whose courage had already taken him through Japanese lines in pursuit of Kapitz's official surrender note. Now, imprisoned behind barbed wire at Tan Tui, he had no intention of staying there for long.

Jinkins had a plan and within days of his incarceration had already ensured that the perimeter fencing could be easily breached to allow him to scout the surrounding area and establish friendly contact with the locals. He had made his position clear from the outset, informing Scott, his commanding officer, that as a POW it was his duty to escape and that he would endeavour to do so at the first opportunity. Scott agreed and promised to support his efforts, but did not want anybody else to know he'd approved the mission. In fact, the CO had seriously considered joining Jinkins himself on the big escape and even accompanied him outside the camp during preparations for the break-out. Second in command Macrae was also among those anxious to leave, but was it right and proper for the two battalion leaders to abandon their men?

Scott could see both sides of the argument. On the one hand he felt obliged to do all in his power to return to Australia with the knowledge he possessed so that he could further assist in the war effort, but on the other he knew his first duty was to remain with his men, to safeguard and protect them from their captors. Undecided about the proper course of action, Scott sought the advice of two fellow officers, Captain Peter Davidson and Lieutenant Denis Smith. He told them that although he was keen to make his own bid for freedom, he accepted that Jinkins was quite capable of taking 'a complete picture and all the information' back to Australia. The two officers were given

24 hours to consider their verdict and were invited to write down their opinions separately and compare notes the following day. Scott had promised to abide by Smith's and Davidson's judgement, whichever way it went, and both men were conscious of the heavy responsibility on their shoulders.

In the end they came to the same conclusion: the commanding officer was responsible to the Australian government for the prisoners of war and it was therefore his duty to remain. They reminded him that they were dealing with a barbarous and treacherous enemy whose mental processes were the opposite of Europeans', and that Scott, given his pre-war experience, had a much better understanding of the Japanese. What was more, in the event of the Australians retaking Ambon – which at this stage was still considered a possibility – as commander he would be in a position to assist any landing force.

It was also decided that Macrae would stay behind. Given that the commanding officer was 'a stranger to the battalion and did not know any of the officers or men, their qualities or their weaknesses, the absence of Major Macrae would deprive him [Scott] of his own counsellor'.[14]

So that was it. The CO and his second in command had no alternative but to keep their promise to stick by Smith's and Davidson's advice, although it wasn't until the middle of March that Jinkins's escape plan came to fruition. In the meantime, half a dozen other men got away under the direction of Warrant Officer Donald Johnson, a 30-year-old Melbourne transport driver, who led them to the island of Dobo and eventually on to Thursday Island. The party included Corporal Ben Amor and his mate Ron McPherson, as well as the brothers Don and Vic Findlay, who got lost on the track and found themselves in the middle of Ambon town early the next morning. They were so embarrassed at their poor navigational skills that they headed back to camp and explained to the quizzical guards that they'd been out to buy tobacco.

Ben and Ron had long given up waiting for the brothers at the agreed jungle meeting point and were anxious to proceed. They'd spent weeks preparing for this escape and weren't going to give up now. Ron had even got a job with the camp cobbler in order to make himself a pair of strong walking boots for the march north. Army ration packs, water bottles and 'anything we could scrounge' were stored in a drain just outside the wire. He had even found a map of the region in a magazine. He traced it with a pencil and put the copy in his pocket.

Australia was just across the water, they reasoned. Such was the optimism of youth that they viewed it as no more than a hop, skip and a jump away. In fact, there were more than 900 kilometres of water between them and Australia, but at least they knew which way to go. The map with its many scattered islands was effectively their passport home.

The date was 10 March 1942, a week before Bill Jinkins's escape party was due to leave Ambon. Much was riding on the success of these missions, not least the survival of the men involved. But there was another issue at stake: if the Australian military knew there was a POW camp on Ambon they might attempt to rescue them and if they didn't – well, at least they'd know not to bomb them if or when the Allies started striking back.

6

'I'M GONNA GET OUT OF THIS BLOODY PLACE'

L IEUTENANT WILLIAM THOMAS Jinkins was scrupulous with his planning, carefully selecting his fellow escapees for their skills and personal qualities and refusing to consider anybody who might be a liability or a malingerer. His team had to be 100 per cent behind the ambitious lieutenant, who was just 30 years old and had a distinguished military career ahead of him.

First he asked his batman, Alec Chew, an Australian-born Chinese, to join him. The two men had already developed a strong mutual trust, so there was never any doubt the 28-year-old Bendigo boy would be keen to go. As Chew tells it, 'I was sitting in the camp and Bill Jinkins came up. He said, "Coming out? You know, get over the wire?" I said to him, "What for?" And he said, "I'm gonna get out of this bloody place." So I said, "Yes, alright."'[1]

Jinkins also approached Gordon Jack, a signals officer with whom he'd become friendly. The Yarraville soldier was told he could choose a mate to go with him and suggested Arthur Young.

If they were to spend much of their time at sea they'd also need men who were familiar with engines and the ocean and Private Cliff Warn, a fisherman who was used to handling a boat, was an ideal candidate. He didn't think twice about the offer. Nor did Private Harry Coe, who hailed from Wonthaggi on the South Gippsland coast and who knew all there was to know about diesel engines after spending much of his early working life maintaining milking machines on his family's farm.[2] The last man to be selected was Roland Rudder, who at 26 was a captain in the transport company, bringing the total strength of the escape party to seven.

Privately, Jinkins believed the group could have been bigger but Lieutenant Colonel Scott, who ruled against it, was worried about how they'd account for seven absent soldiers, especially as three of them were officers. How would the Japanese react once they found the empty beds? So far, camp discipline had been relatively benign but there was no guarantee it would continue that way. In the end Scott resolved the issue with a little sleight of hand or, in this case, sleight of body. He engineered a breathtakingly simple plan whereby they would substitute three volunteers from other ranks for the missing officers.

Although tradition has it that nobody volunteers for anything in the army, the beds of Messrs Jinkins, Jack and Rudder proved surprisingly easy to fill. Sergeants Stanley Piggin and Jim Wilson and Lance Corporal Geoffrey Waring were to impersonate the absent officers by moving into their quarters, assuming their names and numbers and carrying out the normal duties of an officer. Conveniently, this also had the advantage of keeping them off work duties, given the Japanese adherence to the rule that officers should not be used as forced labour.

The deception worked perfectly at first, allowing Jinkins and his party to make good their escape, but the ruse was threatened when the Japanese sprang a surprise roll-call after receiving a tip-off from someone outside the camp (most likely one of the Ambonese). This was the moment of truth. The remaining members of Gull Force were lined up in four ranks for counting in the failing light as the guards commenced the roll-call.

Scott engaged the Japanese in conversation as they walked along the line, while Macrae kept moving men from the rear rank, who had already been counted, further down the line, where they would be recorded again. Both men realised the plan would fall apart if the final tally was not exact, but amazingly the number was spot on.[3] Whatever his personal weaknesses, Scott had shown a surprising measure of courage and ingenuity which undoubtedly saved the day and ensured a speedy and uninterrupted getaway for Jinkins's party.

His quick thinking also compensated for his behaviour the day before, when he reportedly had had a change of heart about the pledge he'd made to stay behind on Ambon. According to Jinkins, the CO insisted on being included in the escape party and only changed his mind after being reminded he was physically unfit to make such an arduous journey. (Apparently he suffered badly from piles and was quite incapable of walking any distance without support.)[4] If the climb down was embarrassing for Scott, his medical condition only reinforced his unsuitability as commanding officer of the 2/21st Battalion.

––––––––

Soon after dusk on 17 March the seven members of Jinkins's escape party assembled on the northern perimeter of the Tan Tui camp in preparation for their departure. For once, the inclement weather turned out to be in their favour, with most of the guards who should have been patrolling outside the wire sheltering in their huts. The men slid under the wire in ones and twos, but after a few hundred yards the drizzle eased and the cloud lifted to reveal a bright moonlit sky which bathed the terrain in a shadowy light.

Without the mist and the rain they could be easily spotted by the Japanese or local informers, but their luck held. The idea was to run up the hill to a house owned by the Dutch police chief Bill Gaspersz, whose three sons had agreed to aid their escape. The family had also offered one of their faithful servants, a young man named Peter, to arrange sailing boats and help them on their way.

In the Gaspersz household the POWs were welcomed with sweet biscuits and coffee, which went down a treat after weeks of simple camp fare. Six locals who had volunteered to act as guides across the Laitimor Peninsula to the south coast of the island were also there. There was no time to waste, given they needed to set sail by daybreak, and thankfully the native escorts were well prepared for the night march, holding aloft hollowed-out bamboo poles containing coconut oil and a wick. 'These were kept alight for the trip across the mountains,' said Jinkins, 'and were only extinguished when we had to pass through inhabited villages.'⁵

By early morning they had made such good progress that they were at the coast, where three outrigger *prahu*s stocked with food, clothing and other supplies were waiting for them. It was 2.30 a.m. and a gentle breeze encouraged them to make for open water, though soon afterwards a squall blew up, driving them back towards the beach. Said Warn, 'We thought we were doing really well and it was amazing to wake up to find we were only a few hundreds yards offshore.'⁶

Undeterred, they set sail again at about 5 a.m., this time openly paddling past Japanese positions in the dawn light after donning Ambonese pyramid-style hats made from woven grass to avoid suspicion. 'We had a lot of luck,' said Warn. 'I'm not a religious man, but I do think that sometimes the Lord does look after you.'

Soon they were heading across the Bay of Paso towards the island of Haruku, to the east of Ambon. It was a tense voyage but by 4 p.m. they'd made landfall and found themselves among friends. The Rani of Haruku, wife of the local Raja, entertained them lavishly in the reception hall, where they were offered much more than they could eat or drink.

The Japanese had so far shown no interest in the tiny offshore communities but the escape party knew they could not stay long, for fear of an informer passing on their whereabouts to the enemy. The Ambonese who'd helped to sail the *prahu*s were also keen to return home with their craft, so Jinkins was forced to negotiate for another vessel to take them across to the main island of Ceram. Only Peter, the Gaspersz family's servant, agreed to stay with them.

What a voyage it would turn out to be. With more than 900 kilometres to go and an unforgiving sea to conquer, the success of Jinkins's escape bid would be down to good seamanship and not a little luck. Only Cliff Warn had the nautical knowledge to see them safely to their destination, although what the rest of the crew lacked in maritime experience they more than made up for in fortitude.

The Rani of Haruku arranged for the hire of a single-masted sailing boat, barely 6 feet long, which would accommodate a crew of nine, including the owner, who made them paddle for fourteen hours to reach the village of Amahai. It was not an easy voyage and the men were exhausted by the time they got there. No wonder they looked for another craft, this time, hopefully, with an engine and a little more accommodation than the last. Fortuitously, a Chinese rubber planter agreed to let them use his 30-foot diesel-driven work boat, on the understanding that they would return it after the war.

Harry Coe, the mechanic, looked it over, gave it the thumbs-up and soon they were loading the vessel with an abundance of local produce and bottles of water. Jinkins and his team seemed to have struck it lucky and were soon on their way to Geser, another island off the far east coast of Ceram.

But their good fortune was about to end in dramatic fashion as the weather took a serious turn for the worse. A week after departing Ambon they were buffeted by a fierce tropical storm. They were seven men and a leaky boat against the wind, rain and mountainous seas and all they could do was bail away frantically to keep the leaky motor launch afloat.

Jinkins and the rest of the crew were dumbfounded by Warn's seamanship and would be forever in his debt. As Jinkins told it:

He took that ship through giant waves, six and eight feet
above us at deck level. He just rode up on the face of the
wave at an angle and then down the back edge of the
wave at another angle, ready to pick up the next one and
go over. We did this for hours and he was at the helm all
the time.[7]

Warn's sailing mastery spared them from shipwreck and
almost certain death as they made their way to Geser over the
next few days. There was great cause for celebration when they
get there, much of it fuelled by the hospitality of the Dutch
controller, who was still in charge, providing ample opportunity
for overindulgence. The amiable Dutchman and his heavily
pregnant German wife were the perfect hosts, and with no
shortage of hard liquor were always up for a party. Said Warn,
'We'd have a few drinks and a few more and end up with a sing
song and the food was excellent too. Everybody was very happy;
you wouldn't think there was a war on.'

In fact, life was so good on Geser that it was tempting to stay,
but Jinkins and his men knew they would be discovered eventually
and hastened to move on to their next port of call, Tual in the
Kai group of islands. After being entertained so generously they
invited the controller and his family, including two children, to
join them on the voyage to Australia, but the Dutchman bravely
declined, insisting that it was his duty to stay at his post until
the Japanese arrived.

Curiously, when the Australians tried to start the engine on
their 30-footer it refused to work, prompting speculation that
it had been sabotaged by the controller, who wanted to keep it
for his wife's evacuation. It was an unsubstantiated theory, but
it cast a shadow on what had so far been an unexpected and
extraordinarily enjoyable sojourn.

Never a man to accept defeat, Jinkins chartered two more
sailing boats, including a large *prahu* called the *Java*, which
was 9 feet in the beam, had a shallow draft and one mast. By

now, other fellow travellers had appeared, including nine Dutch servicemen and two more Australians, all of whom were seeking passage south. The Dutch were given the use of the smaller craft, along with a four-man local crew, while the Aussies and Peter the Ambonese, plus another native helper, stepped aboard the *Java*.

They set sail to the music of 'Beer Barrel Polka' and 'South of the Border', a gentle breeze filling the sails as they made their way out to sea. The weather was kind – too kind. They were becalmed by morning. There was nothing to do but admire the view and savour the scent of the Spice Islands, an intoxicating mix which reminded Jinkins, who was older and more worldly-wise than the rest of his crew, of a lady's boudoir. 'We innocent ones, having never been in a lady's boudoir, wondered what it was like, but he never enlightened us. But the perfume was exotic; it was fantastic,' recalled Warn.

It took a fortnight to reached Saumlaki on the island of Yamdema at the far south of the Kai group, which effectively separated the Banda and Arafura Seas. It was an easy voyage, with the Malay crewman trailing a line over the tiller and everyone tucking into barbecued fish under a starlit sky.

Along the way they called into Tual, capital of the Kais, which was still under Dutch command, although the Australians didn't know that for sure. The welcoming party was heavily armed and for a moment the escapees prepared for a shoot-out, until someone on the quay indicated he was a police officer and they were invited ashore. Once again the hospitality of their hosts knew no bounds as they were treated to wine and a slap-up dinner before continuing their journey.

These were heady times for the young diggers, whose successful escape had imbued them with a new confidence, although their navigational skills had yet to be seriously tested. Each man knew their progress during the first half of the journey had been more through luck than judgement. Indeed, they had only just made it to Saumlaki when the *Java*'s rudder broke off, fortunately as they pulled alongside the jetty. Once again providence had saved them, but they could not be sure how long it would last.

While the mainly Christian population was still free of the Japanese yoke, the radio news suggested it would not be long before the enemy's arrival. No one knew it then, but by July there would be bloodshed as Japanese troops landed on Saumlaki and the Dutch garrison opened fire at close range with their two light machine guns. The Japanese Imperial Navy would reply with several salvos, killing the Dutch commander.[8]

But for the moment Jinkins and his band had more immediate concerns. Realising the *Java* was unsuitable for the long voyage across the Arafura, they searched for a replacement vessel. With great timing, the government supply ship *Aleida* just happened to be in port and somehow the Dutch controller was persuaded to part with her. The 254-tonne diesel-powered vessel came with a crew of seven, a skipper and a navigator, but there was just one problem: none of them was prepared to sail her to Australia.

Once again, Jinkins refused to be deterred and for the next three days joined his men in learning how to operate and maintain the good ship *Aleida*. They also needed enough fuel to get them to Bathurst Island, off the Australian coast, a distance of precisely 650 kilometres as the crow flies, but further given the influence of winds, strong currents and poor navigation.

Jinkins calculated they had just enough oil to get to Bathurst Island on the basis of doing 8 knots in a calm sea, but that was still 80 kilometres from Darwin. With no more diesel available, they decided to chance it, slipping out of the harbour on the night of 22 April 1942, only to be confronted by a heavy swell and monsoonal conditions. Said Jinkins, 'There were huge waves and we were just hitting them head on and getting nowhere.'

Cliff Warn, who was at the helm, decided to head back to shore but in doing so the *Aleida* turned broadside and ran aground on a reef. Come daylight the ship was sitting at a 45 degree angle to starboard, with the sea lapping against the gunwales. 'Two of the boys rowed across to the jetty to tell the controller that we were in a spot of bother.' While Jinkins's capacity for understatement was to be admired, his options were running out. Gordon Jack and Arthur Young got a radio message to Australia revealing their plight and demanding they be picked up as soon as possible, but there was a deafening silence in reply.

Chance would have it that on the same day another vessel arrived at Saumlaki in the form of a well-appointed 48-foot motor cruiser, the *Griffioen*, which was carrying nine women, seven children and four Dutchmen and boasted cabins fore and aft, lavatories and even showers. The diggers hadn't known such luxury since before the war. Unfazed by his earlier nautical disaster, Jinkins tried to negotiate the use of the *Griffioen*, though, not unnaturally, the crew were singularly unimpressed by the Australian's temerity and politely declined.

Bill Jinkins piled on the pressure, promising an Australian warship would pick up the rest of the men, women and children, but the ship's crew were cautious and demanded one of the Australian officers stay behind as a guarantee of their return. Jinkins, who was determined to snare the *Griffioen* for his passage home, was having none of it. With the crew refusing to sail the luxury cruiser and the Australians ill-equipped to handle it themselves, there was no alternative but to hijack the bloody boat and her crew on the grounds of Jinkins's military rank 'and the fact that we're at war', as he put it.

In a final desperate attempt to end the impasse the dogged lieutenant, who was still not 30, called a conference with the crew of the motor cruiser and the island's controller, while placing Harry Coe, Alec Chew and Arthur Young at strategic points around the room. All three were wearing groundsheets over their shoulders. 'We anticipated trouble,' said Jinkins. 'The conference lasted for two hours and no progress was made in persuading the crew to come with us. It was then I disclosed to the Resident that whether they agreed or not, the crew were coming on the *Griffioen*.'

The controller looked surprised and asked how this might be achieved. At which point Jinkins, in a pre-arranged signal, drew a handkerchief from his right-hand pocket and blew his nose. Suddenly the groundsheets fell to the floor, revealing Coe, Chew and Young standing at each entrance, carrying a .303 rifle, .45 tommy gun and .32 calibre pistol respectively.

Much to their consternation the *Griffioen*'s crew, clearly alarmed by Jinkins's bull-headed resolve, were lined up and marched aboard the ship, where they were watched over by armed guards, just in case they decided to dive into the water.

The motor cruiser was almost ready to go, having been victualled earlier, but once again there was concern over fuel supplies. To make up for the lack of conventional diesel, the villagers employed a little native ingenuity by boiling coconut flesh to produce more oil, which they transported to the quayside in hollowed-out bamboo canes. Incredibly, this unorthodox method created enough oil to fill two 44-gallon drums. When the diesel engine had attained maximum heat the coconut oil would take over and, hopefully, be sufficient for the long voyage south. Extraordinary times called for extraordinary measures and the Australians' resourcefulness reflected that.

There were other considerations too, not least the rebellious crew, who could not be trusted to attend to their duties, or even sail in the right direction. Jinkins's description of what happened next, from an interview he gave to ABC journalist Tim Bowden in the early 1980s, demonstrates the lengths he was prepared to go to, to achieve his freedom.

I told the skipper that he had to navigate us to Darwin
and if he deviated from the course more than five
degrees either way he would be shot and thrown
overboard. I had the fear that in the night the skipper
might have been able to turn the ship into reverse and
go back on a 180 degree course and it would have been
very difficult for me to know where we were. But the

sky was cloudless and I was able to mark our course
on stars.[9]

It concentrated the poor man's mind wonderfully and the
skipper stayed awake alongside Jinkins at the helm for the next
72 hours without so much as a momentary nap. Meanwhile,
Harry Coe stood beside the engineer for the same period, keeping
the oils up, while the other Australians monitored the rest of the
crew to ensure there were no acts of sabotage.

Still using the map he'd got from an old magazine in the POW
camp, Bill Jinkins knew he was almost there when definitive
proof of his homeland's close proximity appeared in the shape of
an Australian beer bottle, which he spotted floating nearby. In
fact, they'd sailed into Snake Bay at the north of Melville Island,
requiring them to reverse course and make their way down the
west coast of Bathurst Island towards Darwin.

They were several kilometres off the Northern Territory coast
when something on the horizon puzzled them. What were those
stick-like objects poking out of the water in Darwin harbour?
Were their eyes deceiving them after so many days at sea? They
wondered if it could be a trick of the light, some kind of mirage.

In fact, the focus of their attention was startlingly real, as the
long, thin objects protruding from the water revealed themselves
to be, on closer inspection, masts from some of the ships which
were sunk on 19 February 1942. No one had told them about
the Japanese air raids on mainland Australia.

It was a sobering sight as the 26 Australians, Dutchmen and
native crew made their way into port in the late afternoon of
4 May to be greeted by Chief Petty Officer Chick Henderson.
At sea, the boys from Ambon had fantasised about this moment
for months, mentally savouring the first few beers at the Hotel
Darwin and the slap-up dinner that would follow. Disappointingly
the famous watering hole had been badly damaged in the enemy
attack but, no worries, they were still entertained in style in the

naval headquarters at Winnellie, the same barracks which they'd helped to build a year earlier while awaiting deployment.

Cliff Warn couldn't believe they'd made it.

> It was something I didn't expect to succeed because the elements were against us, particularly on the long trip across the Arafura Sea. It was a long shot, but it was worth trying because if we'd stayed in the POW camp we possibly would not be here today. At the end it's just one of those feelings that, well, we've done it, where do we go from here?

After a night of celebration, Bill Jinkins was interviewed by army, navy and air force personnel who wanted to know about the prison camp on Ambon and how they'd escaped. But while the RAAF and the navy adopted an easy-going style in their questioning the army proved more demanding, with Jinkins handed a block of paper and told to sit down and write a report. 'What they didn't seem to understand was that we were going through quite a trauma of relief – there was no tolerance of that at all,' said Jinkins.

The army's no-nonsense approach might have been because Jinkins was in the hands of officers from the battle-hardened 6th Division, who viewed Gull Force with disdain, the 2/21st having barely left Australia and unable to boast sustained experience in battle. Jinkins described his inquisitors as tremendously proud men, perhaps with good reason, but they had underestimated the importance of the escape of the young officer, who was desperate to get to Melbourne and brief higher authorities about what was happening on Ambon.

Eventually he was flown south by a Sunderland flying boat to report to Military Intelligence, but before then he had one final request of the navy – to rescue the stranded men, women and children he'd been forced to leave behind. The following day an Australian destroyer patrolling in the Arafura Sea received a signal to go directly to Saumlaki and pick them all up. Three days later they all sailed safely into Darwin Harbour.

It had been almost seven weeks since Jinkins and his party had slid under the perimeter fence at Tan Tui but in Jinkins's mind the mission was far from over. Back in Melbourne, still dressed in his tropical gear, he reported to General Sturdee, the Chief of the General Staff, who said to him, 'Welcome home, son. We never expected to see any of you again.' It was confirmation of what the battalion had long suspected: they'd been sent to Ambon on a suicidal mission and no one had expected them to return. 'It took until the scones and tea were served before I got over that,' Jinkins admitted to author Patsy Adam-Smith.

Bill was ordered to go home and spend a few days with his mum – oh, and by the way, get some gear more suitable for the Melbourne autumn, Sturdee advised him. Still in his old khaki trousers and shirt, he returned to the family home in Hawthorn to discover there was no one there and left a note promising to return later. Bill's next stop was Snow's menswear store in Flinders Street, to buy a new cap.

His feet had hardly touched the ground when he returned to Army HQ that same afternoon, to help hatch a plan to rescue his mates marooned on Ambon. Jinkins's plan would take ten days to devise, but its execution would prove much more difficult.

Within 24 hours he had arranged a conference with Sir Guy Royle, First Naval Member of the Australian Commonwealth Naval Board, who was on loan from the Admiralty in London. The plan was to despatch two destroyers to Ambon Bay, where a landing party with Jinkins in charge would free the prisoners, help them board the two ships and then sail back to Australia with them. 'Audacious' hardly does justice to the astonishing proposal, but would it work?

Bill Jinkins, who had no doubt it could be done, would deploy members of his landing party to attack the two Japanese gate posts at either end of the camp while he and two others would walk calmly through the main entrance and muster the POWs in readiness for evacuation. Those who couldn't swim would be towed out to one of the ships by rubber dinghies, while the second vessel would 'blast everything they can get a gun on', he envisaged. The rest would swim the 100 metres and board the ships up climbing nets.

Jinkins based his daring plan on his own detailed knowledge of Tan Tui, acquired during his several weeks of incarceration there. 'I'd taken reconnaissance out of the camp many times [and] I knew what defence facilities the Japanese had. They were not prepared for such a thing. They felt they were absolutely secure.' But wouldn't the two frigates be sighted before their arrival? Jinkins had that covered too, opting for the vessels to take a misleading daylight route away from Ambon, but to change course at night, entering the harbour full blast in the dark.

Support for the bold mission among the military and especially the navy was surprisingly high, with 800 of the 1150 Australians expected to get away. Some might stay behind, some might be killed or injured, but if two-thirds of the POWs made it out, it's 'a worthwhile risk', Jinkins and the top brass concluded. Taking the Japanese by surprise in such a dramatic fashion would also be a huge boost to Australian morale.

With the rescue plan assessed and approved, the Dutch *Tromp* was withdrawn to Fremantle to be re-victualled and the *Arunta* returned to Sydney. Jinkins and his 22-man landing party would join the *Arunta* in Townsville before both vessels made their way north to rendezvous in the Arafura Sea. If this worked, it would go down as one of the most daring and intrepid raids in military history.

Bill Jinkins, who knew there was much riding on the mission, had one more duty to fulfil before departing Melbourne. After missing his mum on that first day back, he knew she deserved a special goodbye. Tellingly, she had no concerns for the safety of her brave son, not through lack of love but because of regular visits she made to a Melbourne spiritualist. Throughout Bill's time on Ambon, 'Spooky', as she was known, assured Mrs Jinkins she'd see her son again. 'Mum had complete confidence I was coming home,' Bill said. That confidence would sustain her for the rest of the war.

7

'BUTCHERY FOR A ROMAN HOLIDAY'

IN THE TWO months since Jinkins's party had left Ambon, conditions in the camp suggested a slow deterioration. While the
absence of the three officers was concealed from the Japanese, the
disappearance of other men who had escaped, or attempted to,
became common knowledge. Sometimes during morning roll-call
more than a dozen prisoners failed to appear, prompting Scott
to convince the Japanese that the missing men were attending to
ablutions or had just strolled down to the village for some tobacco.
There was a limit to how long this excuse would be accepted.

The first indication of a tightening of Japanese security was
the erection of a 12-foot-high, double barbed wire fence around
the camp with machine gun posts installed at strategically placed
angles. There would be no more opportunities to slip out of the
camp unnoticed. From now on, the penalty for breaking out of
the camp or concealing an escape would be death under new
Japanese orders which sent a shudder down the Australians'
spines. The second part of the orders was even more alarming:
for every escapee not recaptured, an equal number of prisoners
of equivalent rank would be executed.[1]

Under the terms of the Geneva Convention the maximum
punishment for escaping was 30 days' imprisonment, but the
agreement held little sway in Japanese-occupied territory. Although

Tokyo had signed the agreement it had never officially ratified it, therefore granting the Japanese military, in its interpretation, the right to conveniently ignore the responsibilities which go with enemy imprisonment.

Scott, not unnaturally, wasn't taking any chances and immediately banned his men from making any more escape bids, including one which had been long in the planning by Captain James Major. Instead, the POWs were advised to obey all orders.

As part of the tighter discipline, surprise roll-calls were instigated. A bell would be sounded giving just five minutes' warning, a signal that provided Ikeuchi Masakiyo, who had helped supervise the mass executions at Laha, with even greater authority to inflict pain and misery on his victims. Emboldened by his new-found power, he was in his element, bellowing orders and keeping a close eye on his charges, who, while unnerved by the interpreter's increasingly frenzied manner, had yet to see him demonstrate his maximum potential for cruelty.

Scott, who reckoned he understood the Japanese better than any other prisoner in the camp, given his pre-war experience, told his men that the only way to obtain the best conditions was through rigid camp discipline. It was part of the Japanese ethos, he explained, and because they insisted upon it themselves, they respected it in others. If this meant serving two masters – the Australian officers and the enemy – the battalion would have to accept it. Indeed, Scott was so adamant about enforcing discipline in the camp that it had unintended consequences, draining the POWs' spirits and encouraging bad elements within the ranks.

Said Scott, 'A few cases of thieving occurred. Some officers were openly jeered at and a day came when fatigues were refused. NCOs attempting to arrange them were laughed at. Discipline was disappearing very rapidly and the bitterness of prison life was beginning to be felt.'[2] It did not bode well for morale but worse was to follow with the CO left in no doubt by his fellow officers about the helpless way things were drifting.

Scott was under increasing pressure from all sides and in an effort to defuse a critical situation called a meeting of every digger in the camp. When they assembled on the parade ground there was such commotion that even Major Macrae had difficulty settling them. His customary call to attention before handing over to the commanding officer had little impact. It was a shambles and Scott was livid.

Unable to control his fury any longer he opened up with both barrels, delivering a stinging verbal rebuke which somehow quietened the crowd. He'd been a soldier far too long to allow any man under his command to dictate to him, he blustered. Didn't they understand his position of being not only responsible to the Australian government for war prisoners, but to the Japanese as well? And just for good measure he made it clear that he considered it his duty to accept the first but was only temporarily compelled to accept the latter.

Scott had caught the men's attention and, warming to his hardline tone, paused for dramatic effect. The entire gathering appeared to turn a sympathetic ear to the CO's final message. 'I will do everything in my power to bring you through this but all orders issued through my officers must be obeyed and the strictest discipline be maintained. Everyone's life may depend on this.' And if they didn't co-operate? If Scott had just achieved the near impossible by gaining what appeared to be their grudging support, he was about to undo it all. Any man who didn't obey would be handed over to the enemy. The boys of the 2/21st Battalion couldn't believe what they were hearing – and it didn't stop there. Those caught stealing from their mates, showing insolence to an officer or refusing to obey orders would also be delivered to the Japanese commandant for punishment.

If some were temporarily imbued with empathy for their CO, others viewed his uncompromising attitude as an affront to Aussie mateship, reasoning that if you couldn't stand by your men under such extreme conditions, you ought not to be in charge.

Scott's tirade was not open for debate or compromise and he would countenance no challenge to his rules. He was determined for the sake of everyone that law and order be maintained, so conscious was he that the welfare, or perhaps the lives, of all could be placed at the mercy of a small minority. This was no empty threat, he warned, as the list of penalties grew. Any offender would also have his pay cut if he ever got home, while NCOs who didn't do their job would revert to the ranks. Evil-doers would know what to expect from now on.

By the end of Scott's parade ground outburst there was complete silence and the men, subdued by their commanding officer's ear-bashing, were dismissed. To say they were stunned is an understatement. Even Scott wondered whether he'd gone too far, later making it clear to his fellow officers that they would not be held responsible for his actions. He alone would be accountable – which was all very well, but the damage had been done. How could he hand a prisoner of war and one of his own men over to the enemy, a policy which struck at the very heart of accepted military practice? Though as subsequent events were to demonstrate, the CO's controversial stance was only the beginning of a much darker chapter in the history of Gull Force.[3]

———

By now the war had reached a new stage, both politically and militarily. The so-called Malay Barrier, a dividing line running down the Malayan Peninsula as far south as the most easterly point of the Dutch East Indies, had been breached by the Japanese and with the fall of Singapore on 15 February the Allied forces were in disarray. The short-lived American–British–Dutch–Australian Command (ABDACOM), which was formed to control a vast area from Burma in the west to the Philippines in the east, now had no role and was dissolved towards the end of February.[4]

The American general and field marshal Douglas MacArthur, who had been forced to withdraw from the Philippines as the Japanese advanced, was Supreme Commander, South West Pacific area, and based in Australia. His command covered Australia, New Guinea and those few areas to the north not already under Japanese control. MacArthur was effectively king pin of the entire south-west Pacific, with Australia playing second fiddle to the Americans.

The immediate challenge was to protect Australia from the perceived threat of invasion by the Japanese. Back in Melbourne, Sturdee, in his capacity as Chief of the General Staff, ordered the 7th Division – now en route to the Far East – and those members of the AIF still in the Middle East to return home. This didn't please Churchill or Roosevelt, but Sturdee, still smarting from the sacrifice of Gull Force, Sparrow Force and Lark Force, was adamant. Either Prime Minister Curtin agreed or he would resign.

Refusing to budge, he got his way, arguing that Australia was the only suitable strategic base where the Allies could build up their strength and take the offensive against the enemy. Accepting the failure of earlier policies in the war against Japan, he noted: 'We have violated the principle of the concentration of forces in an effort to hold numerous small localities.' The failed strategy was of little consolation to the imprisoned diggers on Ambon, and Sturdee would soon be on his way to Washington as the head of Australia's Military Mission in the United States.[5] Sir Thomas Blamey would take over as Commander-in-Chief of Allied Land Forces, a role which brought him into conflict with General MacArthur, who demanded total control and preferred to do things his way.

It was a measure of the power of the United States over Australian operational thinking during these early days that even Bill Jinkins's plan to rescue Gull Force from Ambon might have been subject to American approval. While Sturdee and his fellow officers had given the go-ahead to the operation, doubts had suddenly developed elsewhere. How far this had gone up the chain of command was unclear, but it appeared some Australian politicians were going cold on the idea. It might sound ambitious on paper: two parties of 23 men sailing into Ambon Bay to within 100 metres of the Tan Tui camp, storming the gates, releasing the imprisoned diggers, getting them to swim out to the two destroyers and climbing aboard with the aid of landing nets – but didn't fortune favour the bold?

Not in this case, apparently, because a few days after the plan was submitted the mission was cancelled.

Jinkins never quite got to the bottom of it. At the time he was told the navy weren't prepared to risk their ships, but many years later, at the dedication of the Labuan War Cemetery off the north-west coast of Borneo, a secretary from the Department of Defence told him that Australian politicians had cancelled the operation.

There would be further rescue plans, as well as several even more dangerous missions over the next few years, but this first attempt at liberation was going nowhere. While Australian politicians – possibly under pressure from MacArthur and his team – doubtless saw it as a further waste of resources, the truth was that Ambon wasn't seen as a priority. Given that initial reports from the Moluccas suggested the POWs were being treated well by the Japanese – a view reinforced by Jinkins's debriefing – the diggers would just have to be patient.

If only the truth about the massacre had been known; if only the unfolding horror on Ambon could have been relayed to the outside world.

————

In June 1942 the POWs fell under the command of Captain Ando Noburo, commander of the marine garrison, who was known as 'Handlebars' because of his long, wavy moustache. Sadly, his slightly comic appearance concealed a vicious and spiteful individual who exuded malice. According to Walter Hicks he was nothing less than a sadist. 'He was about five feet four and was a little runt of a man who had a samurai sword that was two thirds of his size. He was one of the most cruel people you could ever imagine.'[6]

Major Ian Macrae, the battalion's second in command, claimed that Ando behaved like a maniac, often foaming at the mouth and jumping up and down on the spot. Lieutenant John Van Nooten, the camp adjutant, accused him of 'almost every piece of bestiality': 'He either started it, goaded it or he certainly did nothing to stop it. He was in on every bit of nastiness.' The Japanese commander, who came from a family of booksellers and spoke reasonable English, had the honorary rank of major but was actually a civilian. 'He was referred to as the *tsukan*, which was interpreter–manager as near as I could relate.'[7]

Ando introduced a raft of petty rules to the camp, banning diaries and most forms of entertainment, cutting back on lectures and ordering all POWs, whatever their rank, to salute Japanese sentries. He was a thug, ably assisted by a team of junior hit men who were only too happy to do his bidding.

The number of surprise inspections increased, allowing the equally despised Ikeuchi Masakiyo to take a particular delight in going through prisoners' belongings. It was irritating and did little to foster relations between the captured and their captors. It also foreshadowed the beginning of a reign of terror over both the Australian and Dutch sections of the camp.

The crackdown coincided with a modest increase in work duties. Some of the men were allocated kitchen jobs, others had to chop the wood, while Eddie Gilbert was made to transport water as there was no connection to the mains within the camp. 'There was a watering point where we had a 40-gallon drum and a cart was built to hold it. We had to fill it up and push it round to various places, including the hospital.'[8] Each day two men were allotted to the task, which was physically demanding but nothing like the hard yakka they were about to endure.

As part of the new disciplinary code all contact with the local native population was forbidden and the Dutch, who until now had enjoyed more generous unofficial privileges in Tan Tui, would suffer most.

In the early days of the Japanese occupation, Ikeuchi, who was running the POW camp like a personal fiefdom, had given the Dutch men permission to write to their womenfolk, who were interned in quarters on the other side of the camp. He offered to collect and pass the correspondence on to the wives, although word from the native villagers suggested the mail was never received. The Dutch POWs therefore decided to write letters by roster and give them to their NCO, who would hand them directly to the Ambonese for delivery.

On 11 July 1942 the unofficial correspondence was discovered when a Japanese warrant officer by the name of Hiroishi found the letters on Sergeant Major Frederick Waaldyk, the Dutch NCO. Much to the horror of the rest of the camp Waaldyk was sentenced to death and placed in the guardhouse for execution the next day. He was told the letter writers had confessed and the Japanese wanted to confirm the spelling of their names. The NCO did so and was given some cigarettes, wine and cake for co-operating. The following day 34 Dutch prisoners, including Waaldyk, nine officers, two doctors and the padre, were assembled in a market hut with their hands tied. At 2 p.m. a platoon of young marines nicknamed the alligators arrived, led by Ando Noburo, the moustachioed commander. On the ground lay a supply of star pickets, lengths of metal piping and pick handles, which the marines seized with relish, terrifying the Dutchmen, who saw a graphic vision of what was in store for them.

The POWs were shepherded unceremoniously out of the hut and ordered to march to the top of an adjacent hill overlooking the Tan Tui camp. Here they were made to halt outside the commander's house, where Ando chose a seat for himself on the porch and ordered Ikeuchi and the alligators to 'commence the punishment'. The official post-war account of the cruel and bloody assault, which happened in full view of the Australian POWs, was deemed a matter for the Dutch and as a result the complete story took a while to emerge. When it finally came to light the world was shocked by its sheer brutality.

The young marines 'fell upon the Dutch like wild beasts and desisted only when every man was unconscious', documents in the Australian War Memorial would reveal.

> Ando then rose and struck each unconscious man a blow
> on the head with a pick handle, entered his car and
> drove off. The sight on the hill was a ghastly one . . .
> and at the conclusion the whole hill was slippery with
> blood. Everyone was filled with horror and fear as it was
> our first experience of the Japanese way of enforcing
> discipline.

An Australian newspaper correspondent, Stewart Legge, reporting from the War Crimes Court sitting on Ambon in January 1946, described how Captain Ando blew a whistle to signal the start of the bashings, with each prisoner suffering three beatings, an hour apart. 'The air was filled with Dutchmen's screams and the yells of the Japanese marines. One officer had his eye knocked out and the socket smashed in. He died. Another Dutch officer had both arms and legs broken and died of tetanus. Others had broken limbs.'[9] Ikeuchi couldn't resist joining in, hitting an officer with wood from a door post, blows which were so severe that the Dutchman died the next day.

Curiously Legge, the Melbourne *Sun*'s reporter on Ambon, quoted Sergeant Major Frederick Waaldyk as one of the first witnesses to give evidence before the War Crimes Court. Somehow the Dutch NCO seemed to have escaped execution, though not the savagery which was inflicted on the entire group.[10]

According to Eddie Gilbert, who witnessed the mass beatings from behind the camp's barbed wire, vicious strokes from pick handles and sundry other weapons rained down on the Dutchmen for at least two hours. 'The sickening sound of those implements hitting and the cries of those being beaten, left an indelible impression on those of us who witnessed the atrocity. It also reinforced the deep hatred we had of our captors.'[11]

Lieutenant Van Nooten was equally stunned by the scale of the brutality inflicted on the Dutch. 'This I think was the first occasion on which we realised how the Japanese could react. It was a kind of butchery for a Roman holiday with those who were performing the acts doing so to show how good they were and the onlookers egging them on and thoroughly enjoying it. It was sadistic and quite horrifying.'

The violence would leave a mental scar on those who witnessed it. According to John Devenish the POWs began to act like zombies or robots afterwards. 'They just did as they were told and didn't talk much to one another. They became things, not people.'[12]

The Dutch doctor who, despite a fractured arm, was the first to recover from the ordeal on the hill attended to the rest of the men as best he could and gave them water. The prisoners, who were so badly injured that few could walk, were carried back to their quarters or to the hospital by stretcher. The final casualty toll was sickening. Three men died, ten were beaten to a pulp but somehow survived, thirteen had single or double fractures, and two suffered fractured skulls. Perhaps realising the marines might have gone too far, Ando sent cake and a glass of wine over to Lieutenant Colonel Kapitz, the defeated Dutch commander, together with a message expressing his regret.

The next day the three dead Dutchmen were buried with full ceremony. At the service, which was attended by some of the top Japanese officers, Ando placed a wreath on every coffin and bowed solemnly. There were times when the conflicting moral code of the Japanese and their erratic behaviour defied all understanding and this was certainly one of them.

It didn't put an end to the daily dose of violence, of course. The Dutch Garden Party was only a foretaste of atrocities to come and once again the alligators would be responsible. Later that month the same marines who had so eagerly inflicted punishment on the Dutch would take over as camp guards. No man would be safe in their presence; few would escape their wanton disregard for human rights and lack of compassion. The Japanese marines, often led by Ando, invariably beat and bashed their captives without provocation.

An early indication of how far he and his henchmen were prepared to go came when the Japanese commander, brandishing a 3-foot-long cane, ran amok in the mess, slashing several men across the face and chest. Captain John Turner was whipped three or four times across the face, severely bruising the cheek bone, and half a dozen times across the bare chest, leaving bruises and welts which took some days to heal. Lieutenant William Chaplin, Captain Mason and one of the camp cooks, Private Williamson, were treated in a similar fashion.[13]

On 8 June 1942 Albert McCoomb was a patient in Tan Tui hospital when the ward was called to attention, Ando walked in and struck one of the senior officers, Major George de Verdon Westley, with his sword in front of the men. 'Captain Ando paused opposite a bed where Major Westley was standing . . . struck him heavily across the body and arms several times with his sword. There was no apparent reason for this action.'[14]

On the same day, country boy Charlie Rivett, who came from Nathalia, close to Victoria's border with New South Wales, was sleeping in the isolation ward when he was disturbed by a visitor. A Japanese officer was standing by the bed. He grunted and then belted Rivett several times across the body with his sword scabbard. 'I don't know why – I was very ill,' he said.[15]

The following month Sergeant Kenneth Lupson, who had just celebrated his 24th birthday, found himself at the wrong end of a loaded rifle aimed by a screaming Japanese guard. 'He motioned to me to salute, which I did – he was still jabbering furiously in Japanese. He then produced an iron bar and struck me heavily across the spine twice. I was caused some considerable pain.' Lupson said the guards, drawn from a detachment of Japanese marines and renowned for their cruelty, were all under the control of Ando.[16]

Sometimes punishments were meted out to dozens of men at a time. During August 1942 a party of 25 Australians who were detailed to dig a drain were ordered by a guard to pick up tobacco, soap and pineapples which had been discarded by some native people. Sergeant Bill Harries, who was in his late thirties, knew this contravened Japanese regulations, but who was he to question the command, so he distributed the booty to his men. Inexplicably the guard, who had just ordered them to retrieve the food and thereby break a camp rule, lined them all up and kicked them hard in the shins and body while punching some of them several times in the face.[17]

To add to the men's suffering, food supplies were also dwindling. By now the Australian stocks which had been salvaged earlier had either been consumed or stolen, leading to severe weight loss. Soon starvation and diseases such as malaria, encouraged by a lack of drugs, would begin to take their toll. Theft, too, became an accepted practice. Those who left the camp on work duties would steal anything of nutritional value, hiding it in their clothes or headgear and pooling it with their mates on their return. Smuggling food became second nature and led to some ingenious methods of carriage. One of the most successful was the lap-lap, cotton pants which men draped around their nether regions in the tropical heat. As Eddie Gilbert recalls:

> It was something like a pillowslip but narrower, with a tie
> at the closed end to go around the waist. The other end
> was brought up over the crotch and tucked into the tie at
> the front. With this item of underwear it was possible to
> carry a small can of meat and perhaps half a carton of
> cigarettes, or if rice was the commodity available, a kilo
> of that.

Inevitably some of the POWS were caught, in which case the entire party was beaten. Yet even the prospect of mass punishment didn't deter the men from devising ever more ingenious ways of tricking the enemy. The smuggled food would help to supplement camp rations, which usually consisted of boiled rice, raw fish and cassava, a potato-like vegetable which became a staple of the prisoners' diet. Anything remaining at the end of meal times would be given to the next person listed on a roster. 'It was rigidly adhered to and everyone knew when their turn was coming up and was ready and waiting for those few extra mouthfuls.'[18]

Coconuts were also available in the first few months and would be stored for future consumption.

Significantly, they didn't steal from each other, at least to begin with. There was honour among camp thieves in the early days, but the strict adherence to communal discipline would not last. To give Scott his due, the men were adjusting to life as prisoners of war thanks largely to his administrative skills. His experience in business between the wars had clearly instilled within him a measure of organisational flair and his propensity for giving orders had never left him.

The Japanese had told Scott and Kapitz from the outset that they would be held responsible for controlling their own men. As part of this arrangement the Australian CO set up his headquarters and allotted officers to each company and platoon. Kitchens were organised and it soon became apparent that the rough shearers who'd grown up in rural Australia were far better at the stove than the army-trained cooks. The country boys were remarkably adept at creating an edible dish from very few ingredients.

Psychologically, Scott seemed to exercise a certain moral ascendancy over the Japanese, especially Ikeuchi, who was making life so intolerable for other ranks. The English-speaking interpreter bowed and saluted whenever he met the lieutenant colonel and was unusually receptive to many of his requests. If Scott's ego, which was rarely dented, had renewed his self-confidence, his moral superiority would soon be tested when he clashed with the Japanese over the need to abide by the Geneva Convention.

The response from the Japanese commandant, who would not tolerate any affront to his authority, left little doubt as to how he viewed Scott's behaviour and gave short shrift to his demands. While the English grammar in the note handed to the CO might be found wanting, the message was clear.

Don't be puffed up
Don't be grow impatient
Don't be grow vain
Don't be intrusive
Don't be too forward
To say such a haughty protest for our orders to work by
   you Australian.
Shut your mouth better.[19]

———

In mid-1942 Australian morale was sent sky high by the stirring sight of RAAF Lockheed Hudson bombers flying low over Ambon. The roar of their engines sent a frisson of excitement through the camp as they dived down on shipping in the bay, raising hopes of an early end to the war. Said Eddie Gilbert, 'They flattened out, dropped their bombs and with little between them and the water, continued up the bay past our camp, pursued by some Mitsubishi Zero fighters.' Eddie never discovered how successful the bombers were in sinking or hitting their targets, but their presence certainly boosted camp morale.[20]

If the Hudsons gave cause for bursts of elation the reality of life in Tan Tui quickly sapped any remaining optimism. The increased discipline, the random bashings and the shortage of food continued to take their toll, prompting some of the diggers to resort to ever more desperate and dangerous measures. Despite the threat of execution for those who tried to escape, a few of the POWs became so hungry that they made nightly trips under the wire in search of food from villagers. With such blatant disregard for the rules it was inevitable they'd be caught. Sure enough, the guards found out about the midnight food missions and in early November grabbed four men as they attempted to re-enter the camp.

Retribution was swift, with the group taken up to Japanese headquarters and beaten savagely until dawn. In the morning Ikeuchi announced that the entire camp would be punished unless all the other men who'd gone out on night food searches confessed. A few owned up, having been assured they would receive light punishment, but the Japanese were not satisfied with the number who'd come forward. The following day the Australians were lined up before a group of villagers who were ordered to identify the guilty ones.

For Eddie Gilbert it was hard to convey the degree of fear and apprehension that gripped the prisoners as the local men fixed each Australian with a lingering stare and slowly made their way along the line. 'Not being part of the "escapade" myself I trembled at the thought that one of the villagers would identify me to avoid being punished himself. It was a truly nerve-racking and terrifying experience.'

Eddie's fear was more than justified, as 25 men were identified and made to join the other four being held at Japanese headquarters. For the next eleven days screams echoed through the camp as the prisoners were beaten to within an inch of their life in a frenzy of violence and torture. As Eddie described it:

> With their wrists tied together they were suspended from
> branches of a large tree with their feet barely touching
> the ground. On and off during this time they were
> savagely beaten with pick handles, steel pickets, steel
> rods – anything the guards could lay their hands on. At
> the end of the day they were tied together around the base
> of the tree.[21]

Sometimes their genitals were kicked or parts of their body burned with cigarette ends. Once a day they were given food and water by the other POWs, only for the beatings to resume soon afterwards. Three days after the nightmare began some of the men were allowed back to camp. Others were also released over the next week but eleven failed to return.

Those who survived took weeks to recover from their internal and external injuries, while others who were never seen again were taken away by truck and beheaded. The mass punishment lasted eleven days and by the end it felt as though the entire strength of Gull Force had been beaten into submission. It was hard to believe their plight could get any worse, but even darker days lay ahead as death, disease and the ever-present threat of the Japanese sword cast a Stygian gloom over the 2/21st Battalion and its accompanying units.

8

VOYAGE INTO THE UNKNOWN

F EW HAD HEARD of the island of Hainan when the 3048-tonne
freighter *Taiki Maru* set sail from Ambon on 25 October
1942. Indeed, the ship's destination hadn't been revealed when
Ikeuchi the interpreter announced that 263 Australians and 237
Dutch were to be sent to a convalescent camp which was much
better equipped to deal with the sick and injured. The 500 men
represented a third of the diggers on Ambon and all the Dutch
prisoners.

Most of the men who were selected for the voyage were
already sick, which gave credence to the Japanese explanation for
the transfer. Because of their condition they'd be accompanied
by almost every member of the Australian Army Medical Corps
unit, which, although demonstrating concern for the men, left
Ambon with only one trained doctor, an Australian by the name
of Peter Davidson. It wouldn't take long for the lack of medical
personnel to have serious consequences for the health of the men
left behind, and it wasn't the only Japanese decision to leave the
battalion baffled.

To add to the sense of uncertainty, fourteen Australian officers
were also assigned to the 'convalescent' camp, including Scott
and his second in command Ian Macrae. Those who remained
on Ambon would now be under the command of Major George

de Verdon Westley, whose authority would be so undermined in the grim years ahead that his reputation would be permanently tarnished.

Some of those chosen for the voyage into the unknown were reluctant to go, including Fred Crane, who was among more than a dozen POWs from the Swan Hill area of Victoria and reckoned better the devil you knew. Fred, 24, found a pair of mates who'd been split up in the transfer and were keen to exchange places so they could stay together. 'The Japanese didn't know I swapped. They just bundled us off and I stopped [behind] with the hope that I might get rescued early, which I didn't.'[1]

There were many false assumptions and unfounded hopes about who was going where and why in the days leading up to the ship's departure. The men were given the impression they were destined for a holiday camp, a tropical resort to the north where they could see out the rest of the war in relative comfort. Nobody seriously believed the propaganda and Captain Ando's farewell reinforced their suspicions.

The vessel was due to sail at 11.45 a.m. Just before it weighed anchor the marine commander couldn't resist giving the last man aboard, Captain John Turner, a swift blow to the body. Turner, who was clearly relieved to see the back of Ando, was now even more determined to maintain a detailed record of everything that happened. His meticulous notes would provide damning evidence against the Japanese after the war and a comprehensive picture for military historians.

First impressions of the ship they were on did not bode well. The upper holds, which contained most of the men, including the sick, were 'very crowded and ventilation was almost nil', but there were adequate tinned rations and plenty of water and the Japanese crew seem 'fairly co-operative', Turner noted. Indeed, the discipline on board appeared so lax that there was even talk of taking over the ship and heading for home. Ron Leech reckoned the idea was 'entirely feasible' as there were several Dutch naval officers among their ranks. 'However as we were under no illusion that such a course of action would have disastrous effects on those remaining on Ambon and possibly the whole Pacific area, we decided against the plan.'[2]

Thus any thoughts of mutiny were soon quelled. The *Taiki Maru* hit the tail end of a typhoon, causing heavy seas in the first few days, but apart from seasickness it was a largely uneventful voyage.

By now the POWs had been told where they were going, even though they weren't sure what to expect. Word had got around that Hainan was an island off the south coast of China nearly 1000 kilometres south-west of Hong Kong and about the same size as Formosa, later known as Taiwan. It was 16 kilometres due south of Lui Chow Peninsula and 313 kilometres east of northern Indo-China. To the north was the Hainan Strait, to the west the Gulf of Tonkin and to the south-east the South China Sea. The geographic location meant little to the country boys of the 2/21st, most of whom had never set foot outside of Victoria, so it might as well have been in the middle of nowhere.

Hainan was rich in iron ore and coal which, together with rumoured deposits of other valuable minerals and oil, explained Japan's interest in the island.[3]

On 4 November the ship's skipper sent for Captain Turner and, pointing to a speck on the horizon, declared: 'There is the island of Hainan where there is much hard work for you all.' The 33-year-old St Kilda–born officer told the skipper that all those on board were sick men and therefore incapable of hard labour, but if Turner was hoping for a sympathetic hearing he was disappointed. Instead, his remark was met by gales of laughter from the ship's captain and his first officer. It was the first confirmation that the Australians' new home was going to be nothing like what they'd been promised.

Ten days after leaving Ambon they called in at Sama, on the south coast of Hainan, where they were inoculated for cholera and typhoid. On 5 November they disembarked at Bakli Bay, where they were met by Captains Ida and Mishima, Adjutant and Quartermaster of the Japanese Naval Landing Party, and marched to the prison camp, about 6 kilometres away. Those who were fortunate enough to survive would be held there until the end of hostilities.

Along the route they were jeered at by Japanese civilians and coolies working on the wharf. It was a dark and depressing welcome, made worse by the revelation that they would also be treated as coolies from now on. As for the island of Hainan itself, unlike Ambon the coastal region offered little to commend it in terms of vegetation or terrain. As Scott put it, 'The outlook was deplorable – a barren, sandy island with nothing but a little cactus here and there, a hot wind and no convenience of any kind. This impression was shared by everyone.'

The Hashio prison camp, which covered about 4 hectares and was surrounded by a low barbed wire fence, consisted of four barracks about 70 metres long by 9 metres wide. The buildings were constructed from pine boards and had wooden shutters in lieu of windows and a roof made out of corrugated iron sheets. The men soon discovered that the barracks, which were of a primitive style and originally designed for the use of Chinese coolies, were not waterproof. The barracks' centre aisle was made from dirt with a sleeping platform at each side and, contrary to earlier reassurances, bore no resemblance to a holiday camp.

The Australians were assigned one building and the Dutch another. There was a kitchen which had few utensils and the water, which came from two wells, was undrinkable unless boiled. The sick were bundled in with the healthy, which really made little difference as there were neither beds nor nursing equipment and all ranks slept together on straw mats (two for every three men). The latrines were antiquated, with excrement bailed out every night into a container and buried nearby, leaving a foul smell which hung around all day. Increasing the likelihood of disease there were no drains, so waste water would quickly form a stinking pool, attracting malarial mosquitoes and other creepy-crawlies.

A diary kept by Sergeant Maloney described how the huts were infested with bugs, cockroaches, rats, lice, fleas and ants:

> The Japanese were quite indifferent to the whole state of affairs and no assistance was given despite repeated requests. Men ate and worked in filthy conditions inhabited by natives and imported coolies. No soap, brooms, scrubbing brushes, cleaning materials of any description were provided during the imprisonment. The camp was a quarter of a mile from an old swamp which was an ideal breeding ground for mosquitoes.

The day after their arrival Captain S. Kondo, Commander of the 4th Yokosuka Special Naval Landing Force and the man in overall charge of Hainan, assembled the prisoners and read a proclamation from a rostrum. The Australians and the Dutch, already demoralised by living conditions which were far inferior to those on Ambon, looked on anxiously. Surely the news couldn't get any worse?

Kondo started with a vision which he hoped would both comfort and reassure the POWs, telling them that they were no longer regarded as the enemy because they had surrendered. 'So you can serve your duty here without any need of anxiety. We feel very much sympathy for you and treat as well as our regulation permits, but ... even a small act of opposition must be severely punished.'[4]

At this, the men shuffled uneasily, and rightly so. They were told that a great city was being built and the Australians were expected to join in, especially with road work. At first the prisoners thought they'd misheard it. There was no interpreter at this stage so language difficulties made it difficult to understand the Japanese captain. Scott moved to clear up any misunderstandings by making it plain that all his men were sick.

'That's most unfortunate,' the commander replied, 'but you must do your best.' Oh, and by the way, there was another small problem, the Japanese officer added. 'We don't have much food to give you, so the daily diet will consist mainly of rice' was the essence of his message.

Lieutenant Colonel Scott would be in charge of discipline and if they all behaved they'd be treated as well as regulations permitted. While the men couldn't fully understand the speech, the Japanese commander's demeanour was not lost in translation: if you don't like it, too bad, and beware the consequences.

While the living conditions left a lot to be desired, at least the Japanese adopted a fairly benign attitude in those early days. Captain Turner described their policy towards prisoners during the first two months as one of 'relative reasonableness', but sadly it didn't last.[5]

The POWs' first task was to clear prickly pear from the route of a proposed road. Everyone was expected to pitch in, including the officers, because it was good for their health, Lieutenant Takai, Hashio's first camp commandant, told them. They must live a simple life like the Japanese and be earnest and diligent. The Australian officers, who until now had been excused work duties, weren't happy with their new role, prompting Scott to take the matter up with Kondo. Cleverly, he pointed out that if the officers were compelled to do manual work alongside the men they would lose face, although he would be happy for an officer to accompany each work party.

Scott's thinking was that this would provide a buffer between the guards and their prisoners, but when he handed a letter to Captain Kondo over Takai's head, detailing his position, Takai himself lost face. The result was a change in his attitude from one of reason to extreme hostility. As tensions grew, Lieutenant Takai finally lost his patience with the Australians' failure to co-operate, punishing them by increasing their workload and even forcing the sick to get out of bed. Said John Turner, 'All men, even if suffering from beri-beri, who were not in hospital, engaged in work parties.'

The pressure on Scott was also taking its toll. On one occasion he lost his temper during an exchange with Kondo and two Japanese judges who were visiting the camp. A few days later he was ordered to sign a paper agreeing to co-operate with his captors to build a new East Asia. The stakes were high but, courageously, both Scott and Turner declined, knowing full well that they risked being shot if they stood their ground. Faced with the Australians' intransigence, Kondo was forced to take a different tack, hinting that there would be reprisals for the entire camp if they didn't put pen to paper. It did the trick, with Scott informing his second in command Lieutenant Macrae (later to become a major) that under the circumstances he had had no alternative but to sign.

While the decision defused the immediate crisis it did nothing for the mental well-being of Scott, who appeared to be on the verge of a nervous breakdown. An appendix to the official post-war report on Hainan claimed the commanding officer's health was 'cause for the gravest concern'. Scott himself felt equally concerned for the emotional well-being of his men, saying in his post-war report:

The duplicity of the Japanese in sending all the sick men
to such a dreadful spot, the total absence of facilities and
drugs for the treatment of urgent cases, lack of proper
food, bitter resentment and complaints from the men
who faced a dreary future of hard manual labour under
appalling conditions, all took toll mentally.[6]

Such was the concern over the CO's mental state that Lieutenant Macrae arranged separate quarters for Scott, 'to prevent his complete breakdown'. A hut just over 2.5 metres square built out of second-hand iron was erected by the men about 30 metres from the barracks and it seemed to do the trick, for Lieutenant Colonel Scott's condition began to improve.

The same could not be said for the rest of the camp, whose

general health was deteriorating rapidly. By 24 November 1942, no fewer than 40 cases of beri-beri had been diagnosed. The following month, morale plummeted further as the men began to suffer severe hunger. The quartermaster appealed to Scott, who by now had been ordered to vacate his hut by a furious Lieutenant Takai, to press the Japanese commander for more food. Perhaps suggesting he was still mentally unbalanced, Scott disregarded the quartermaster's plea, insisting he was satisfied with the cooking and distribution and the POWs ought to grin and bear it. 'Remember you're Australians and behave like men,' he ordered them.

Scott, who by now was overwhelmed by the weight of complaints which he was asked to pass on to the Japanese, believed it made more sense to keep his requests to the minimum and only approach the camp commandant on very serious matters. Fellow officers failed to comprehend his attitude, reinforcing the perception that the CO was not looking after the best interests of the battalion. Yet, unexpectedly, the policy bore fruit, with Kondo treating Scott with greater respect and occasionally acceding to his demands.

On Christmas Day 1942 there was even a little extra food and a tot of prickly pear juice to help them celebrate and drink to the King's health. It was hardly a typical Aussie Christmas but at least it lifted their spirits for a few hours. Tom Pledger missed out on the treats because he'd contracted a bout of dysentery and had lost a couple of stone. He'd also developed beri-beri, but that didn't prevent his culinary imagination from working overtime. 'Won't it be lovely to get my teeth around a good slab of steak and half a dozen eggs.'[7]

Nineteen forty-three dawned with little hope of an early end to the war. The Japanese insisted they were poised for victory but the men of Gull Force, with no reliable news to hand, didn't know what to believe. The sickness, the poor food and the growing sense of despair now triggered a breakdown in community standards that had so far kept the battalion as one. Some of the men started to steal, others to sell their clothes and watches to buy tobacco or a little additional food, and a few were so desperate they almost gave their possessions away. Even the tradition of supporting and helping your mates, so long a fixture of military life, was being undermined. Said Ralph Godfrey, 'There was absolutely no Australian mateship for 18 months – it was every man for himself. If he got something he kept it, he didn't share it with anybody.'[8]

There was also the issue of suppressed sexual appetite, which was not openly discussed until after the war when Scott revealed that a case of sodomy occurred. These were young men, after all, and while their sexual drive might have dimmed under the conditions in which they were living, some clearly had difficulty containing their carnal instincts.

The controversial allegation in Scott's official post-war report did not sit comfortably with the experience of others, who maintained that the men didn't have the energy or inclination to think about sex. As George Williamson said, 'It just didn't enter your mind. If you don't get the vitamins and the right food into you, you just lose all interest in sex because you just don't have the drive.' As for accusations of homosexuality in the camp, he said, 'It never happened. People ask me was there any male rape or anything like that? Well, there was none of it went on. I know that.'[9]

These were sensitive questions. Whatever the truth, there was little doubt that temptation in its varying forms was beginning to pose a serious threat to the orderly conduct of day-to-day life in the camp. Scott moved to nip the looming crisis in the bud by calling a parade of all ranks, ordering them to maintain their self-respect. Cases of stealing, refusing to obey orders and insolence to officers would be dealt with personally by him and he would have no compunction about delivering offenders to the Japanese for punishment.

The warning was virtually a carbon copy of his speech on Ambon, only this time there was even more at stake. To survive in such a hostile environment they had to pull together, he told them, and theft and other forms of criminal behaviour would not be tolerated.

> Hard as the task of maintaining order was it had to be done. It was no use threatening men with punishment when the war was ended. Crimes had to be stopped at once and the type of man who would not respond to appeals for honesty and decency must be ruled by fear.[10]

As if conditions in the camp weren't bad enough, far worse would follow, as the Australians and the Dutch were soon to find out. Many of the POWs wished they were back on Ambon with their mates, though they did not know about the mass bashings of the Australians a few weeks after they had left or the sickness and starvation that would soon lead to many more deaths. Life on both Ambon and Hainan was about to enter a new and much deadlier phase.

The names Scott and Westley would also dominate this cruel and bitter chapter as they struggled to maintain discipline among the men, while appearing to acquiesce to the enemy. The way Gull Force reacted would become part of battalion folklore. What happened when officers and men turned against each other would ricochet through the post-war decades and into the 21st century.

———

While the POWs on Hainan and Ambon remained ignorant of events in the outside world, there was evidence that the tide was beginning to turn in the Pacific theatre of war. These were early days, but the Americans, so taken by surprise at Pearl Harbor nearly a year earlier, were now on the offensive.

In August 1942 US marines came ashore at Guadalcanal and secured the airfield. The battle for the Pacific island became one of the bloodiest battles of the Second World War and would tie up American forces for the next six months, until the Japanese finally evacuated in February 1943. Over much of the same period Australian and Japanese forces were engaged in an intense battle for control of New Guinea. The initial Japanese attack, which began with an assault on Rabaul in January 1942, posed a serious threat to the Allies and would engage Australian forces in the pivotal Kokoda track campaign for many months.[11]

Back on Ambon, Allied air raids on military installations and shipping in the bay provided an encouraging sign that the war in the air was far from over. Occasionally, Allied bombers flew unnervingly close to the camp itself, but the Australians reckoned the Yanks knew about the camp and would never drop their load on innocent men and women. Within months, events would prove how wrong they were.

The island's prison population had also grown in the latter half of 1942. A group of nine Americans escaping from the Philippines had been captured during a hair-raising voyage south. They included Edward Weiss, a member of the US Army's Signals Corps. Weiss's escape from Corregidor as the Japanese moved in on Manila during February 1942 was to become an epic story of survival as he sailed and island-hopped his way down towards the Dutch East Indies with fellow radio operator Clyde Rearick.

Along the way they were joined by other Americans who were equally determined to avoid capture, including men such as Lieutenant Bob Grainger, a deeply religious man who would have an impact on the lives of many both during and after the war; Ensign 'Red' Carson, a career naval officer aged about 30; and fellow Ensign 'Mac' McGibony, in his late twenties. They were mostly entry level commissioned officers. Six-foot-tall Lieutenant 'Swede' Jensen was a reserve officer who'd been called up for duty, while 'Pappy' Hunter was a chief quartermaster and an expert navigator. Captain 'Lars' Nelson, 60, the oldest of the group, was a civilian engineer in the Philippines and on the outbreak of war had been commissioned in the US Army. The only civilian in the party was Ed Kincaid, in his thirties, who made a living in the import–export business.

Facing incredible dangers as the might of the Japanese war machine moved relentlessly south, they risked their lives in remote jungles and storm-tossed seas for months on end in pursuit of freedom. Ed Weiss obtained a leaking *banca*, a hollowed-out tree with outrigger, for part of the voyage, while at other stages the group used an 18-metre sailboat called the *Maria del Pilar*, which they'd purchased on the Philippine island of Negros. It was a sturdy vessel with a 12-metre mast and a small cabin. The plan was to sail her to the neighbouring island of Cebu and on to Mindanao, the Dutch East Indies and finally Australia.

Apart from dealing with unpredictable weather they had several close shaves with Japanese patrol boats whose crews luckily mistook them for native fishermen, but it was inevitable that their good fortune would run out. Six months after the Japanese declaration of war on the Philippines the intrepid Americans sailed into the small community of Tobelo on the island of Halmahera in the Dutch East Indies, unaware that the white-suited harbourmaster was now in the employ of the Japanese.

'White suit', as he was dubbed by Ed Weiss and his mates, asked about their nationality and where they were headed. They explained that their destination was the United States. The Dutchman asked whether they had a pass from the Japanese and Swede replied, 'No.' White Suit then asked, 'Will you please come with me and be my prisoners?' Swede replied, 'No, we will not.'

The Americans then started asking him questions. Swede asked, 'Who are you working with – the Japs or the Allies?' White Suit replied, 'Before I worked for the Hollanders, but now for the Japanese.'

It confirmed what the men already suspected. Their cover was blown – it was only a matter of time before their location was passed on to the enemy. Swede told White Suit to get off his boat, but it would not be the last Ed Weiss saw of him. Three years later their paths would cross in very different circumstances.[12]

On 10 August 1942 a Japanese patrol boat appeared nearby, with two of the crew crouching behind a machine gun on the deck. They opened fire in the direction of the *Pilar* and in an impulsive gesture of defiance the Americans raised the Stars and Stripes. Hopelessly outgunned, they realised there was no escape. They'd sailed and drifted about 3200 kilometres since leaving Negros on 28 June only to have their hopes of freedom dashed just north of the equator.

Ed Weiss wondered whether they'd be shot or taken prisoner as four or five Japanese marines jumped onto the deck of the *Pilar* and tied the Americans' arms behind their backs. Instead, they were herded aboard the patrol boat, ordered into a storage hold and the hatch closed, leaving the nine prisoners in ink-black darkness. Later they were transferred to a small freighter where they were joined by about 25 Dutch civilians. They then set sail for a small island further south named Ambon.

On 16 August they arrived in Ambon's deepwater bay, which was alive with warships and other Japanese military activity. It was their first sight of the island the Americans would call home for the next three years.[13]

Soon they would be joined by five more Americans who had also made the perilous voyage south. By coincidence, Ed Weiss had trained with three of them – Mike Maslak, Stan Kapp and Irv Stein – in Signal School at Fort Monmouth, New Jersey during 1939. The remaining two were George Lindahl, a Captain in the Field Artillery, and B-17 radio operator and gunner John Biss. What a story, what an incredible adventure they had shared as they attempted to make their way to freedom. After walking more than 160 kilometres through inhospitable terrain on Mindanao, they had sailed nearly 1600 kilometres on a sea-going *banca* to an island off the north-west tip of New Guinea. Reassured about their safety by friendly natives who sheltered them for several days, they were eventually exposed by the Muslim village chief, who turned them over to the Japanese. Now they were also bound for Ambon.

Since the Japanese invasion in February, Ambon's civilian population had also increased as more Dutch men, women and children were shipped from other islands within the Dutch East Indies. Peter Koop, who was about six at the time, had grown up with his family at Manokwari on the north coast of Dutch New Guinea, now Irian Jaya. His father was the local police chief there and his mother a teacher. They were transferred to Ambon in early 1943 and spent the next two years there, much of it behind barbed wire. Sometimes they were allowed out to the beach, but conversation with the guards or the locals was strictly forbidden. Said Peter, 'We were reasonably fluent in Indonesian but they didn't want us to talk and I remember a number of times being punished for that.'[14]

On one occasion his mother Fje stood up to the Japanese after Peter was made to balance on his leg holding a stone above his head in the baking midday sun. The Japanese ordered her back to school to teach, but she refused, saying, 'Not as long as my kid is standing in the sun.' 'The guard tried to force the issue,' said Peter, 'but she didn't budge. In hindsight, it's amazing how this very ordinary woman stood up to them.'

It was not the only test of the Koop family's endurance as they settled down to life on Ambon. Soon they would be thrust into the front line of battle.

For some months the Japanese had been using part of the camp for storage of household goods in open-sided sheds along the main road, close to the hospital and opposite the Dutch compound. But in an ominous departure, they decided to use the sheds for storing bombs as well. By the close of 1942 there were an estimated 200 000 pounds of explosives in the camp which, if ignited, would inevitably cause untold death and damage. The Australian officers whose quarters were barely 5 metres away were understandably concerned and asked Major Westley to make an official protest to Ikeuchi, but it made no difference. To the

Japanese, the POWs had no rights and even a request to paint a red cross on the hospital was dismissed. The camp interpreter told them he assumed the Yanks knew they were there – so why worry?

In reality, no one could be certain whether the US Air Force was aware of the Allied prisoners held on Ambon because the POWs couldn't be sure whether any of the escapees had made it back to Australia to inform the authorities. The diggers could only keep their fingers crossed that the Americans knew the truth and would give the camp a wide berth on bombing runs. It wasn't until 15 February 1943 that the stark reality emerged. Just before 11.30 a.m. a menacing drone was heard in the distance. The US Air Force had Tan Tui in its sights.

It was the 90th Bombardment Group's 319 Missile Squadron, led by Captain Charles E. Jones, who had taken off from Fenton Airfield at Hayes Creek, about 50 kilometres south of Darwin, hours earlier.

Walter Hicks was out on a work party and had just got back to camp when the air raid siren sounded. 'Within a matter of minutes a squadron of US Liberators came in from the south straight across the island and over the sea plane base,' he said.[15] Originally there were nine planes on the mission but Captain Jones's B-24 was forced back to base because of engine trouble, leaving Lieutenant Paul C. Johnson in command.

Walter, who was watching the action from the road, saw the group turn left towards Ambon town where they dropped their bombs, before one of the aircraft made an unexpected manoeuvre to the left again. Walter didn't believe what he was seeing as the Liberator headed directly towards the camp. Didn't the pilot know they were there?

Eddie Gilbert had also heard the air raid alarm and looked up to see the B-24s flying towards the harbour. 'Their route took them past the camp – not directly over it but close enough.'[16] He was pretty safe, he assured himself, assuming they'd never bomb their own side. What he didn't realise was that he was about to become a sitting target, as a stick of bombs appeared from the belly of one of the planes and hurtled towards the camp. 'We were like rats in a trap.'[17]

Momentarily transfixed by the aerial display, Walter counted the Liberator's lethal cargo, bomb by bomb. Four bombs fell outside the barbed wire perimeter, a fifth landed on a sentry box, another fell onto the women's hut in the Dutch compound and a seventh careered off and neatly positioned itself between a stack of bombs in the storage sheds. 'Have you ever heard bombs dropping?' he asked. 'It sounds like galvanised iron being ripped up like paper – the sound was almost deafening.'[18]

Surprisingly, the storage depot did not explode immediately. The rogue bomb had merely set fire to the thatched roof and injured an engineer who was carrying out maintenance work. Most of the men were safe for now, but they knew they had to get out smartish before the whole dump went up. Said Walter:

> The anti-personnel bombs were in wooden cases so it was only a matter of minutes before one would go off and when one went off the whole lot would. Of course when we got to the gates the Japs wouldn't let us out. We were stuck in the camp behind the wire. I didn't feel happy. Not happy.[19]

The Dutch section had taken a direct hit. Peter Koop was sheltering under a bed with his mother, aunt and elder brother, Robert, when the bombs fell. Mrs Koop seized her two boys, put Peter under her arm as he was smaller, and made her way down to the beach to escape the explosions. In the ensuing panic people were walking, staggering and running in all directions, but where was Dad? Then, in the distance, Peter saw the familiar figure of Archibald Koop racing towards him. 'I remember him coming in from the other side, waving to us and telling us to keep running because he was trying to find my aunt.'[20] But it was too late. Peter's aunt was already dead, killed by a fatal shrapnel wound to the head.

Archibald Koop arrived in the Dutch quarters just as another blast demolished the building and in the force of the explosion he was badly wounded. As he lay unconscious, debris tumbled onto his crumpled body, fracturing his legs.

Peter Koop's vivid recollection of that appalling day has never left him, nor has the respect he holds for his mother. 'We don't hear much about the women but when you have two kids to look after in that kind of environment, it's always made me think dearly about my mother.'[21]

The engineer who was injured by the rogue bomb was Lieutenant Parkin Campbell, Section Officer of No. 3 Section, 2/11th Field Company, who was only a few yards from the actual bomb dump and badly needed assistance. With a total lack of concern for their own safety Captain Peter Davidson, the island's only senior medic, and Private Maurice Atherton, an Englishman who'd grown up in northern New South Wales near Inverell, rushed to his aid. It was, according to Sergeant Don Baker of the 2/12th Field Ambulance, 'Morry's greatest and noble day ... It was a suicide rescue and they knew it, but it did not stop them. As they reached the injured man the dump went up with terrific force.'[22]

Irish-born Davidson, who had grown up in Queensland, was dead at the age of 42. Atherton was badly burned and in a severe state of shock, but at least he was alive. Sergeant Baker pulled him out of the rubble but Morry refused any medical attention until Davidson had been seen to first. Don Baker viewed Maurice Atherton's actions that day as 'an example to us all of courage, fearlessness and self-sacrifice'.[23] Morry took some time to recover, but miraculously he did so, eventually returning to work and somehow finding the time to grow vegetables in a small garden – not for him, but for his sick comrades. Sadly, he would not endure the hardships to come.

In the pandemonium that followed the latest blast, other men rushed in to clear the area. Jack Panaotie saw a sheet of flame followed by a terrific explosion. 'The whole place was on fire and all the huts were flattened. Under the debris someone yelled, "Help", and we got him out.'[24]

Jack turned to see a pair of hands protruding from another pile of rubble. It turned out to be the padre, Charles Patmore, nicknamed 'Chewing Gum Charlie' because he was always offering PK to the men. Les Hohl, who was also nearby, shouted to the padre to hold on while he found some other men to help pull off the timber. He went away to grab some blokes and as they returned a raging fire fuelled by the *atap* thatching swept across the ruins, engulfing the trapped clergyman. They reckoned he must have died in seconds.[25]

As the flames continued to crackle across the dump, at least half the bombs were yet to explode. The fire had to be extinguished quickly if further casualties were to be avoided. With no running water the only alternative was a human bucket chain from the beach to the fire. American marine Red Carson bravely took control, standing amid the wreckage to direct operations. 'Over here!' he bellowed, ordering the men to tip their buckets over the unexploded bomb crates on which he stood. The others reckoned the American was either heroic or foolhardy, but disappeared down to the shoreline sharpish. Les understandably concluded there was no point in hanging around the bomb dump longer than necessary.

Carson, however, seemed oblivious to the danger as he continued to shout his orders. 'Hey, guys, there's a bomb over here. Keep it cool, keep it cool, man. Hurry, soldier, keep that one cool.'[26] Slowly the immediate danger passed, and only then did the full scale of the carnage emerge. The explosion had left a hole some 12 metres deep, 60 metres wide and more than 100 metres long.

Ninety per cent of the camp had also been flattened, leaving much of it a smouldering ruin, but it was the human toll among the Australian POWs and the Dutch civilians that was the greatest tragedy. An estimated 27 Dutch women and children lay dead and ten Australians, including six officers, had been killed. Among them were the adjutant, Captain John Hooke, who had been so effective as a buffer between prisoners and guards.

According to Lieutenant John Van Nooten, many more were also injured, a lot of whom died later. 'It was a huge blast that was just beyond your powers of registering,' he said. 'How it did not kill more we will never know.'[27]

That night as whiffs of smoke and the smell of burning timber drifted through what remained of the old barracks, some survivors pondered their good fortune, while others began to ask questions among themselves. How could this have happened when the Americans must have known the camp was there? And if they didn't know, surely the pilots must have seen them, as they had flown so low.

Sapper Sydney Prince decided it was the bomb dump they were after. Charlie Norman agreed, but it didn't explain the reckless loss of innocent lives. 'How could they bomb our camp?' he said. 'They must have known we're here, or have they forgotten about us?' Doug Phillips took a more cynical view. 'Perhaps the top brass know we're here but they're keeping it to themselves and not telling the pilots in case they won't bomb.'[28] 'That's it,' said Charlie, 'I'll bet that's it. I'll bet they didn't tell the pilots we were here. I can't see why they'd bomb us otherwise.'[29]

How closely Doug's and Charlie's views reflected the truth remained unclear but it was a credible explanation. Were the Allies prepared to risk endangering the POWs in a bid to destroy the bomb dump? Was this simply one more sacrifice the men of Gull Force would have to make? Or had the Australians simply failed to share their information with the Americans? Had there been a serious breakdown in the intelligence structure between the US and the Australian military or was it merely friendly fire, a poorly executed bomb run by a pilot who had no idea what he was targeting?

Ed Weiss, the American POW who spent much of the war on Ambon, was and always would be left wondering how his fellow countrymen came to bomb the camp when the Allies should have known of its existence. 'You'd have thought that when they were planning the mission the flight crews would know it was there. I've heard from different sources that they did and they didn't. I've also heard they bombed it by mistake but who admits it I don't know.'[30]

What was without doubt was that the Australian military knew about the camp, because Bill Jinkins had briefed them fully after his escape, but had the information been passed on to the US Air Force? 'I would assume it was shared with the US military,' said Ed Weiss. 'However, the question remains how far down the ladder did this information go and was it part of the briefings given to the crews that were going on a mission to Ambon?'[31]

If it was a stuff-up, the mistake was clearly costly. Despite Ed's repeated attempts to uncover the truth, the complete files from that bombing raid were never recovered. Reflecting on the tragedy, and perhaps driven by a sense of duty to those who died, his enquiries continued.

Even at the age of 91 he had trouble erasing the image of a teenage Dutch girl who was mortally wounded in that terrible blast. At the time he thought she was dead, but when he spoke to her she opened her frightened eyes. Ed knelt beside her and clasped her hand to reassure her. 'Because her face and head showed no sign of wounds I lifted the blanket covering her. A bomb fragment had torn through her stomach and she was bleeding badly. There was nothing I could do to help her.'[32]

The dying girl pleaded for a drink of water.

I had been told that you never gave anyone with a
stomach wound a drink of water, no much how they
pleaded for one [but] her pleas were too much to bear.
I ran to my hut to get my water canteen. If I could have
cried I would have. This innocent, lovely girl had become
a victim of the madness of that day. I too had become a

victim. I was losing the ability of a human to outwardly display human emotion.[33]

By the time he returned the young woman was dead. He wiped the sweat off her face with a damp cloth and covered her body again with the blanket.

Those who died in the bomb dump attack were kept overnight in the camp hospital, which was conveniently close to the cemetery. By morning, a series of wooden crosses appeared at the head of every grave, bearing the name of each victim – 16 February 1943 was the most sombre day the camp had known. The funerals for the Dutch and Australian victims eclipsed so many other tragedies during the preceding twelve months that it was difficult to see how life could get any worse.

It was just over a year since they had been herded together at Tan Tui, yet it transpired that this was only a taste of the level of suffering to follow.

Later that morning a large white banner bearing a red cross was placed on the roof of the hospital by the Japanese, following a request from Major Westley and his newly appointed adjutant Lieutenant John Van Nooten that the site be marked as a POW camp in the hope that Allied bombers would avoid it in future.

It seemed to be a rare display of compassion by the Japanese, whose photographers eagerly took pictures of the banner while snapping the damaged buildings. But if the men of Gull Force interpreted the gesture as the beginning of a new understanding with their captors, they were mistaken. Two days later 'Handlebars' Ando ordered that the sign be removed. The Red Cross banner had simply been a propaganda exercise, devised for the benefit of the Japanese cameramen.

9

STRANGERS IN THE NIGHT

THE EXPLOSION OF the bomb dump on 15 February 1943 was a defining moment in the history of the camp, with men differentiating their time on Ambon as before or after the blast. For the rest of the war they would regard Allied aircraft with the same misgivings as the Japanese military, each posing a serious threat to their safety. Said Eddie Gilbert, 'From that day on we were no longer able to comfort ourselves with the belief that we would never be bombed by our own planes. We started digging air raid shelters.'[1]

While the sight of US bombers over Ambon sent ripples of trepidation through Tan Tui, their presence also acted as a reminder that the tide of war was turning. It provided the only incontrovertible proof the Australians had that the Americans were on the offensive. Deprived of radio contact with the outside world, the POWs had no reliable information about the progress of the war. Japanese propaganda proclaiming the fall of Darwin and the subordination of the Australian people was never taken seriously, but without clear evidence to the contrary such rumours were demoralising to the men.

Since the bomb dump went up there had also been a noticeable crackdown on the camp, with the Japanese toughening their stance and demanding more POWs for work parties. The hardest jobs were on the wharves, where coal burning freighters had to be refuelled while other vessels were unloaded by hand. It was back-breaking toil, made all the more exhausting by the prisoners' poor physical condition.

Even more arduous was shovelling up large quantities of gravel from the beach and carrying it by basket to waiting trucks. Two men supported each basket, which was slung on a pole between their shoulders, the sheer weight of their cargo consuming every ounce of their energy. This was slave labour in the extreme. Backwards and forwards they staggered for hours under the heat of the tropical sun until the job was finished, and all this on a daily food ration of 480 grams of rice and maybe a little fish or some fruit or vegetables if the Japanese were feeling generous.

Food was becoming an obsession as empty bellies groaned and rumbled through the long night and men lay awake talking of little else. Even sleep was difficult, given the rudimentary nature of the facilities. As Eddie Gilbert described it, 'Bed for me was three wooden planks, each about eight inches wide, with about six thicknesses of hessian for a mattress.'

With food so scarce the men were forced to adopt desperate measures to survive, including so-called scrounging, which involved men pilfering anything edible they could find. Some of the work parties were particularly adept at pinching foodstuffs while unloading Japanese shipping, while others secreted stolen rice or cigarettes about their person by concealing them in their lap-laps. Such behaviour carried major risks – anyone caught with contraband in their pants would be beaten – but it didn't stop the petty theft. Instead, the men devised ever more ingenious methods of smuggling their ill-gotten goods into the camp. Tiny squat stools used as seating in the Japanese army trucks which transported the work parties had false bottoms built into the seats for storing illegal booty. Sacks ostensibly used for carrying sago palm tops also came in handy for hiding rice stolen from a storage shed.

Most of the time the guards suspected nothing, although occasionally they carried out surprise checks, resulting in a swift bashing for anyone unlucky enough to be caught. On one occasion the guards decided that everybody on the same work party would be punished. 'There would have been about twenty of us,' said Eddie Gilbert. 'We were lined up in two rows and told to raise our hands above our heads. The guards, armed with pick handles, made their way along the rows systematically thrashing us on the buttocks.'

They were all left badly bruised and shocked by the experience, but while some might have thought twice about their actions in future, the scrounging continued. Until now the accepted policy of the men was to steal only from the enemy. This wasn't regarded as theft but as unofficial appropriation of what they considered was rightfully theirs and if that meant a slight bending of the rules, so what? To use the POWs' terminology of the time, food was 'captured'. Anyway, this was war, wasn't it, and they were slowly starving.

As 1943 evolved, a new and more disturbing trend emerged. Because the climate and fertile soil made it easy to grow cassava and other root vegetables, the men started vegetable plots to supplement their meagre diet. Eddie Gilbert grew a small bed of peanuts and waited patiently to harvest them, but when the time came someone else had got there first and taken the tops off the plants. 'This shattered me somewhat,' he said, 'for not only did I grieve over the loss of what might have been a valuable supplement to my diet but I was confronted with the reality that when men were hungry great strains were placed on their moral code.'

It wasn't an isolated occurrence and soon the theft of root vegetables had its own nickname, 'bandicooting', named after the Australian marsupial that digs by night for delicacies in the soil, leaving the tops in place.

Many POWs who had spent months tending their crops woke to find they'd been a victim of bandicooting, which embraced all forms of horticultural theft. Even the officers' garden was raided, which, given they didn't share their produce with the rest of the men, was, perhaps, to be expected. As Eddie said:

> It was a matter of survival. The officers kept the fruits of their labour. They didn't share it with the rest of the camp – no, it went to the officers' mess. So it was pretty understandable, you'd agree, that when they got their chance at night time, someone would go and bandicoot.

Stealing other men's food, especially the officers' veggies, also raised discipline issues. But how did you punish a starving soldier? How did you enforce a moral code with men who were hungry, sick and weary? These were serious questions for which Major George de Verdon Westley had no immediate answer, though harsh measures were clearly necessary if the situation was not to deteriorate further. The battalion's commanding officer on Ambon, a man who ostensibly seemed all for a quiet life, was still some months away from ordering the most controversial action of his career, but as prison life unfolded between 1943 and 1944 his mind would be concentrated.

So far, the relationship between officers and men had not broken down entirely and for many POWs the 24-hour cycle was almost bearable. Work, sleep and simple pleasures, such as reading and cards, were now just part of the routine and as long as you remained fit and avoided a bashing, life went on.

Stuart Swanton's detailed record of his existence behind barbed wire provides one of the most comprehensive accounts of 1943 to emerge from Tan Tui. As an experienced typist and stenographer before the war, he was able to write his secret diary in coded shorthand. When it was eventually transcribed, readers would virtually hear, see and almost smell the camp, as Swanton shared the minutiae of daily life as a prisoner of war.

Corporal Stuart Mill Swanton, born in the Melbourne suburb of Elsternwick in December 1913, wasn't in the best of health and often found himself on light duties, doing odd jobs around the camp, as revealed in his entry for 9 March. 'Spent most of the day pulling out nails out of Atap roofing for the bootmakers.'[2] Two days later he suffered a recurring bout of malaria. 'Had a little rice for breakfast but had to lie down straight afterwards.' By 13 March he was no better.

> Went on sick parade and got a couple of aspirins. Hospital was full so there was no chance of getting in there. Returned to bed in the hut. At about 12 o'clock I got another attack of the shivers which was a most weakening experience and this was followed by a high fever. Just the same as the day before, still no treatment.

Sometimes he left the camp to work in the Japanese head-quarters. 'We were chopping and carrying wood all day. I was very annoyed with a couple of our boys because they were trying to pinch things from the Japanese store all the time. If they were caught we would have all been up.'

More law-abiding than some of his mates, Stuart wanted to get through the war in one piece and took a dim view of the malcontents and light-fingered. Brought up a devout Baptist and a former street preacher in Melbourne, he was a man of high moral values who expected the same standards of others. Since the death of Chaplain Charles Patmore in the bomb dump explosion he had also become acting padre in the camp, performing last rites and conducting burials. As an accomplished pianist and viola player, he had a remarkable ability to reharmonise hymns with each new verse, which might have helped to relieve the sense of hopelessness in the camp.

There was no escape from the boredom and homesickness the POWS had to contend with, but it was amazing how the human spirit refused to die. Sometimes there were concerts in the evening, although the Japanese were quick to remind the men that fun inevitably came at a cost. A scrap of paper found on the floor earned each man a slap across the face from the camp commandant during one performance.

On 1 May more prisoners were shipped to the island and this time they had a particular accent which was familiar to the Australians. They were Pommies. 'Twelve hundred Englishmen arrived from Java. They marched from Ambon town to a camp ten miles away but we don't know what they were going to do yet as they were army prisoners.'[3] The British POWs were mainly Royal Air Force personnel who had been captured in Singapore and taken to Ambon and the neighbouring island Haruku to build air strips. They fared worse than the Australians over the ensuing months and years, with another unnamed diarist noting: 'They were in very poor health compared with us – collected tobacco and gave it to them.'[4]

A fortnight after the British were spotted, Stuart recorded the first Australian death since the bomb dump went up. Jimmy Duncan, who had had his leg amputated after a tree fell on him, died at 4.40 a.m. on 16 May. A month later Corporal Swanton celebrated (if that was the appropriate word) his third anniversary in the army, but with little opportunity to mark it in the traditional manner, he spent the day typing up notes for the commanding officer. With demand for Stuart's keyboard skills growing, even the Japanese employed him to type a roll showing the name, rank, age, occupation and address of all ranks – 526 men in total.

Throughout this period the Allies continued to pound Ambon from the air. 'Air raid alarm at ten o'clock at night. It was very cloudy but clear enough for a plane or planes to drop bombs over Laha amid a pretty barrage of ack-ack.'[5]

Food supplies were also dwindling and by late June Gull Force was getting little other than rice and cassava. The poor diet lowered the men's resistance to the bugs and diseases floating around the camp, with some catching dengue fever or dysentery. Others, like Stuart, were always fighting off malaria. July began with Stuart 'feeling very wretched and feverish. Had a dreadful morning for my head was splitting and I knew, even if the doctor did not, that I had malaria.' Fortunately there was still some quinine in the hospital, though not much.

The next day Darky Lee was given five days hard labour breaking up stones and concrete with a sledgehammer. Stuart did not reveal what he'd done to receive such punishment, but pointed out that 'he was very lucky to get away with his life'.

And so the days turned into weeks as the men of the 2/21st Battalion, weakened by ill-health and lack of food, continued to labour and hope that one day they would be free. Meanwhile, there were domestic chores to attend to. Stuart found the simple act of washing his clothes rather therapeutic, taking his mind off deeper concerns. There was also sport, but when the men organised a basketball contest few had the energy to play for more than a few minutes. One Sunday Stuart was given the afternoon off and did some gardening. He planted some peanuts and pumpkin, cooked more cassava for tea and went to church in the evening.

It was through these small gestures of personal commitment to the future that Corporal Swanton maintained the will to survive, though just as quickly the mood could change.

He heard a rumour that the Japanese had landed in Australia and got as far as Pine Creek, near Alice Springs. This sort of propaganda could sometimes do as much damage to a man emotionally as Japanese brutality could do to his physical well-being, but after due consideration the rumours were invariably dismissed.

The seemingly constant presence of Ikeuchi, the camp interpreter and all-round bovver boy, meant that no one could relax their guard. In fact, nobody was safe, including the locals and even other Japanese. On one occasion Ikeuchi knocked out the Japanese sergeant major for being late. It was a vicious assault which resulted in the man appearing with a bandaged arm and black eye the following day.

Native fishermen also found themselves targeted for perceived wrongdoings, such as paddling their *prahu*s too close to shore when passing the prison camp. As Stuart Swanton recorded, 'When they were brought in they were bowled to the ground with a rod of steel tube and taken to Japanese headquarters.' The men themselves knew when to get out of Ikeuchi's way, although that wasn't always possible, given that he often lashed out with no warning.

Some days were more bearable than others, with Stuart noting that the interpreter's hate campaign must have waned temporarily, because he had only struck a couple of prisoners. How much longer could the insanity continue?

By mid-year, sickness was taking an even heavier toll, with a lot of men now suffering from beri-beri, a painful condition caused by a vitamin B1 deficiency. It's triggered by a lack of thiamine, more particularly a diet of polished white rice, which the men were fed at Tan Tui. First it attacked the nervous system, which led to severe lethargy and was usually followed by complications affecting the cardiovascular, muscular and gastrointestinal systems. It was one of the most feared and disabling illnesses in the camp, partly because of the swelling it caused to parts of the lower body, including legs and genitals. Apart from the difficulty in walking, victims could also suffer a loss of sensation in the hands and feet, mental confusion, involuntary eye movements and vomiting.

Beri-beri was easily cured by large doses of thiamine hydrochloride or a return to a thiamine-rich diet, but neither was available to prisoners on Ambon so patients were simply left to suffer.[6]

Even a hospital bed did not guarantee much in the way of care or comfort if Stuart's experience was anything to go by.

It's very wearying in hospital and the time seems to drag. There are about twenty beri-beri cases here at present. Legs and limbs become numb and they lose the power of their legs. Had a visit today by the Japanese doctor but he just passed through and did not examine any patients.

On another inspection by a Japanese officer eight patients were immediately discharged and ordered back to their huts. One man was told he needed the exercise, otherwise he would end up going to heaven.

Others escaped the daily grind by daydreaming, conjuring up memories of life back home. Stuart admitted to sudden flashbacks of his childhood in rural Blackwood, 'frolicking around the hills'. And there were important dates he had to remember. 'July 27 was a special day for me as it was the anniversary of my engagement with Leonie. Three years!! How much longer I wonder?'[7] Stuart's fiancée, Leonie Marshall, or Leo as he often refers to her, would have to wait another two years before she knew whether they'd ever be married.

Astonishingly amid the death and disease camp concerts still continued but the style of comedy was not to everyone's liking. While cutting comments about the officers went down particularly well among the men, those who were targeted did not always get the joke. Soon Major Westley had banned all gibes against officers and insisted on the right to censor all scripts. The army bureaucracy clearly lacked a sense of humour.

There were good and bad days in the camp. Sometimes the chickens which Stuart was raising produced a few eggs, which helped to supplement his and his mates' diet. Often the mundane would rub shoulders with the tragic, with the relative insignificance of one incident having no more or less importance than the other. On Wednesday, 11 August Swanton recorded: 'At last I'm out of hospital. One of our boys, Jim Harvey, was in again with a nervous breakdown and was very bad. I noticed amazing difference in growth of my chickens.'

Then two days later:

Jim Harvey died last night. No concert. Carried about two barrow-loads of soil to my garden during the day. Also cooked some cassavas, paw paws, greens and had them all for tea. Kept some cassava for supper and had it with a tin of salmon which Arch had brought home. It was simply beautiful.

And so the death of a mate was dismissed in one short sentence while the subject of what had been on the menu for that evening dominated that day's entry.

Random acts of cruelty also got a brief mention in Stuart's diary and served to illustrate the kaleidoscope of drama during an average day. A Japanese officer killed a dog 'by bashing out its brains against a fence and then asked our boys to bury it because the poor dog had died', he wrote.

By now Swanton was fit enough to go on work parties, shovelling baskets of wet clay and filling blast walls in the wireless station. As always, the work was arduous and the guards unpredictable. 'One drunken Japanese soldier wanted to fight me and kept saying, "Come here please." Later, in contrast, a navy soldier passed and nodded and smiled at me.' The work parties, especially those that involved unloading shipping, provided ample opportunity to 'capture' foodstuffs and other small luxuries. On 26 August Corporal Swanton spent the morning transferring drums of oil from a ship in the coal wharf and was able to nab a bar of soap in the process. In the afternoon a Japanese soldier went down the hatch and brought up a case of meat, which he left with the men before disappearing. Within a few minutes the meat had also vanished, the wooden packing case in splinters.

Throughout this period there was no let-up in aerial bombardment, with groups of Liberators appearing every few days, only to be met by a heavy barrage of ack-ack from destroyers anchored in the harbour. Some of the bombs fell dangerously near the camp. Seven months after the attack on the bomb dump which destroyed much of the camp, the Americans still hadn't got the message. On 2 September Stuart reported:

Plenty of hot metal flying around us. Bombs landed at Ambon 1000 yards from the camp. A piece of ack-ack shell landed within 50 yards of us and fizzed for a while and we thought it was an incendiary bomb. The 'all clear' was given and ten minutes later another bomber came over and dropped more bombs. Ended welcome way of celebrating four years of war.

The Second World War, which effectively began in Europe in early September 1939, still had nearly two years to run in the Pacific theatre, as the men on Ambon would experience to their cost.

While Swanton's diary offers a unique insight into life as a prisoner of war, it also provides an intriguing reference to what conditions were like on the other side of the barbed wire. On 4 September he went out on a work party to build an air raid shelter for a Japanese brothel on the island. It was no more than a casual aside in his diary but given that bombs had landed about 30 metres either side of the building only the night before, there was obviously a degree of urgency about the matter. The 'comfort women' who staffed the so-called gardens of pleasure were drawn from overseas as well as Ambon itself.

Walter Hicks, who was by now employed as a houseboy by the Japanese, knew about the brothel and how it worked, with its different standard of facilities depending on rank.

They had brothels for the Japanese officers, the sergeants, warrant officers, petty officers and men. They brought some Japanese women but they also had plenty of volunteers among the Chinese and Indonesian girls. The Japanese treated them well and paid them well – it was not a shameful thing to do.[8]

Although Walter's memory is based on what he witnessed, others had a different view of the comfort women's employment. A former Japanese navy paymaster who was stationed on Ambon claimed comfort women were hunted down and confined. On several occasions he heard young Indonesian women screaming and in tears. 'It made me feel terrible every time,' he wrote later.[9]

In mid-September more Australians arrived. Stuart was down on the wharf when he spotted one of them, an airman, lying on a stretcher surrounded by Japanese. Apparently he'd been shot down over Tanimbar, south-west of Ambon. There was no chance to talk, but his name was Graham and he came from Melbourne. He was one of two men rescued but there was no sign of the second.

Back in the camp more men were falling sick from disease and starvation and the death toll was rising. On 14 September George Laton succumbed to dysentery and beri-beri. He was buried the next day. Private Viv Warne, who was 27, died the morning after. Stuart helped carry the coffin to the cemetery and as soon as the burial was complete returned to his hut to cook some home-grown pumpkins for tea. It was another typical day in Camp Tan Tui.

Remarkably, in spite of the appalling conditions and the stench of death which pervaded the compound, the POWs still made merry given the opportunity. Stuart, no mean player on the string bass, teamed up with a couple of guitarists and two ukulele players for an impromptu concert the following day. It wasn't exactly the Trocadero but Stuart and his fellow musicians certainly cut a dash in their green pants, white shirts and bow ties. At least it kept their mind off the hunger and disease surrounding them.

Another camp stalwart, Private Bill Tibbett, from Footscray, died from dysentery on 1 October. He was only 23.

Around this time a second group of airmen were spotted in the camp, this time Americans who'd been forced to ditch their planes. The Australians were forbidden to talk to the Americans, who were identified only as 1, 2, 3, 4 and 5. The Japanese described them as 'bad men' who should only be served cold meals.

November was also marked by the departure of 'Handlebars' Ando Noburo, the Japanese marine commander. Another naval captain called Shirozu Wadami replaced him, but he had little interest in the camp and handed much of the day-to-day control over to the vicious Ikeuchi. The interpreter's reign of terror would soon know no bounds.

With the daily rice ration down to 280 grams per man, plus a little cassava or fresh fish if they were lucky, the Australians realised that they had to help each other to improve their chances of survival. Mateship, which had been so sadly lacking in the past, was now imperative. A new spirit of mutual co-operation developed as the men formed small syndicates to pool resources and share what they had. Sometimes the groups of four to eight men were mere 'marriages of convenience', as Eddie Gilbert put it, while others were based on long-standing friendships.

Eddie had three staunch mates, Eric Stagg, Allan Martin and Jack Morrow. They had all enlisted on the same day in June 1940. They hadn't known each other before but they become bosom buddies in the camp. Any spoils would be shared and if they could give each other a hand on camp or work duties, they would. One man's needs was the rest of the syndicate's responsibility. Joining forces and supporting each other was the only way they'd survive this hellhole, they reasoned. As Eddie Gilbert later wrote, 'It was this more soundly-based type of syndicate which was the more likely to endure.'[10]

But did providence share his optimism? As conditions worsened even the syndicates would be undermined.

Apart from food, what most men wanted was news from home. The Japanese knew this but used the occasional arrival of letters from the Red Cross as another form of torture. Just before Christmas news leaked out that a batch of mail was in. It was the first correspondence from home in nearly two years and gave the men a tremendous boost.

We waited impatiently to see who the lucky recipients would be, but as the days turned into weeks our excitement turned into bitter resentment. To this day I do not understand why this delivery of mail was withheld in this way, unless it was another way our captors chose to torture us mentally.[11]

Now and again a letter would be handed to a soldier on his deathbed but often he was too ill to read it. What senseless disregard for the dying.

Private Oswald 'Ossie' Uren, just 25 years old, would doubtless have appreciated a message from home in Fish Creek, near Wilsons Promontory, had he been compos mentis. But he died from a combination of dysentery and malaria a couple of weeks before Christmas. Even those without disease weren't safe from death's embrace. The day after Ossie died a man identified in Swanton's diary as Norman Tulip but almost certainly John Norman Tullett drowned while working in the shipyard unloading logs on 8 December 1943.

The men of the 2/21st were fading fast. The next day Carlton boy Private Charles McCusker died from dysentery and malaria. Charlie, who was well liked and had a reputation for always talking, was buried with due ceremony in the graveyard behind the hospital and was remembered for a morbid parting groan as he was laid to rest. As George Williamson told it, 'When we were laying him in the ground he bent with the rope around him and went arghh – the wind coming out of his soundbox. One of the chaps said, "You can't even shut the bugger up when he's dead."'[12]

It wasn't meant unkindly but merely reflected the growing fusion of black comedy and tragedy in Tan Tui, where even the macabre was sometimes funny.

Yet amid the daily log of crippling illness and human decay, small snapshots of island life would remind the men that love and tradition were not a distant memory. On their way to Paso in a construction gang, Stuart's work party passed a native wedding ceremony taking place. 'The bride, bridegroom and bridesmaids were in conventional westernised costume and it was a thrill to see it.'[13] Incongruous though such spectacles must have appeared to the men, at least they proved that life went on – though not that long for some.

Sapper Charlie Coombs, who had been ill for some time and had lost his sight, died from dysentery. He was 43 and belonged to the 2/11th Field Company. He was described by Stuart as a very brave man to have lasted as long as he did.

On Thursday, 23 December Corporal Swanton celebrated his thirtieth birthday with two fried eggs, which his mates served up as a present. The POWs were privately hoping they'd have a special dinner on Christmas Day. The guards knew it was an important religious festival and gave them an easy time. In the evening the men tucked into a plate of rice, pork stew, baked cassava and a bun, followed by fruit salad. It wasn't much by Australian standards, but it made a change.

––––––––

Nineteen forty-four began with no positive sign of an imminent end to hostilities. The air raids continued, the lack of food suggested the Japanese were having trouble shipping supplies in and the atmosphere in Tan Tui remained bleak.

New Year's Day dawned with some sore heads among the guards after a night of heavy partying. The noise had been deafening and the Japanese were 'pretty well blithered', Stuart wrote, although interestingly it wasn't only the guards who'd hit the grog. 'Some of our fellows were in the Japanese quarters on New Year's Eve and had to be carried back to the camp drunk – everyone was ashamed of them.' Fraternisation with the enemy was rare. Which Australians had inveigled their way into the party and how had they done it? Swanton's diary revealed no more but clearly some POWs were on better terms with their captors than others.

For the majority of men the relentless round of working, sleeping, dodging bombs and beatings became hard to bear and many Ambonese felt sorry for them, dropping little packets of food and clothing for them along the track at great personal risk.

Then in March word came down from the Japanese that the camp gardens would no longer operate as private enterprises. Each man would have to hand over their produce to the communal kitchen. Stuart recorded: 'We expect that our fowls will be taken from us next – the Japanese say there must be no individualism.'

It was a bitter blow for those who relied on their own hard work to supplement their meagre rations and part of a broader Japanese crackdown that would see an even harsher regime emerge under Ikeuchi's more brutal rule. No one was spared. One native who stole something from the army store was bashed with a board for ten minutes before being tied to a post and left in the sun all day. Wrote Stuart, 'What a sight it was to see the poor fellow standing there practically unconscious and Japanese soldiers standing round reading a notice pinned to him.' It reminded him of a picture of Christ on the cross with the Jews looking on.

Death was now an almost daily feature at Tan Tui. On 16 March Private Ted Warner, from Melbourne, died at the age of 28. No further details were given. Two days later Bill Grant succumbed to a long illness. By 4 April the number of deaths since the POWs entered the camp had reached 48. No one dared contemplate the future, but the figure would go much higher.

Sergeant Pat Russell, born in Port Albert in 1917, was the next to go. Like so many of his mates he was only in his mid-twenties when he died from dysentery. On 24 April four men – mentioned in Stuart's diary as Williams, Harbruther, Brown and Mac – died, also from dysentery. To make matters worse, two were from Stuart's hut and he knew them well. In the afternoon he joined a grave-digging party with eleven others in the teeming rain. Two days later four more men died – Robilliard, Bailey, Lather and Jack Malloy.

Food rations were also dwindling by the day. The rice issue was getting smaller and fried fish was only an occasional luxury. Stuart noted ominously that the poor diet was having a very marked effect on everybody's health. Fortunately he was not a smoker. Tobacco had become the main camp currency and was used almost exclusively for trading food. 'Every day one sees heavy smokers sacrificing their much needed meals for smokes. In fact men are now dying every few days from malnutrition.'

Apart from food and tobacco, the other valuable commodity was news. This usually came in the form of unsubstantiated rumour but just occasionally rare nuggets of fair dinkum reporting from the outside world filtered through.

In early 1944 six more US airmen were imprisoned on the island after their B-24 was shot down during an air raid over Ambon. They were surviving members of the crew of the *Paper Doll*, which belonged to the 529th Squadron of the 380th Heavy Bombardment Group. Attacked by Japanese fighter planes as it flew south of Ambon across the Banda Sea, the *Paper Doll* lost power and was forced to ditch about 190 kilometres south of Ambon. Three men were killed in the crash and another died as a Japanese aircraft strafed the wreckage. The seven survivors managed to inflate two life rafts and drifted for six days until an enemy plane spotted them and opened fire, claiming the life of a fifth man. Now they were down to six.

Twelve days after their B-24 hit the drink the Americans washed up on the Kai Islands, nearly 700 kilometres south-east of Ambon. Natives provided sanctuary and even offered to take them to Australia or Port Moresby, but it was an empty promise. In fact, they betrayed the US airmen to the Japanese, who transported them to Ambon, the target of their earlier bombing raid. Held incommunicado inside a hut outside the main camp at Tan Tui, their arrival did not go unnoticed by fellow American and POW Ed Weiss, who realised they would have important information about the progress of the war. But how to make contact without drawing attention to himself? That was the Pennsylvania boy's challenge and he would not be thwarted.

It took him some days to formulate a plan which involved an empty lipstick holder, a bucket of tea and a little daring.

Ed knew food and drink were taken to the Americans' barbed-wire-encircled hut every day by an Australian and the idea was to place a note, spare paper and lead from a pencil into one of the metal containers. The Aussie, however, wanted nothing to do with it so Ed swapped places and delivered the message himself. All went well until he returned to pick up the empty containers only to discover the lipstick holder had gone unnoticed. With the guards only a short distance away he could hardly speak out loud. Instead, he tilted the tea bucket slightly, creating a barely discernible rattle in front of one of the airmen. The American got the message and in one deft movement removed the lipstick tube.

Ed told the Americans to leave their reply hidden in a basin at the bathing spot. A day or two later he saw the US contingent taken down to the wash area and then marched back. It was time for him to strike.

As Weiss was now in charge of distributing water supplies around the camp, none of the guards was suspicious when he carried a bucket down to the tank and twisted a few valves before fiddling with a wash basin. Sure enough, the lipstick holder, which had earlier been 'liberated' from the Dutch civilian compound, was there awaiting collection. Hurrying back to camp, Ed could hardly wait to read the contents, which revealed that North Africa and most of Italy were under Allied control, Russian troops had driven the Germans back to the 1939 Polish border and American and Australian forces were making headway against the Japanese in New Guinea, New Britain and the Solomons.

While the news from the European theatre was encouraging, Ed couldn't help feeling disappointed by what he perceived as a lack of progress in the south-west Pacific. If ground fighting was still going on around 2000 kilometres east of Ambon, how long would it take the Allies to reach the inhabitants of Tan Tui?

There was another alarming revelation at the end of the US Air Force officer's scribbled note. In what appeared to be an apology, the American airman admitted they hadn't known the POW camp was there. How could this be? It was more than a year since the Allies had made the mistake of attacking the bomb dump, killing dozens of Dutch and Australian prisoners in the process. Surely news of the Ambon prison camp had been passed on to the Liberator crews by the Australian military by now? But if, for whatever reason, the intelligence had not been shared, it did not bode well for the future. Tan Tui would remain a target and Allied lives would continue to be threatened by their own side.

In fact, all the aerial activity had become something of a running joke, prompting a dash of black humour among the men whenever they saw a Japanese plane. As John Van Nooten said, 'We'd see the big red dot and say it's alright – it's one of ours. We knew that the island was a big base . . . we knew it had to be attacked. We were glad it was being attacked but we kind of wished they knew we were there and just missed us.'[14]

The fate of the Americans who briefed Ed Weiss via the lipstick holder was unclear. About a week later the small group of unnamed airmen disappeared from the hut on the hill, leaving Van Nooten to ponder what would happen to them next. 'I'd hoped they'd been taken to another POW camp,' he said, 'but I felt that was unlikely and they were in all probability executed.'[15]

In fact, it would take several decades for Ed Weiss to establish what had really happened to the men he called 'the strangers in the night', and finally meet the young officer who reached into the bucket of tea to retrieve the lipstick holder.[16]

———————

By now the Allied offensive was taking its toll. American and Australian aircraft were pummelling the Japanese on land and sea. Much of the air activity was being orchestrated from the Darwin area, where Lockheed Hudson bombers were charged with tracking down enemy naval forces. On 27 March 1944, RAAF Squadron Leader John Scott and his crew of three took off from Hughes Airfield, south of Darwin, on a reconnaissance mission over the Banda Sea some 500 nautical miles to the north. It would take them dangerously close to the island of Ambon, where Japanese Zero fighters waited at the ready to combat any aerial incursions.

Scott, who was 30, was already a veteran of these sorts of flights, which were regarded as something of a milk run. His strategy was to climb to an altitude of 30 000 feet and hide in the clouds before heading for home. He knew that the .303-calibre Browning machine guns on board would offer little protection against the much faster and well-armed Zeros, which meant he needed to keep a healthy distance from enemy aircraft.

Sadly, his luck would run out on this day. Together with Flying Officer Donald Beddoe, 27, from Melbourne, Flight Sergeant Bob King, the 21-year-old Perth-born navigator, Flight Sergeant Bruce Wallace, also 21, from Melbourne and the plane's wireless operator and gunner, and Flight Sergeant Keith Wright, from Brisbane, at nineteen the baby of the crew, he would be shot down somewhere over the Banda Sea. Miraculously, they survived, though it is unclear whether they were forced to ditch in the water or crash-landed on Loeng Island, just east of Timor.

Whatever the circumstances, they managed to survive on Loeng for two months with the help of friendly natives, until one of them betrayed them to the Japanese. They were then transferred to Saumlaki in the Tanimbar Islands to the east, where Beddoe was shot dead while trying to signal to an Allied aircraft. Eventually the survivors were sent to Ambon, where they were interrogated but obstinately refused to give much away. All Scott would confirm was his name and place of birth. He had grown up and lived in Adelaide, where he had attended a commercial college. One of the interrogators was Ikeuchi, who would later testify that the men were confined in a solitary cell outside the main POW compound so they couldn't communicate with other Australians.[17]

The Japanese were tiring of the RAAF crew's silence and on 15 August 1944, their fate was settled. Yoshio Miyazaki, deputy commander of the naval garrison, decided to sentence them to death. Another officer, Sub-Lieutenant Hideo Katayama, ordered Warrant Officer Shigeo Uemura, who was in charge of the guards at Tan Tui, to arrange the airmen's execution for the following morning.[18]

Word leaked out about the presence of the air force personnel when they were seen in the back of a truck which pulled up outside the guardhouse late at night. Most assumed they were Americans who'd been forced to bail out or crash-land. The following morning another truck arrived, as well as four of the camp's most feared guards: Frill Neck, Grey Mare, Giggling Gertie and the Black Bastard. Shovels and picks were retrieved from the storehouse and placed on the vehicle. Minutes later, the four airmen were herded on to the flat-bed truck. Ed Weiss watched the grim, unfolding drama from only 9 metres away as the doomed quartet were driven off. They were never to return.

The four were beheaded on the site of an Ambonese cemetery near Galala. The exact details of what happened and who was responsible would take years to emerge, as would the identities of the executed men. Their fate and that of their executioners would constitute one of the most troubling episodes of the war and its aftermath.

Katayama, who was one of the executioners, the adopted son of a Methodist minister, would later claim that he was under the impression the four had been legally tried, found guilty and sentenced at a temporary court martial. The facts would continue to fester for decades and wouldn't be put to rest until the latter part of the century.

———

Allied fighters and bombers were a regular sight in the Ambon sky, but until now Tan Tui had escaped largely unscathed since the February 1943 disaster.

On 28 August 1944 a squadron of Lockheed P-38 Lightnings, the celebrated American fighter planes nicknamed 'the fork-tailed devil', appeared overhead in what Van Nooten described as 'a softening-up process'. 'They put on a real Hollywood type production of shooting up everybody and frightening the hell out of the Japs.'[19]

Eddie Gilbert, who was out digging tank traps, suddenly found his work party being machine gunned. One man was injured, but thankfully there were no fatalities. The P-38s vanished as quickly as they had appeared and everyone thought the attack was over. Then they heard the distant drone of the B-24s.

John Van Nooten reckoned he counted 250 and was sure 'somebody's going to get it today'. Ed Weiss assumed they were going to bomb Laha airfield, but to his horror they turned sharply left and headed towards his side of the island. There was complete mayhem as he attempted to find shelter in a dirt trench. Several bombs exploded on the cobblestone road, throwing him about 15 centimetres into the air before slamming him down again. Breathless and heavily concussed, he lay there enveloped in black, acrid smoke. 'For several seconds I thought I'd died and felt as though I were floating to heaven. When the black smoke cleared I stood up, and in exhilaration of being alive, I extended my arm and clenched fist skyward and shouted, "You bastards, I've survived, I've survived!"'[20]

An Australian he'd befriended, Sergeant Norman Balcam, from the Melbourne suburb of Yarraville, believed he was suffering from shell shock and pulled him back down. Both men followed the B-24s as they circled the island, wondering what would happen next. They couldn't believe their eyes. The Liberators had re-formed and were heading straight back in the camp's direction.

This time the bombs spewing from the plane's belly were smaller, but equally deadly. They were anti-personnel bombs, which fired thousands of metal pellets when they hit the ground. And still it wasn't over. As the B-24s departed, a new formation of North American B-25s arrived, attacking the shoreline and dropping parachute bombs, which often took days to explode after being caught up in trees.

By the time Eddie Gilbert got back to Tan Tui with his workmates, much of the camp had been flattened. 'We were greeted by the news that two men had been killed immediately, sixteen were wounded and one died later,' he recorded in his diary.

'Before the first bombing in 1943 we were supremely confident that the camp would never be attacked by our own planes. That confidence evaporated.'[21]

It's possible the Allies' target was a radio transmitting and receiving station a few hundred metres away from the camp, as well as anti-aircraft guns positioned just outside the compound. Whatever the reasoning, it was yet another blow to Gull Force and its dwindling numbers.

There were only five huts left to accommodate them now, but more significant than the damage was the change in Japanese policy. As Eddie Gilbert observed, 'The attack on Ambon that day heralded a further hardening of our captors' attitude toward us and, more seriously, a further reduction in the already meagre rations we were receiving.'[22]

10

'THE SICK WERE THE FAT LADIES OF THE CIRCUS'

Back on the island of Hainan conditions during 1943 and 1944 mirrored the plight of the POWs on Ambon. Disease, starvation, punishment and physical exhaustion plagued most of the Dutch and Australian soldiers who'd been shipped there in November 1942.

Far from being the convalescent home they'd been promised by their captors, the Chinese island offered little in the way of medical facilities, food or basic comforts. Instead, the Japanese and their Formosan guards imposed a level of savagery so extreme that even those who survived would bear the scars for the rest of their lives. It was Captain Bill Aitken, an Australian Army Medical Corps doctor attached to the 2/21st, who summed it up most graphically. 'Our treatment by the Japanese and their attitude towards us was so disgraceful and inhumane as to merit the severest condemnation of any civilised person.'

Aitken, Coburg-born and in his late thirties, became one of the heroes of Hainan as he struggled to care for the men in the face of wilful obstruction and continuing brutality by the Japanese, as well as the lack of food and drugs.[1] Morale continued to plummet, the result of sickness, poor food and lack of news from overseas. With the Japanese insisting they were close to victory, Lieutenant Colonel Scott admitted that most of the men were in a 'low mental state bordering on despair'.

The Japanese were also cracking down on discipline within the camp, which was still under the control of Captain S. Kondo, commander of the 4th Yokosuka Special Naval Landing Force. In February 1943 six Dutch prisoners escaped but returned after a few days. The repercussions were extreme. Days off were cancelled as the POWs began six weeks of non-stop work. As Scott pointed out in his post-war report: 'This was the start of our downhill run in so far as health went, as nobody was in the condition to stand hard work without a rest from the intense heat and on the food that we were receiving.'[2]

But the punishment didn't end with an increased workload. Much to the horror of all the POWs the six Dutchmen who had tried to escape were taken away and executed. It was an act of retribution which would have implications for the entire camp.

Captain Ida, the Japanese adjutant, assembled the POWs on the parade ground and warned them that from now on all escapees would be executed. What's more, the officers and sergeants would be held responsible for any future escapes. A night watch would be maintained from 2000 to 0600 hours and if there were any further attempts to break out the officers would know what to expect. The chilling warning was followed by a demand that everyone sign an agreement pledging not to escape. Captain Mishima and Lieutenant Nichiara handed the document to the CO, but in a welcome demonstration of solidarity with his men, Scott refused to accept the order.

The Japanese officers stormed off in a rage, threatening Scott and Captain Turner with death by firing squad. The two Australians had taken a massive but calculated risk, yet amazingly it seemed to work. Their decision to make a stand paid off and after further negotiations over the document they were spared.

By mid-1943 few were in the mood to escape. Ill-health, in particular beri-beri, was taking its toll, with at least 143 men suffering from the debilitating condition and many more less-severe cases recorded. St Kilda–born Captain John Turner, soon to celebrate his thirty-third birthday, was sent up to the guardhouse to remonstrate with Captain Ida about the medical situation. Unless there was an immediate improvement in food and drug supplies 'things would shortly be very serious,' he said.

Ida pointed out that there was a severe shortage of food and medicine but agreed to give the men a pig to share. It would not go far between 500 men, but at least it contained vitamins A, B and C, which might help to counter the beri-beri. If the Japanese offer of a pig was a joke, it wasn't very funny. At least five Australians had already died of beri-beri and several more were close to death.

Dr Aitken's graphic account of conditions in the hospital suggest a scene of suffering and squalor akin to Dickensian London. 'Every bed held a man with complete oedema [an excessive build-up of fluid] of the whole body and gasping for breath. Others in the same condition were being nursed on the floor propped up against the wall.'[3] To make matters worse, the sick were herded into work parties, regardless of their physical state. The Japanese demanded 120 POWs for each party – men who, according to Aitken, were 'scarcely able to stagger to work at which they were flogged and kicked'.

Each night the worst cases were carried back into camp by their mates, only to be subjected to ridicule by visiting Japanese officers, who laughed at the scale of their deformity. (Some had such swollen testicles that they had to carry them around in their hands.) It provided the Japanese medical officer, Captain Ichiro Kikuchi, and his non-medical friends with considerable amusement, the more grotesque cases triggering gales of laughter. 'The sick were the fat ladies of the circus,' Bill Aitken remarked – a source of continuing entertainment for any passing Japanese.

The irony was that the beri-beri could easily have been treated. There was ample Vitamin B on the island, much of it unloaded from ships and widely available to both the military and civilian populations. Even the POWs managed to obtain small supplies by trading with the locals. Had it not been for this illicit business a far greater disaster would have occurred, Aitken concluded.[4]

While beri-beri was the principal camp ailment, other diseases were also striking men down. Malaria and dysentery, as well as influenza and skin diseases, were sweeping the camp. Apart from sickness there was the random brutality and ever-present fear of sudden death. The Japanese were so unpredictable that the men could not be certain of their safety or survival from one day to the next and it wasn't only the Allied prisoners who were targeted.

On the morning of 17 July 1943, some 120 Chinese, under heavy guard and with their hands tied, were brought to the camp entrance in several lorries. What they had done was unknown, but their troubled countenances suggested they feared the worst. Made to sit in the sun without food or water for much of the day, the Chinese couldn't help noticing the arrival of another truck containing a contingent of young Japanese soldiers with fixed bayonets. Several officers drew their swords and demonstrated their prowess with the weapons in front of the Australian and Dutch POWs who looked on. Among the Japanese officers was the dreaded medico, Captain Kikuchi, the so-called senior surgeon, who was by now notorious for his callous treatment of sick prisoners and his arrogant manner.

At 6 p.m. the trucks formed a convoy and drove off, disappearing over a nearby hill to an area of sandy desert where the Chinese were ordered to dig a long trench by Lieutenant Takai, the camp commandant otherwise known as 'The Black Snake'. Private Courtney Harrison, who later wrote a detailed exposé of the terrible conditions on both Ambon and Hainan, recalled that Kikuchi was in a joyful mood. 'He was wearing a pistol strapped to his waist and he brandished his sword in front of his prisoners. He took part in the massacre with other officers and guards, pushing the bayoneted and beheaded coolies into the trench. Many screamed in terror before they were killed or buried alive.'⁵ The Japanese guards and officers returned to the base about an hour later, having bayoneted and buried the Chinese.

None of the Allied prisoners witnessed the mass slaughter but it was confirmed a few weeks later when Lieutenant Colonel Scott and Lieutenant Smith were allowed out of the camp and strolled over the rise to find a trench-like grave which had been freshly filled in. It was just another day in enemy-occupied Hainan, where the Japanese viewed compassion as a human quality without value, and life itself was even cheaper.

The senseless daily torture continued as work parties who failed to perform their duties were punished accordingly. On 28 July 1943 a group of POWs under the command of Lieutenant Ronald Green, from Caulfield, was carrying sandbags up a steep railway embankment to an anti-aircraft position when Private Ivo Fishwick tripped and fell. Lieutenant Takai screamed at him and struck young Fishwick on the back with his fist as he lay on the ground. Shortly afterwards another man, struggling under the intense weight of the sandbag, also collapsed, prompting another unprovoked attack from Takai, who kicked him four times in the back, ordered him to stand up and then bashed him twice in the face with his clenched fist.⁶

This was standard procedure. In the same month Lieutenant Edgar Tanner had been in charge of a sand moving party on the beach at Hashio when he politely asked Chin Tze Ping, the Japanese interpreter, if his men might take a short rest, given the high temperature. Chin, a Tokyo-educated Formosan, was in no mood to sanction breaks, accusing the Australians of being bad men while attempting to hit Tanner in the face and throwing him to the ground.⁷

A few weeks later Chin, who had a sadistic streak to match the cruelty of the most brutal of guards, was up to his old tricks again, bullying a group of sick men carrying sandbags down on Hashio beach, punching them in the face, hitting them with sticks and even threatening them with shooting. As the work party leader, Lieutenant Tanner suffered the same treatment. 'Many men collapsed during the day, several were helped home at the end of the day and on return to the camp ten were admitted to hospital.'[8] Doc Aitken continued to plead the case of the sick, the exhausted and the dying but his entreaties fell on deaf ears.

Tom Pledger, who in August 1943 had just marked three years in the army, watched over many of his patients in their final hours as he performed his duties in the hospital. In a letter to his mum, Katherine, he wrote:

> Ten of our chaps have died mostly from beri-beri and it's been very disheartening for us as we have not had a single success with any of our bed patients. It's very hard to sit there and see them gasping for breath for about 24 hours before they pass away.[9]

There was little likelihood of his mail being delivered and Tom knew it, but somehow it was therapeutic to put pen to paper.

> Oh mum, I would give all my money to get a line home to you, to show you I am still alive, but the Japs don't seem to think it necessary. This is the time you long for a nice mum's meal, a good bath, then curl up in a chair and switch on the wireless. Oh when will it come true?[10]

Meanwhile, the bashings continued. Chin, who had forged a grim alliance with fellow master-in-crime Lieutenant Takai, the camp commander, believed he had the right to strike his charges for even the slightest perceived misdemeanour. Most days he laid into work parties with a heavy piece of wood. When Clive Newnham, the Hawthorn-born captain, who was in charge of a group of men on a construction job, tried to explain that his blokes were too sick to push a heavy truck, Chin flew into a rage. Half a dozen men were given six to ten blows each, including one who was a hospital patient but had been given a day's try-out at work. By the time Chin had finished, one soldier was left with a badly lacerated elbow, another an injured back and most of the rest were covered in bruises.[11]

Sometimes the guards were too lazy to do the job themselves and ordered the Australians to beat each other. Warrant Officer Edward Norman was in charge of 50 POWs unloading a ship in the harbour when the Japanese quartermaster, Captain Mishima, handed him a heavy stick. Norman was ordered to beat up the Aussies working in the hold but refused to do so. Mishima gave the implement to one of his own guards to do the job. The Australian warrant officer protested and tried to intervene, but Mishima merely threatened him with the same treatment. Said Norman, 'The men were worked to the ground in terrible heat and bad conditions . . . and didn't get home until 21.00 hours.'[12]

Remarkably, and in spite of everything, a semblance of social life was maintained throughout this painful period. Occasionally, those men who were fit enough organised cricket matches on the parade ground and even those who were too exhausted to play enjoyed watching them. It was on such a day in February 1944 – a Sunday when the Japanese, by all accounts, had for some reason looked kindly on requests to observe the day of rest – that the sight and sound of leather on willow saved the men from a potential tragedy.

Without any warning a large American bomber appeared over the roof of a nearby building, not 12 metres above the ground. The motley crowd of players and supporters looked up in surprise to see a machine gun trained on them. They were sitting targets and there was nowhere to hide. Thankfully the crew realised these were not Japanese sportsmen – not with their slouch hats and Caucasian faces – and the machine gun remained silent. There was a mixture of relief and jubilation among the Australians who now knew their presence on Hainan would be reported back to the US military, as Scott's official post-war report on the camp confirmed. 'It was a tremendous thrill for we knew that there was a good chance that our camp would now be known as a POW camp. Japanese do not play cricket and this would be known.'[13]

The camp guards, astonished by the American plane's low altitude and the crew's temerity, were in shock and herded the men back into their huts at the end of bayonets and with sticks flying.

It gave the men a tremendous lift, knowing the Allies were on their way, yet how long would it take to liberate Gull Force, whose troops had been variously incarcerated on Ambon and Hainan for the past two years? How much longer could they endure the sickness, starvation and brutality, which worsened by the day? It was the unpredictability of life that added to the strain, not just the near-death experiences suffered at the hands of the Japanese or in the hospital, but also the threat from extraneous elements who were not the traditional enemy.

Chinese guerillas had already made their presence felt on Hainan, including through a daring raid on the camp itself. What made them particularly worrying was their seeming inability to differentiate between the Japanese and their captives. Communist or nationalist guerillas, neither seemed to worry about the colour of your skin. If you weren't one of them you were the enemy. Now the Australians were about to find that out for themselves.

It was Lieutenant Ron Green, a Litchfield boy in his mid-twenties, who first sensed trouble. He was the officer in charge of a work party employed to build a road from Hoban to a Chinese village about 8 kilometres to the north. Hoban was about 25 kilometres inland from the prison camp at Bakli Bay. There were 40 in the party. Twenty-four would work on the road while ten were employed on wood-cutting duties about 1.5 kilometres away. The rest stayed at Hoban on camp duties.

Green asked the Japanese commandant, a man by the name of Okabisi, about the threat posed by guerillas, asking if there were any hostile Chinese in the area. 'Yes,' came the emphatic response. The young lieutenant wasn't happy. 'I objected to the fact that POWs were forced to work in such an area exposed to this danger, but he merely laughed and replied that his guards would afford sufficient protection against the Chinese.'[14]

The road-building team left by truck every morning at about 9 a.m., accompanied by fifteen Japanese and Formosan guards. Normally, Lieutenant Green would have joined them on 8 April 1944, but he was suffering from a bad dose of diarrhoea and stayed behind in camp. Private Robert Smith, from Berwick in Melbourne's east, heard the first rifle shot. Luckily he was some distance away with the wood-chopping party and wasn't too concerned, given that gunfire was a common sound on Hainan. His mood changed several minutes later when another soldier he recognised as Private Cyril O'Donnell staggered out of the scrub on the left-hand side of the road with a bullet through his shoulder. Breathless and in pain, O'Donnell muttered something about a Chinese ambush on the road-building party and that he'd 'made a bolt for it'.[15]

In fact, the attack had happened just after the truck carrying the men had been driven over a rise. It was coasting down the hill when a single shot rang out. The driver slammed on the brakes, causing many of those standing in the back of the vehicle to topple over. For a moment there was total confusion, followed by the sound of a bugle being blown. John McMahon, a country boy from Cullulleraine on the outskirts of Mildura, was used to hearing shooting back home on surrounding farmland, but nothing prepared him for what followed.

There was a sudden volley of rapid gunfire from the roadside, striking down guards and prisoners indiscriminately. The truck driver leapt out of the cab and ran for his life, hotly pursued by two Chinese boys in their early teens who each appeared to be carrying an ancient weapon similar to a blunderbuss. Fortunately, their aim was poor and the driver escaped unharmed. Three of the Australians sought shelter under the chassis while others ran to the roadside and took cover behind some trees. Private McMahon had no choice but to remain in the cab, as he was wedged between the bodies of Japanese guards.

Frankly, he didn't know what to do but he was momentarily comforted by an apparent lull in the fighting. Then came the menacing pitch of whistle and bugle which he'd heard minutes earlier. Johnny McMahon peeped over the bottom of the window to see a swarm of Chinese charging down a ravine towards his lorry. 'I ducked my head and the next thing I knew they were all over my truck. They stripped the dead Japanese guards and took their arms. I lay quiet beside Private Cornell and pretended to be dead.'[16] McMahon's acting skills were pretty convincing as he closed his eyes and heard the Chinese guerillas rifling through Leslie Cornell's pockets, while ignoring him. Two of them were talking and he vaguely heard the word 'Indo' mentioned. Then came a shot. McMahon felt Private Cornell's body stiffen alongside him.

Private Alan Murnane, in his twenty-ninth year, hid behind the dual wheels at the rear of the truck. Next to him Sergeant Kelvin Gilder, who was a year younger, suffered what turned out to be a fatal shot to the buttocks. Murnane, from Terang on the road to Warrnambool, decided to make a break for it. 'A Formosan guard, fully armed, was following. I called to him to get out of the way, knowing that he would draw fire.'[17] And that's exactly what happened. About five Chinese who were lying in the middle of the road opened fire on them at a range of about 25 metres. It was then that Private O'Donnell was hit in the shoulder. Murnane, who must have had a guardian angel that day, somehow avoided injury and fled into the scrub.

Private Fred Hillier, who was pinned down by other bodies, opened his eyes and saw blood pouring from Private Leslie Cornell's mouth, nose and ears. Up in the cab Johnny McMahon maintained his death-like pose. 'I lay still while they pulled my water bottle from around my neck. Another bugle call sounded and they all left.'[18] Only then did he look up and cast an eye around the truck, which was a scene of utter carnage. Bodies littered the rear tray and roadside, blood oozing from bayonet and gunshot wounds. Sergeant Gilder's lifeless frame was slumped under the truck and several Japanese and Formosan guards, some dead, some wounded, lay scattered nearby.

The only other sign of life among the POWs came from Private Hillier. With typical Australian understatement McMahon whispered to him, 'How'd you go?' Hillier replied matter-of-factly: 'I've been bayoneted three times.'[19] McMahon helped his injured comrade out of the truck and lowered him into a seat taken from the cab.

Back with the wood-chopping group Private O'Donnell was recounting how he had been shot in the shoulder as the gang of Chinese appeared over a rise on the road. He had run for about 200 metres and hidden behind a tree stump while several other Australians marched towards the guerillas with their hands up. Among them were Private Arthur Chenoweth, who hailed from St Peters in South Australia, and Private Freddie Stokes, from the Melbourne suburb of Fitzroy.

McMahon was a lucky man. So was Hillier, whose bayonet wounds, surprisingly, did him no serious harm.

Soon word of the attack filtered back to Hoban. The Japanese were humiliated by the success of the ambush and over the next few days searched the area for the bandits and possible survivors. Lieutenant Green was worried about the men who'd been left behind and, fearing they were lying wounded in the scrub, asked permission to launch his own search. He was told to wait.

Bob Smith, who had been working in the wood-chopping party, was eventually allowed to accompany Green and some Japanese to the scene of the bloodshed and collect the dead and injured. The two Australians made a brief search, calling out to the missing men, but there was no reply and they were ordered back to camp. Two days later, much to Green's astonishment, one of them, Corporal John Nelson, walked into Hoban with hardly a scratch on him. Nursing only a small wound to his right shoulder, he revealed how he and the other missing men, including Chenoweth and Stokes, had been captured by the Chinese. After marching several kilometres Chenoweth and Stokes, who were also slightly wounded, were separated from the rest of the men and accompanied Nelson to a Chinese village, where they were apparently well treated. The next day Nelson had resolved to return to the camp, leaving the two others behind because they were too stiff to walk.[20]

Subsequent attempts by the Japanese to locate the Australians failed, though Nelson claimed the eight men they were separated from were invited to join the guerillas and become soldiers. 'I don't know what their answer was. At any rate they went away with them.'[21]

The fate of the missing Australians remains one of the biggest mysteries of the entire Hainan experience. Were the guerillas communist or nationalist? Did the Australians accept the invitation to become soldiers in a bid to escape the Japanese? Crucially, were they still alive? These were questions which would not be answered until after the war was over.

The events of the past few days had left Gull Force in no doubt that the enemy took several forms. Apart from the Japanese and marauding bands of Chinese guerillas, there was also the growing problem of Lieutenant Colonel William Scott. While not the enemy as such, his actions had certainly prompted the men to wonder whose side he was really on.

Aitken's post-war report was scathing in its condemnation of the man who was supposed to look after the battalion's interests. Accusing him of often 'aggravating' the situation, the doctor claimed the commanding officer was 'selfish, weak and near-sighted'. He was too conciliatory to his captors and too ready to accept a course of action that would obviate his personal conflict with them.

> He often gave his own personal likes and dislikes preference in matters affecting the welfare of the whole camp. No firm stand was taken against the policy of the Japanese to send sick and convalescent men on work parties. On the contrary Lieutenant Colonel Scott actually ordered that no men were to be rested and appeared to

be anxious that as great a number as possible be sent
to work.[22]

These were damning allegations that would haunt the CO
for the rest of his life – and they did not end there. Captain
Aitken claimed Scott was so desperate to keep out of trouble with
the Japanese that he rarely lodged complaints about the men's
condition. He showed little concern for the sick and dying and
his lack of interest in the hospital was 'very marked and often
commented on'. But of all the criticism levelled at the commanding
officer, the greatest would be about the way he handled discipline,
culminating on one occasion with the near death of a man whom
he decided to hand over to the Japanese for punishment.

Aitken was particularly irritated that members of the
Australian Army Medical Corps (AAMC), who were classified
as non-combatants, were disciplined by being sent out on work
parties. Scott disregarded their status, thereby cutting back on
the number of men available to tend the sick in hospital.

The barrage of complaints against Scott was made all the more
credible by its principal source. Captain Aitken was respected
throughout the camp and helped to save many lives. Yet the
CO wasn't without support. His second in command, Major
Ian Macrae, remained faithful throughout, although there were
occasions when that loyalty would be subject to intense strain.

It was the case of Private George Roy that became Hainan's
cause celèbre, striking at the very heart of Scott's authority and
creating such controversy in the camp that even the officers would
eventually question their CO's sanity. Deniliquin-born Roy, a
boxer before the war, was known for his hot temper; he often
spoke before he thought. On this particular day his lip got the
better of him and he offended one of the officers.

The young private, who was sick in hospital at the time, had
decided to freshen up with a shower. The camp showers were
hardly more than a jam tin which you filled with water to pour
over yourself, but they did the job. There were special times for

washing, depending on rank, work duties and physical condition. Hospital patients were allowed to slip in after the officers and before the work parties came back. On this day Private Roy, who had no watch, nipped into the shower five minutes early and was spotted by one of the officers, who asked him why he was there. Roy explained that he'd traded his watch for food and had no idea of the exact time. The officer took umbrage and an argument ensued.

Once again Private Roy's tongue was to get him into trouble as accusations flew about the officer's conduct under fire. Fellow squaddie Roy Harris said his mate reminded the officer that he had disappeared during the Japanese invasion on Ambon. 'I happen to be one of your men and we wouldn't find you when the action was on, so don't talk to me . . .'[23] George Roy realised what he'd said and buttoned his mouth before he accused the officer of outright cowardice, but the damage was done. His act of insubordination was reported to the colonel and soon he was facing a court martial.

Lieutenant Denis Smith, whose official account of the whole unseemly episode was based on his own diary records of the time, described the incident as a 'particularly bad case, and to make matters worse it occurred in the sight and hearing of a Japanese guard'. If camp discipline was to be maintained Roy would have to be made an example of. Scott decided to hand him over to the Japanese for punishment, not appreciating the degree of violence that would be meted out on the hapless private.

Dr Bill Aitken reminded the commanding officer that Roy was still under his care and could not be released from hospital for punishment. Scott agreed to let him to stay there until he was recovered sufficiently to face Japanese justice. Roy stayed in bed for the next three months, no doubt privately hoping that the matter would be forgotten come his release. But Private Roy, when he was deemed fit enough to join a work party, had not bargained on the CO's long memory. While the men were being counted that night, he was spotted by Scott, who demanded to know: 'Are you ready for your punishment?' George Roy nodded, unsure what to expect but clearly apprehensive.

Overnight Scott came under pressure from some of the other officers not to go through with it. Lieutenant Smith, a Londoner by birth who was perhaps more familiar with British military justice, urged the commanding officer to reconsider his decision, even if it posed a threat to the control and welfare of the camp.

> He promised to consider this and on the following day he informed me that he had spent a sleepless night thinking the matter over. Great as the temptation was he considered it his duty to maintain order. He owed a responsibility to the whole force, but in particular to his officers and he must protect them if the welfare of the whole camp was to be considered.

By now Private Roy was a very worried man. Desperate to avoid an appointment with the Japanese bully boys, he pleaded with Ian Macrae to intervene. The second in command, keen to show support for his commanding officer, remained unmoved and told Roy that he 'richly deserved whatever he would get'.[24]

Marched up to the guardhouse, George Roy was handed over to the Japanese NCO commandant, who, when told of the nature of the offence, took it very seriously. According to Roy Harris he was given a number of choices, including having his thumbs tied to a horizontal bar while being belted with a pick handle or having a wire tied from his thumbs to his toes via his private parts and having the current switched on while being doused in water.[25]

He chose the horizontal bar. There were differing accounts of what followed – the official version and the other ranks'. Lieutenant Smith claimed the adjutant, Captain Clive Newnham, tried to intervene to stop the flogging. But Roy Harris insisted that after the beating had started and 'they'd given him 15–16 cuts with the pick handle', George turned to the adjutant and said, 'Look sir, you'd better stop them or they'll kill me.' And that Newnham replied, 'You should have thought of that before – carry on.'

By the time the Japanese had finished with Private Roy, Captain Aitken took one look at his bruised and bloodied body and declared, 'I can't do a thing for this man – they've pulped him from the kidneys down. He's got Buckley's.'[26]

Harris's blow-by-blow account of the punishment and its aftermath was not based on hearsay. He was there, and helped to carry George Roy back to his bed.

Amazingly Private Roy survived the ordeal, but the severity of the beating and the fact that Scott himself had instigated it did not sit well with the Australians. In later years, even Major Macrae admitted that his superior had gone too far. 'We all wished to God it never happened, most of all Scott. I think it was a miscalculation of Scott's. He didn't think anything as bad as that would happen.'[27]

The vicious attack on Private Roy and the commanding officer's role in it shocked the entire camp and further undermined the CO's authority. If there had been whispers about his suitability for office in the past, concern among the officers and men had now reached a climax.

The following day four officers called a meeting of their colleagues to protest Scott's actions. Dr Aitken, never a man to hold his tongue when provoked, said he wanted to disassociate himself from everything that had happened. The fact that he'd released the soldier from hospital hadn't meant that he was fit to take the punishment, he made clear. Two other officers and a junior colleague asked the CO to alter his policy of handing men over to the Japanese.

Smith conceded in his diary that it was a dreadful situation.

The whole thing seemed quite appalling. The commanding officer was beset on all sides because he had attempted to do what he thought was right. Some of those who had tried to protect him had turned against him and the attitude of the men could be well imagined, although there was very little comment in the lines.

Scott knew he had lost the support of his battalion and, under pressure from his fellow officers, agreed to discontinue the controversial policy. He alone would take responsibility for what had happened and none of the officers would be held accountable.

If Lieutenant Colonel William Scott wasn't a broken man, he was close to it. As Denis Smith recorded in his diary: 'He . . . left the meeting in a state of mind that one can well imagine.'[28]

And that was putting it kindly.

11

THE CAGE

WHILE LIEUTENANT COLONEL Scott was facing a crisis coping with his force on Hainan, Major Westley had challenges of similar magnitude on Ambon.

The POWs on both islands were not only sick, starving and demoralised, but camp discipline was now posing such a serious threat on Ambon that Westley was forced to countenance the unthinkable: erecting a second jail within the Japanese prison for those men deemed to require additional punishment. This prison within a prison was aimed at controlling the hard-core element of petty thieves and malcontents who stole and cocked a snook at authority at every opportunity.

As food supplies deteriorated vegetables disappeared from garden plots and even the kitchen stores were raided. Of course, it was understandable that hungry men might resort to desperate measures to fill their stomachs, but it could not be tolerated when their greed impacted on the greater well-being of others. Every prisoner was entitled to equal rations, and those who were too greedy to respect the system would need persuading, by force if necessary.

Hitherto, camp punishments had proved to have little deterrent effect. The threat of docked wages, loss of rank and even physical discipline had had little effect on serial offenders, who saw Westley as a spent force. Not for nothing was he known, unkindly, as 'the swamp ghost' by members of A Company, which he commanded. He'd worn the epithet since his days in Darwin, when he reportedly got lost on manoeuvres on one occasion. And his reputation wasn't enhanced when the Japanese invaded Ambon and A Company found itself marooned in Eri, at the southern end of the Laitimor Peninsula. Westley and his men were forced to surrender before they had any opportunity to fight. While the situation was not of Westley's making, this lack of action would further undermine his authority when the time came to take over from Scott on his departure for Hainan.

Rightly or wrongly, an officer who'd seen no combat would inevitably see his standing eroded in the eyes of the men he led.

It hadn't always been like that. Those who'd served alongside Westley when he was a staff officer in the militia before the war remembered him as competent. He'd also been successful in civvy street, carving out a career for himself as an estate agent in Melbourne, where he grew up. But now, at the age of 34, the Hawthorn-born officer appeared to have taken on more than he could handle. The responsibility of command was weighing heavily on his shoulders and he found it difficult to gain the respect of his men. Without the overall confidence of the Australians for whom he was responsible, how could he enforce discipline?

It was against this background that Westley came up with what would prove to be one of the most divisive and ill-considered measures in the history of the Australian military.

The cage, or 'the boob' as it was originally called, was devised as a deterrent and approved by the Japanese. Anyone found guilty of contravening camp rules, particularly those who pilfered food, would find themselves held overnight in the 2 metre square holding pen, which had no roof and was initially made out of native materials. There were differing recollections of the boob's construction, which some insisted was wreathed in barbed wire and so uncomfortable that to spend a night there was sheer torture.

Later, a roof was placed on top to protect prisoners from overnight rain. Walter Hicks remembers the cage as half the size of an average room with 'barbed wire around it and a tin roof'. 'If a man hit an officer or stole from the officers' quarters they would slam him in the cage with minimum rations. Usually a term in the cage was so horrendous that they'd never risk it again, so in some ways it was effective.'

While Walter had mixed views on Westley's decision to maintain control by such controversial means, he could understand the CO's thinking. 'I could see the purpose of it because some of the fellas were incorrigible. They wouldn't learn.'[1]

On one occasion a prisoner literally grabbed another man's food while queuing up in the mess line, swallowing it immediately. That day's ration consisted of a piece of sweet potato and a cake about the size of a small vegetable coated in a thin layer of fish sauce. There was no more to go round, so the other guy went without his meal for the day. The offender himself was charged and thrown into the cage for his greediness. 'He deserved it,' said Hicks. 'I would have given him a thrashing.'[2]

While the boob was a convenient way of punishing men for minor transgressions, most POWs were deeply troubled by Westley's style of home-grown discipline. Many were disgusted that an officer should mete out such treatment to his own men. Les Hohl, a sapper in the 2/11th Field Company, Royal Australian Engineers, was persuaded by his mates to confront the commanding officer and urge him to dismantle the boob.

> Sir, all the men in the camp consider that this cage is the most cruel and barbaric punishment any person could impose on another. It is a disgrace to Australia in the eyes of the Japanese and the Ambonese and everyone in the camp. Sir, I request that it be dismantled.[3]

Ailsa Rolley's account of Sapper Hohl's confrontation with Westley records that the commanding officer was unmoved, saying: 'I am responsible for discipline in the camp and it is the considered opinion of the officers that the only way to stop theft is to make the punishment so harsh that no one would steal again.'

Les tried to appeal to the CO's sense of justice. People committed crimes even when the penalty was death, he pointed out. 'Surely, sir, the punishment should fit the crime – in this case it is just out of all proportion.'

By now Westley was quietly seething at the sapper's perceived insubordination and he was not prepared to budge. 'As I said before, it is the considered opinion of the officers that this is the way to handle stealing. We have the welfare of the whole camp to consider. Stealing must stop. It is the only way to survive,' he told Les before dismissing him with a curt wave.

In his diary Stuart Swanton observed that it was hard to know how to deal with the habitual lawbreakers. 'A barbed wire cage has been constructed on the main camp road and offenders are locked up there as punishment.'[4] The decision to erect the cage was backed by the Japanese and it was not long before they started using it themselves. Stuart revealed the Japanese were also using the boob 'for any of our chaps with whom they have trouble, but they usually dock them a few meals into the bargain'.

Interestingly, in later years there was a degree of selective memory among officers over the presence of the cage, with some denying it ever existed. But among the men there remained a clear and unqualified mental picture of this cruel and barbarous contraption, which would haunt Westley for decades to come.

Eddie Gilbert has never forgiven the CO for what he did.

The idea was that if anyone got caught pinching stuff during the night, when they came home from their work party they were put into this wire cage and kept there, irrespective of the weather. What I hold against Westley more than anything was his going to the Japanese because he was worried about fellas going out at night and stealing stuff. But we were hungry![5]

Private Jack Morrow, from Lawson in New South Wales, was one of Eddie's two great mates in the camp. They'd formed a syndicate and looked out for each other. Morrow was also one of the early occupants of the boob. He'd got into the officers' garden and stolen some cassava, a root vegetable that was native to Ambon. Four years older than Eddie, Morrow was not in the best of health and the last thing he needed was a few nights in the boob, where he tossed and turned in the limited space, drenched by a tropical downpour. After being fed minimum rations he was released in the morning to rejoin his work party.

A few nights in the cage had devastating consequences. 'He was already on starvation rations and that wire cage – well, he didn't die directly afterwards but I hold that man Westley to blame for shortening my mate's life,' said Eddie, who continues to seethe with indignation at the way the officers behaved. 'There were a few we'd admire and respect, but as a body, well, you see they didn't go out to work so they had all day to create a garden and to nourish it. Then they'd eat it on their own, not sharing. It didn't leave a nice impression.'[6]

The true extent to which the cage contributed to Private Morrow's decline can only be guessed at, but within a year he'd be dead. Eddie Gilbert would never forget or pardon the man he held responsible.

Years later, when George de Verdon Westley turned up at a battalion reunion Gilbert looked him in the eye and said, 'I don't want to talk to you.' 'I turned my back on him and never saw him again.'[7]

While it was easy to be judgemental about the cage, it was important to remember that such appalling times did not make Westley's job easy. In the latter days of the Australians' captivity on Ambon the theft of food and other petty crimes could not go unpunished. Wasn't it better to deal with it 'in-house' than to hand offenders over to the Japanese, who would undoubtedly inflict far greater pain? The CO had a duty to enforce law and order for the good of the entire camp and in retrospect his response might not seem unreasonable, given the extraordinary conditions of the time.

Yet there was no denying that many saw this as an affront to the spirit of mateship. Didn't Westley's decision strike at the very heart of the Australian military tradition of looking out for each other, ensuring each other's welfare and showing compassion? Mateship was valued in Australian culture and held up as a virtue in the Australian military code, alongside loyalty, teamwork, duty and honour.[8]

Westley was also faced with deteriorating food supplies, making it imperative that the meagre rations be shared. The starvation diet had already taken its toll, with many more POWs falling victim to disease.

To make matters worse, the Japanese increased the workload, culminating in what became known as the Long Carry. It was one of the most physically demanding and senseless episodes of the 2/21st's entire incarceration on Ambon. The Japanese introduced the new work party towards the end of 1944. It required the men to haul heavy bags of cement weighing nearly 45 kilograms over 13 kilometres of rugged jungle track between two villages on the south-east coast of the island. John Van Nooten later described the work party's route from Batugong near Paso to the village of Hutumuri as 'indescribably difficult country. Up hills, down hills, through a jungle and around a track that goats could just walk on.'[9] To make matters worse, Japanese soldiers beat the men with pick handles as they struggled to carry the cement, often on all fours.

The Long Carry lasted for several weeks and also involved work parties taking 113-kilogram bombs along the same track. Two men carried a bomb on a bamboo pole between them, each staggering inch by inch up and down the rugged trail, knowing that one false step might ignite their deadly haul. 'After blokes had done that, that really put most of them on the skids,' Jack Panaotie recalls.[10]

Come the final days of the Long Carry, most of the Australians were so sick and exhausted that it was difficult to muster a functioning work party. One man collapsed on the road, prompting Ikeuchi to go in search of replacements.

> Ikeuchi went through the huts and there was a fellow, as he thought, in bed asleep. He started belting him with a stick and saying, 'Get up.' And the bloke was dead. He'd go through the hospital where the blokes were dying like flies and he'd say, 'You get out of bed. You get out of bed. You're alright, nothing wrong with you.' The mongrel bastard.[11]

To add to the men's despair, the Long Carry turned out to be a totally pointless exercise. The bombs and cement, which were never used, could easily have been transported around the coast by barge. This reinforced the theory that the entire exercise was designed as a punishment. Certainly that was the view of Westley, who later told the War Crimes Commission that it was a 'particularly drastic form of torture . . . deliberately instituted in my opinion to break down morale and kill off the weaker prisoners'.[12]

With the Japanese daily food ration now down to about 230 grams per man, the POWs' average weight had fallen by nearly 20 kilograms, and beri-beri, malaria and enteritis were rife. Most of the men had also developed tropical ulcers, some up to a foot long. Said Westley, 'They were usually on the legs. One man had an ulcer which stretched from the ankle to the knee.' Also known as jungle rot, tropical ulcers develop as an open sore on the skin, eating into the muscle, tendon and sometimes even the bone. If left untreated they can be intensely painful.

And still the poor devils were ordered to work. 'I have seen men on crutches and sticks forced to work by the Japanese,' said Westley. 'I know of some cases where men were so weak that they had to be lifted on to the trucks, being forced to work.' Even Westley, who as the CO should have commanded a degree of respect from his captors, was struck hard on his ulcerated leg by a stick-wielding Ikeuchi. 'The part that hurt me most was that it was done in full view of the troops. He never lost any opportunity to humiliate me.'

Westley often protested about the treatment of his men but he never got any redress. 'Even those complaints which I lodged in writing to the commander-in-chief of the island were not accepted. Very often they were screwed up and thrown in the adjutant's face.'

During the course of their imprisonment, the POWs were often ordered to engage in near-suicidal work practices, particularly involving explosives.

As bombing raids become more frequent, the Japanese decided to build several tunnels in which to store their food and other essential supplies. Along with shovelling their way though coral rock and removing the rubble, the men had to line the tunnels with coconut logs to stop the walls and roof from caving in. It was back-breaking work, but it did not have the same high level of risk as handling the explosives used to blast the rock away. Foolishly, the Japanese ordered the men to extract the picric acid from aerial bombs that could no longer be used. 'We had to chip it out with a hammer and chisel, break it up, then hammer it on another surface to make it into a powder,' Eddie Gilbert remembers. The powder was then stuffed into a hole in a bamboo rod and placed by the rock face. It was a disaster in the making, given picric acid's tendency to be detonated by a sudden shock or spark.

'Inevitably, it happened one day. A spark was caused and the bomb exploded. That was the most frightening work party of all because we all knew it only needed a tiny spark. I hate to think what it must have been like when that one went off.'[13]

Fortunately, Eddie wasn't working that day, but the blast killed one man instantly and caused shocking injuries to three others. Within a few days they were also dead.

———

Food, health and living conditions continued to deteriorate on Ambon. By October 1944 the daily ration had been reduced to about 40 grams of rice and about 200 grams of tapioca flour. It was barely enough to sustain life, particularly for those engaged in hard physical labour.[14]

The Americans, who had their own quarters in Tan Tui Barracks, were also finding the going hard. Ed Weiss, still in charge of water distribution, lugged 10-gallon buckets and a cart to the hospital, the cooking huts and other strategic points around the camp. The American crew, comprising Mike Maslak, Clyde Rearick, Irv Stein, John Biss, Stan Kapp and Weiss, dubbed themselves the convict gang. It was a fair description, given the nature of their duties and the hard labour involved.

The water cart had two iron-rimmed, wooden-spoked wheels and an 80-gallon drum secured on a wooden platform. Weiss still remembers it vividly.

A six foot wooden T shaft protruded forward for pulling, pushing and tugging. It required all our physical strength to get it up the slope of the main camp road. While four of us struggled with the cart, the other two, each with ten gallon buckets of water suspended on a pole or yoke, would follow along and help fill the drums spotted throughout the camp. After a painful period of time we all developed calluses on the back of our necks and on our shoulders. To this day I still have the scars.[15]

After delivering the water the US group spent the rest of the day chopping wood for fires in the Japanese guards' kitchen and the camp cook hut.

It was during this period that the Americans suffered their first loss. Mac McGibony, who had sailed south in such high spirits with Ed and the others on the good ship *Pilar* in 1942, died of dysentery. Some of the convict gang were assigned to grave digging and devoted much of the next morning attempting to carve a hole in the coral undersurface deep enough to hold his body.

Mac's slender frame was wrapped in a blanket and carried up the hill by Ed, Clyde, Red Carson and Bob Grainger, who read a verse or two from the Bible. The men were deep in thought as they performed the simple ceremony and began to fill in the grave. As they started to make their way back to camp, Weiss hung around for a few moments and muttered, 'So long, Mac.'

The number of Americans on Ambon now stood at thirteen. Who would be next? they must have wondered. How much longer could they endure the pain of POW life? Would they ever find their way home?

In fact, what the Allied prisoners at Tan Tui didn't know was that an audacious plan to free them was being given active consideration by the Australian military. Code-named Project Anchovy, the initial idea was to land a guerilla force on Ambon with a view to rescuing some, if not all, of the POWs. Through its native agents on the island, Australian intelligence had already compiled an impressively accurate picture of life on Ambon and the conditions at Tan Tui.[16]

It knew the number of guards on duty in each of the two watchhouses, which were connected by telephone, and how the lights were extinguished at night. Watch was kept by about 75 men, who lived in the western part of the camp in wooden houses with thatched roofs. Intriguingly the spymasters also knew about a radio located in a pit some 5 metres outside the fence, although how it was used and by whom was not revealed. The source of this information also provided a detailed description of Ambon town, which was labelled 'filthy'. 'Food refuse, fish heads and offal lie rotting in the streets and are a breeding ground for flies. There appear to be no organized sanitary services . . . and education appears to have been neglected due to more pressing needs.'[17] Native policemen were encouraged to act as informers, but Christians who had been subjected to Japanese persecution were not keen on the idea and treated the local population leniently.

There were also unsettling reports about the plight of the POWs, whose condition was described as 'very emaciated'. 'They were stated to have been badly treated, being forced to work hard on insufficient food and beaten if they did not please the Japanese.'[18] The informant also revealed that the locals 'appear to have had a liking for the Australians and frequently tried to pass them food, tobacco, even at the risk of a summary beheading'.

While the news was not all bad, the intelligence available to the Australian military by early 1945 could make an observer wonder how long they'd been holding on to it. If they knew so much about Tan Tui now, did they also know about the camp before it was bombed? Whatever the truth about the past, it was the present that dominated talk among those who were planning Project Anchovy, which was rapidly taking shape. The idea was to despatch an SRD Country Craft towing a Wellfreighter submarine from Darwin to a point south-west of the Laitimor Peninsula on Ambon's east coast.

The Wellfreighter was a midget submarine which resembled a motorboat when not submerged. It could carry up to eight personnel and was ideal for clandestine reconnaissance operations. Once in position the midget sub would land a four-man team, a rubber dinghy and enough food supplies to last them eight days on Ambon. While in hiding they would attempt to make contact with some of the POWs or sympathetic locals to gain further information, in readiness for an all-out rescue. At least, that was the plan, but like so much of the effort that went into Ambon before and during the war, it would come to nothing.

There were only two Wellfreighters in Australia and not one could be spared. 'There was a possibility of undertaking this project with two Wellfreighters but it was not possible to commence within three months of approval.' The decision, signed by Major S. Bingham, CC, Group D, was dated 30 May 1945. Within three months the war would be over. Project Anchovy was already dead in the water.[19]

12

ESCAPE FROM HAINAN

MORE THAN 3000 kilometres to the north, on the island of Hainan, the rest of Gull Force had had their daily rations cut to a mere 340 grams per man. In such circumstances even rats had become a delicacy. There were rumours of imminent rescue by Allied forces and talk of escape among some of the officers. There was also the unspoken fear that the Japanese would resort to mass execution of the POWs if the island was invaded.

Ever optimistic, Tom Pledger thought the war would be over by Christmas. 'We do nothing more than to talk about our home and homecoming,' he wrote in his diary on 8 September 1944.[1]

> Of a night we sit outside – Les Pyers, Allan Brownley and myself – and as we were all from the north coast recall old faces and places and try to work out what will be our last few moments before we hit home. Hopes were high but the tummy was empty as the food was very poor and scarce again. Oh to be able to dip into the old cupboard and get a scone or slice of cake.

Then, come October, he admitted there were moments when you wondered if you could carry on.

The monotony of it all, nothing to see but faces you know off by heart. You know just what they'll say and you feel like screaming at them and having a go at the Japs by yourself. But then comes the despair. What good would you do? You'd only get belted to death. And so reason takes its place and you start to dream. Oh there was never a dreamer in the world like the 210 in this camp. Home, mothers, wives, sweethearts, good times before and after. That was our life and so it carries on one day after another . . .[2]

Apart from the lack of food, the mistreatment of the inmates only added to their woes. Captain Bill Aitken said Japanese officers, NCOs and guards were forcing the men to work harder by kicking them, hitting them with rifle butts and flogging them with shovels, pick handles, iron bars and sticks of wood. 'This treatment imposed a great deal of mental strain on all men and in addition to three fractured limbs many other injuries requiring medical attention were inflicted.'[3]

The POWs' emotional and mental state contributed to their weak physical condition as much as the poor diet and slave labour. Said Aitken:

There were many reasons for depression – bad food, trying climate, lack of news and tobacco, hard monotonous work, boredom and lack of amusement, plus the prospects of a long and dreary confinement in most uncomfortable circumstances with daily life hampered and made more difficult by many minor and often unnecessary restrictions.[4]

From January 1945 food rations continued to decline, with the average daily calorific intake dropping to 1640 in February and falling to 1470 the following month. Most adult males require at least 2500 calories a day to maintain a healthy weight, while those engaged in hard physical labour need more.[5] It was no wonder that Aitken was shocked by the Australians' appearance.

> Most of the men presented a ghastly picture, walking around like skeletons with pot bellies and oedematous legs and faces, and with various sores and boils, dressed with any old scrap of rag. We were all extremely weak and I don't think a single man was capable of running 100 yards and it took the greatest of effort to carry out the normal functions of life, let alone any necessary extra duties. The serious effect of malaria, diarrhea and influenza etc. and the difficulty in treating these in this type of patient can well be imagined.[6]

Aitken's memory of the men's grotesque physical state would reinforce the evidence he later provided to war crimes investigators, and he had no doubt who was responsible. Captain Ichiro Kikuchi, the camp's chief medical officer, had to be held accountable, if not for actual murder, then for manslaughter due to wilful neglect, he insisted.

For those looking after the sick and dying – men like Jimmy Morrison of the 2/12th Field Ambulance unit – the pressure was intense. Not only were they forced to work with limited facilities and few or no drugs, they were invariably ill themselves. Jimmy, who by early 1945 was only in his mid-twenties, was rarely without malaria and would often suffer bouts of shivering and shaking while caring for his patients.

Some of the sick were rendered almost senseless by their condition. One day Jimmy was treating Joe Capon, a 30-year-old private from Geelong, who was so hysterical that it took eight men to hold him down. 'Quite a few others walked around like zombies, but Joe just went blood red. It was dreadful,' he recalls.[7] Sadly, in the struggle Joe hit his head on the floor and died – just another innocent victim of a crazy world that must have seemed like bedlam.

Ian Macrae, who had garnered much respect during his period as second in command to Scott, was also not immune to personal suffering, though as a man of action he was often a factor in his own undoing. On 17 February 1945, he was detected by a guard trying to leave the camp at night. The 40-year-old Melbourne-born major had spent much of his incarceration planning his escape and had slipped under the wire on countless occasions, with a view to gaining intelligence from local villagers about the Chinese nationalists on the island. Macrae was arrested and ordered to stand to attention outside the guardhouse for three days and nights. Privately, because of the warnings that had been issued previously about escapes, he had expected to be executed but after two-and-a-half days he was released, following the intervention of the commanding officer.

Quietly relieved about this unexpected reprieve, Ian Macrae did not give up his quest for freedom, but it would be another couple of months before he made a second attempt, and this time he was determined to succeed. On 24 February a small group of Dutch prisoners made a successful escape, which may have helped to inspire him, but it was a comment from a friendly Formosan guard that really concentrated his mind.

Word was that American forces were expected to land any day, and that if or when this happened the Japanese planned to execute the POWs en masse. The grim warning clearly added even greater urgency to Macrae's plans for escape.[8] The Japanese also decided to erect an electric fence at about this time, making it harder, though not impossible, to leave the camp. Macrae intended to assemble an escape party of no more than six men and had informed Scott about his plans. The CO, who was the only other person to be told about the operation, readily agreed, but there would be two months of intense preparation before the men left.

Apart from Major Macrae the rest were Sydney-born Staff Sergeant Ron Leech; Private Stuart Campbell, 24, who had enlisted at Toorak; Private Tom Lockwood, who was the same age and from Glen Iris; country boy Private Myles Higgins, aged

30, from Drouin in Victoria; and Fred Perrin, about whom little was known.

Interestingly, Leech later suggested that he helped to instigate the escape plan and that Macrae asked to join them at the last minute. They accepted him, but only on the understanding that he would no longer have command over them once they left the camp. He agreed and never once tried to pull rank. Such egalitarianism – if the story was true – could only work among Australians.

What was certain was that on the night of 16 April they lifted up the bottom wire with a log of wood, allowing Leech and Macrae to crawl through the gap, tossing their packs ahead of them. Apart from the danger posed by the electrified fence, there were prickly pears to crawl over. 'It was not my idea of a pastime but we got out and blundered around.'[9] Suddenly all hell broke loose as an air raid siren began to wail. Thinking they had been spotted, the men dug themselves into a potato patch and hid. It looked like the escape mission had failed before it had begun, but the cause of the commotion turned out to be a surprise attack by US aircraft, which lit up the night sky by dropping phosphorus flares.

Amazingly, the Japanese guards, who were madly firing at the planes and partially dazzled by the glare, failed to see the Australians. By now the rest of the men were under the wire and made good their escape. After three hours of walking they bedded down in some bracken, only to discover later that they were almost back where they had begun.

They didn't realise it at the time but their temporary refuge was at the base of what turned out to be some kind of Japanese fortress, a mere 45 metres from the prison camp. Leech – an ex-professional cyclist who had just celebrated his twenty-seventh birthday and went on to write a detailed account of the escape and the adventures that followed – spent the next day hiding with his mates in the 60-centimetre-high vegetation while desperately trying to avoid being seen by the Indian guards who peered out

Informal portrait of officers of the 2/21st Battalion in Darwin, prior to their departure to Ambon in December 1941. *Left to right*: Lieutenant Rodney Gabriel, Captain Charles Patmore, Major Mark Newbury, Lieutenant John Davis, Lieutenant Noel Thomas, Lieutenant William Aitken, Lieutenant Colonel Len Roach, Commanding Officer. *AWM P03156.003*

Tom Pledger and Jessica, 1940. *Photo courtesy of Tom Pledger*

Max Gilbert, December 1940. *Photo courtesy of Max Gilbert*

Six members of the B Company mortar detachment, 2/21st Battalion, and three Ambonese youths, shortly before the Japanese attack on Ambon. *Left to right*: Corporal Austin Carr, Private John Robertson, Private Alfred Mason, an Ambonese youth named Simon, Private Maric (Eddie/Max) Gilbert. *Front row*: Two Ambonese youths, one named Janis Lopulalan, Private Robert Williams. This photo was taken on Eddie Gilbert's Kodak Baby Brown camera. He destroyed the camera when the Japanese attacked but concealed the undeveloped film until he was released in 1945. *AWM P07476.001*

Laha airfield.
Photo courtesy of Ed Weiss

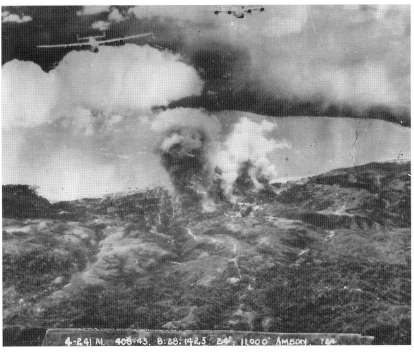

Laha airfield under attack, taken from the leading B24 Liberator at 11,000 feet.
Photo courtesy of Ed Weiss

The Tan Tui POW camp, Ambon. Four-fifths of the prisoners died in this camp.
AWM 118253

Bakli Bay, Hainan Island, c. 28 August 1945. General view of the POW camp hospital.
AWM 030365/02

Survivors of Gull Force were evacuated from Ambon and brought to Morotai by RAN corvettes for hospitalisation at the Australian POW reception group camp. Here stretcher cases on the wharf wait for ambulances. *AWM 115775*

Bakli Bay, Hainan Island, c. 28 August 1945. Lieutenant Colonel W. J. R. Scott stands beside graves of men of the 2/21st Battalion who died in the POW camp. *AWM 030368/02*

Stuart Swanton, circa 1940.
Photo courtesy of Lloyd Swanton

Ed Weiss, September 1945, Morotai.
Photo courtesy of Ed Weiss

The camp interpreter of the Ambon POW camp, Ikeuchi Masakiyo, standing with
members of 1st Australian Armoured Division Provost Company on Morotai.
AWM 115780

Top left: Charles Shaver and Ed Weiss, 28 November 1993. *Photo courtesy of Ed Weiss*
Left: Walter Hicks, June 2012.
Above: Max Gilbert, June 2012.

Ralph Godfrey, April 2013.

Jim and Emily Morrison, November 2013.

Members of the Gull Force Association at the Honour Wall, Kudamati, Ambon, in 2013. Sue Head is second from right, back row. *Photo courtesy of Sue Head*

Tom Pledger marching with the Gull Force banner on Anzac Day, 2013.

from the top of their lofty outpost. Come dusk, they slid down from the grassy mound where they were hiding and headed for a distant mountain range. None of the group was in good health. Macrae was seriously incapacitated with beri-beri and Leech, who was also suffering from malaria, wasn't much better.

With little water and not much in the way of food supplies the six men staggered on and arrived in the mountain foothills by the second night. Their aim was to make contact with the Chinese nationalists who were headquartered in Hainan's hinterland but nothing prepared them for the arduous journey to come and the natives they met along the way. 'Before dawn Tommy Lockwood and I were looking for water and when we come back to the other four we found them surrounded by the wildest look of brigands you've ever seen in your life,' said Macrae.[10] The scene which greeted them was both bizarre and almost incomprehensible. It was as though they had stepped back in time, according to Leech.

Unknowingly we were about to enter and traverse a land peopled by the Miao, Lois and southern Han tribes, all at war with the Japanese, Chinese and each other, unseen by white people, unchanged for a century. While the world killed each other with the latest methods of destruction, these people believed that the world was flat, fought with six foot bows and arrows, old French muzzle-loading blunderbusses, had no use or knowledge of money, tattooed themselves with blue dye, bound their hair forward in a unicorn cone, while worshipping, to us, unknown gods and demons.[11]

Fortunately they were friendly, which was more than could be said for the Japanese the men had left behind in the POW camp. The workload expected of the men had reached a new intensity, with guards inflicting regular beatings on those Australians who fell short of the guards' requirements. Scott talked of 'frightful' violence and 'unbelievable' cruelty. 'It was very difficult to

understand why there was not a very heavy death toll as a result,'
he admitted in his post-war report.

Some of the Australian officers volunteered to be in charge
of the work parties, in the hope of improving conditions for
the men. Lieutenant Ronald Green, who was acting adjutant at
the time, was beaten insensible for his efforts. Private Harold
Beamsley, 32 and Malvern-born, was to suffer even more. He
was so viciously assaulted that he suffered a fractured arm. As
he almost fainted from the pain the Japanese guards twisted
the broken limb and hit him about the head. It was cruelty so
extreme that Scott was prompted to deliver a strong protest to the
Japanese district commandant, Lieutenant Yoshida, who agreed
to visit the injured man in hospital.

The Japanese officer was clearly embarrassed, for he apologised
for the ill-treatment of the Australians and ordered a three-day
holiday. It was the men's first day off in eight months, but it did
not signify an improvement in living conditions.

The POWs were locked inside their camp, encircled by the
barbed wire fence, which was now electrified. They would
remain there indefinitely, all strength and will leaching slowly
from their emaciated bodies. The only upside was that the work
parties were suspended, which brought an immediate end to the
slave labour. It was an unexpected bonus and one which would
inevitably help to spare lives.

However, with the men restricted to the camp for days and
weeks on end, discipline took another turn for the worse, forcing
them to take punishment into their own hands. Once again it was
stealing food which prompted the crackdown. The padre even
delivered a sermon in an effort to convince offenders to mend their
ways. With every member of Gull Force barely receiving enough
to live on, 'any man who stole food under present conditions
may well be guilty of murder in the first degree,' he said.[12] The
appeal made little difference.

With the commanding officer at a loss to know how to control
his men, an unlikely turn of events occurred. As Scott described

it, 'The men themselves decided to take a hand. They organised themselves into a Vigilance Committee, detected offenders, tried them and administered punishment.'[13] Offenders were subjected to a beating, sometimes severe, and although it was intended to cause no long-lasting injury, there were subsequent reports that some men died. Roy Harris from Mildura claimed the so-called vigilantes got out of hand, with a few men 'belting anybody for the least little thing'.

A mate who picked up some dry leaves from a tomato garden to smoke was reported to the committee and he was made to strip off and was then put over a desk. 'They held their own court martial, sentenced him to 27 smacks with a cane across the backside – that killed that man. And there was another man who was the colonel's batman – an Englishman, a wonderful man – he got belted for some paltry turn out and died.'[14]

These were not isolated incidents. Jack Devenish said he saw as many as eight men punished, and not always for stealing food.

> It could arise out of almost anything. For instance if you had a difference of opinion with somebody and got a bit punchy and hit someone, the committee had the power to punish you for that. It was always done the same way with anything from six to ten lashes with a pick handle on the bare buttocks. They were careful to avoid hitting the spine, but it left shocking blue, bruised areas on the buttocks. The thing that staggered me was to see our own boys inflicting this sort of punishment on their mates. God knows they were in enough trouble without having to suffer those sort of things.[15]

While the pain was extreme, it was the humiliation of the beating that had the greatest impact. Said Scott, 'It had the effect of greatly decreasing and finally causing trouble of this nature to practically cease. This system of control continued until the end of our period of internment.'[16]

Where Scott and Westley had failed so miserably in their attempts to instil discipline, the other ranks had succeeded. While the method was controversial, and clearly not countenanced by military law, the result was to restore order in a community whose lives were being threatened by the actions of a few. Clearly, tough measures were merited, given the level of disease and starvation in the camp. Between January and April 1945 there had been 55 cases of malaria and 27 cases of beri-beri. Said Scott:

The health of the camp was in a dangerous condition.
There were serious cases of starvation. The average weight
on April 27th was eight stone and the loss in weight
between February and April was about sixteen pounds.
Without an increase in drugs and food a large number
would die.[17]

Meanwhile, the escape party had survived their first 24 hours with the blunderbuss and bow and arrow–wielding locals they'd encountered on their journey, and were keen to move on. The Chinese indicated there was a village not far away and the Australians formed a motley column, with the gunmen leading the march and the bowmen at the rear.

On arrival at the village they were unnerved to find the Chinese wearing Dutch uniforms. How had they got them? Were they taken from Dutch escapees and, if so, what did it say about the possible fate of the Australians? There was no alternative but to trust their luck, which had served them well since they had slipped under the barbed wire a couple of days earlier.

They need not have worried. The rag tag bunch were soon being introduced to the headman, who wore a revolver around his waist. Later they were offered plates of chicken and rice, as well as sake to wash down the food. At last Ron Leech and his mates began to relax, as they spread themselves out on a dirt floor in a village hut. For the first time in years the pangs of hunger had disappeared and, more importantly, they were free.

As Leech put it, 'I suppose never again will one night be filled with such simple pleasure. We had made it, despite the search planes, despite being lost, against thirst and hunger. We had reached a seemingly safe haven and we were content with our earthen floor.'[18]

Despite the relative home comforts of their newly found refuge, the Australians were still on the run and they needed to get as much distance as possible between them and the enemy. There was a narrow escape the following morning when some Japanese wandered into the village, but the POWs, dressed in Chinese clothes and rubber-tyre thongs, hid under their bamboo hats. Ron hoped no one noticed his ginger fringe.

Bad weather and nearby military activity delayed their departure and the men were forced to wait for several days. Poor health, including dysentery and frequent bouts of malaria, also weakened them and they realised they had to improve their fitness if they were to negotiate the narrow mountain tracks and fast-flowing rivers to reach the nationalist headquarters. The journey was expected to take at least fifteen days and nights.

There was also the problem of wild Indians, or Indos as they were known by the Chinese. These indigenous people seemed to pick fights with everyone, regardless of creed or colour, and were known to have a taste for human liver, which they regarded as a cure for malaria. Not wanting their vital organs to end up in a cooking pot, the escapees were keen to make headway as soon as possible. Eventually, sixteen Chinese guards assembled in the village to escort them to the island interior, where most of the nationalist troops were based.

It was to be a wearing and dangerous trek, a march that would put further stress on already severely aching limbs. Away from the village huts the mountainside rose steeply, a dirt track winding its way 900 metres up, or more. It was the first stage of their journey and the demanding terrain did not bode well.

Within a few hundred yards Tom Lockwood collapsed, declaring he was already spent. There was no room either side of the narrow path for two men to support him, so Ron Leech and Fred Perrin encouraged him forward with a tree branch stuck firmly in his back. The next man to fall was Myles Higgins, who was reduced to crawling on all fours up the steep gradient. Once again, his mates helped him to his feet and provided him with a stick to aid his walking.

It was night by now and the Chinese guards at the head of the column were out of sight. Ian Macrae, who was staggering behind them and suffering acutely from beri-beri, stumbled. Leech went to his aid only to discover that he was lurching blindly in the pitch-black conditions. When the rear guards caught them up, they took the danger in their stride. What's the problem, they enquired? Why worry? What will be, will be. Their doctrine of fatalism might not have sat comfortably with the Australians, but it provided partial relief at an otherwise stressful moment.

If they were caught by the Japanese they'd be shot or beheaded. If they weren't, they could be robbed, killed or eaten by the wilder elements of the Chinese. Or, just possibly, they might survive. No one dared to ponder such optimism right now, but if they made it to the Chinese nationalist headquarters they might live to tell the tale.

Thus the long march continued, through valleys of dazzling beauty and mountain paths with dauntingly severe gradients. They encountered lush jungles, crossed raging rivers, witnessed exotic bird and wildlife and met fascinating people, many of them natives who seemingly had nothing but were happy to share what little they had. It was as though the indigenous population was on another plain of consciousness. On one occasion the men passed beneath a lone Chinaman sitting naked apart from a loin cloth in the fork of a tree, his hair fashioned into the now familiar unicorn-style twist. Ron Leech observed that the man did not deign to look at them, preferring to commune with nature or his gods. 'I felt deeply that we of the twentieth century were entering a time long gone, but wondered at progress. For we were at war and he was at peace.'[19]

There were also moments of light relief – for some. When Macrae fell off his horse while crossing a river, the Chinese burst into laughter. The fact that he nearly drowned didn't seem to bother them.

And then there was the silence. There was the rustling of leaves and distant bird song but little conversation as the party meandered through agrarian scenes which had remained largely unchanged for centuries. Water flowed down terraced hillsides where cattle grazed and women thrashed their rice. Was there really a war on in this Shangri-La? The men might be forgiven for concluding they were among peace-loving people, but every now and again there were ugly reminders of the fierce conflict going on between the Chinese and those who had occupied their land. A group of Japanese soldiers were caught, tied up with ropes and several big dogs let loose on them. Each man died from the injuries sustained in the mauling. Two Formosan deserters were summarily executed by the nationalists for demanding money. And word was out that British soldiers who were caught were worth 30000 shillings if handed in to the Japanese. The Aussies hoped the bounty hunters could tell the difference.

Occasionally there were buildings to sleep in and meals of pumpkin, meat and rice, washed down with coffee. It was almost civilised, yet the constant threat of Japanese discovery meant they could never relax. They were also debilitated by regular bouts of high fever, the pain and discomfort of beri-beri and the sheer physical demands of walking through such difficult terrain. Myles was the sickest and often had trouble maintaining a foothold on the craggy tracks. Apart from suffering from the usual conditions, he had a badly infected foot which forced him to crawl along with only his bare hands for support. The other men were extremely concerned for his welfare as he was well liked and never usually complained, but he was clearly weakening by the day and his foot was badly swollen.

Macrae's beri-beri was also getting worse and he was very shaky. A pony was provided to aid him on the journey but the party was making slow progress and, to add to their worries, Japanese troops and forts were spotted nearby. But there were also encouraging signs that their destination was getting closer. They were offered proper beds to sleep in and even a haircut and a shave. Rice wine was produced and the Australians, who had been teetotal for so long, consumed more than was good for them. This was strong liquor and there were several sore heads the next morning.

The final climb along a high mountain ledge proved to be one of the most difficult days since the journey began and there were still 42 kilometres to go. Eventually they reached another village where one old man could speak English. He told them about the failure of the rice crop because of recent typhoons and spoke pessimistically about the war continuing for another three years. However, there was more comforting news when it emerged that there was a radio operating within the village, and even a bank. This was genuine civilisation compared with where they'd travelled during the past few weeks.

They had hoped to reached the nationalist HQ the next day, but come morning most of the men had gone down with malarial fever. Myles, Tom and Fred were all in a bad way and Macrae, who could hardly walk, was told that his pony had escaped. To make matters worse, they discovered they'd made little headway. Yet, undeterred, they limped out of the village, with Ron Leech gently prodding the walking wounded with a wooden pole.

Incredibly, they managed to clamber up the remaining steep hill, and from there they gazed out to Wuzhi mountain, at 1840 metres the highest peak on the island. It was one of the most glorious sights of their long march, for it meant they were only a short distance from their goal. As they staggered down into the valley which separated them from the nationalists' base, they were met by armed soldiers, who ordered them to stop. Had they taken a wrong direction? Had they wandered into enemy territory? Thankfully not. The troops were guards despatched from nationalist HQ to ensure the escapees' safe passage on the final stage of their marathon march.

Sadly, fate had one last act of cruelty to impose upon the men, just as they reached safety. For Myles Higgins, who had put up such a brave struggle through weeks of suffering, salvation had come too late. As the Australians were welcomed into the camp and escorted into a hut to rest awhile, Myles collapsed. His endurance was exhausted, his body at the point of meltdown. After achieving the near-impossible for a man so ill, Myles departed this life at precisely 8.45 p.m. on 13 June 1945.

Death offered the sort of escape many other POWs must have been pondering, but it was not Ian Macrae's chosen route to freedom. There was work to be done and a war to be fought.

13

THE BEGINNING OF THE END

IF MACRAE'S MAD dash for freedom on Hainan suggested it was worth the risk, there was a grim reminder of the danger of being caught outside the fence on Ambon.

In March 1945 two Australians who were desperate to escape from Tan Tui slipped under the barbed wire one night and were reported absent a few days later. Private James Elmore, from Korumburra, in Victoria, who had just celebrated his twenty-third birthday, and his mate Private Frederick Schaefer were so determined to flee their living hell that even the likelihood of certain death in the event of capture did not deter them. Schaefer managed to stay on the run for about two weeks before being caught and handed over to the Japanese, who took a sadistic delight in parading him through the streets with a noose around his neck. His fate was assured and he was duly executed shortly afterwards.

Jimmy Elmore stayed hidden for longer, managing to seek sanctuary in a tiny Ambonese village just across the bay from Tan Tui. By the time he was found by enemy soldiers he was suffering acutely from dysentery and died the next day. It was a merciful release, for had he survived longer he would almost certainly have endured the same fate as his mate Schaefer.

It was a measure of their desperation that the Australians were willing to take such risks. The American Ed Weiss had contemplated going under the wire but thought better of it when the harsh reality sank in. How would he survive without adequate supplies of food and water? How would he communicate with the locals without the language skills? More presciently, how could he endanger the lives of his fellow Americans if he were caught? The Japanese warning that they would kill ten POWs for every prisoner caught might or might not be an idle threat, but he couldn't chance it.

As the final year of the war dragged on and the prospect of defeat seemed unavoidable, the Japanese were becoming increasingly edgy. By April, theft from military stores was a capital offence. When the Japanese suspected that food stocks hidden in a tunnel near the camp were being pilfered by the Australians they followed the footprints back to Tan Tui. Inside the barracks they found the Aussies cooking rice and tinned fish that had been stolen from the tunnel. The notorious Tokkei Tai military police were sent in to interrogate them and identify the culprits. Two days later, four men confessed to stealing food from the storage tunnel and were immediately taken out and bayoneted to death.

If the daily threat of execution wasn't bad enough, many of the inmates also became human guinea pigs in a controversial inoculation trial carried out by Japanese medics. Ostensibly, the idea was to test phials of vitamin B1 on about a hundred prisoners in an effort to cut the incidence of beri-beri, though many of the POWs suspected the Japanese had more sinister motives. They were partially right. After the war it emerged that the camp medical officer wanted to test the effectiveness of a typhoid vaccine which was out of date.

The effect of the injection varied with each man. Some reported even greater loss of energy and shortness of breath, while others emerged unscathed. Whether the jab caused a serious deterioration in the men's health was difficult to establish because most of the human guinea pigs were dead by the end of the war, but there was little doubt that this was a medical experiment that fell far short of Geneva Convention guidelines for the treatment of prisoners of war.

The accumulated impact of poor diet, starvation, disease and physical exhaustion was also taking a terrible toll. Over the first four months of 1945 51 more POWs died. Another 47 succumbed in May alone. The men were dying like flies. With a death rate like this it wouldn't be long before the camp's entire Australian population would be exterminated – but then perhaps that was the idea.

Some of the members of the so-called convict gang, Americans Ed Weiss, Mike Maslak, John Biss and Irv Stein, were assigned to grave-digging duties. Now minus their old buddy Mac McGibony, whom they'd already buried, they were ordered to return to the cemetery. Ikeuchi, the camp commandant, who was behaving ever more irrationally, had accused them of being responsible for the increase in deaths and said that they should therefore bury the bodies. While the logic behind this was hard to follow, the Americans had no alternative and resigned themselves to spending their afternoon in the graveyard, chipping away at the coral which lay just beneath the superficial covering of soil.

Usually they got through three or four burials a day, not only digging the hole but also carrying the corpses up the hill for burial. There, an Australian officer recited the 23rd Psalm, a mixture of rock and soil was scattered over the body and the plot was marked by a stake identifying the dead man. While the solemnity of the occasion was not lost on the men, the ritual was now being performed so frequently that survivors become inured to the unfolding tragedy.

June was no better, with a staggering 72 Australians falling victim to either beri-beri or dysentery, the latter almost certainly the result of poor sanitation. By now most of the men did not have the energy to make their way to the latrines, a wooden construction built over the seawater and dubbed the Bridge of Sighs. Instead, slit trenches were built for the men to use outside their huts, the sewage dribbling through the camp and attracting swarms of blowflies. No wonder so many inmates were going down with the trots.

It became more imperative to dispose of the bodies as quickly as possible, which placed even greater pressure on the convict gang. They didn't have the time or the strength to dig the graves deep enough, which forced the Americans to lay the dead to rest in a hole barely 30 centimetres deep. That was hardly enough to hold the blanket in which the remains were wrapped.

Another American, Bob Grainger, a deeply religious man, tended to the sick and dying, wandering the makeshift hospital and reading passages from the Bible to those who were near their end. Ed Weiss, who recalled him reading a verse to a dying Australian, admitted the sadness of the situation sometimes produced uncontrolled bursts of anger. 'I said to him: "Why don't you let these men die in peace?" "Ed," he replied, "that is what I am trying to do."'

Each month it got worse. In July, 94 Australians and one of the grave-diggers died. The American was Irv Stein, who had quite simply lost the will to live. Ed and the others urged him to hang on, but he breathed his last on 26 July. Said Weiss, 'We dug his grave a bit deeper and as Bob Grainger intoned, "Man that is born of woman has but a short time to live and is full of misery", we gave Irv Stein his freedom.'[1]

It was a month that Weiss described as a period of abject fear and sense of utter hopelessness 'that tested my sanity almost to the breaking point'.

And still the horror continued. During the first ten days of August another 29 Australians and one American were buried. Swede Jensen, who had been the captain aboard the *Pilar*, finally yielded to a combination of beri-beri and dysentery. It was desperately upsetting for those who knew him well, as he never got to see his son, who had been born after Jensen left the United States.

Who would be next? Weiss, who tried to be meticulous with his own hygiene, especially after burying so many bodies, also contracted dysentery. It was not surprising in the circumstances and for a day or two he believed his time was up. But he persevered, eating ripe bananas, which he'd been told was the only food that could be tolerated by those afflicted with the disease. It seemed to work because by day five the stomach pains and fever began to ease. 'It was one of the few times I can remember saying, "Thankyou God",' Ed Weiss recalled.

There was little else to thank the Lord for. Even apart from the number of deaths so far that year – 296 in all – the Japanese were showing no mercy to their captives. An Australian POW who was the last man to be recaptured after escaping from Tan Tui was bayoneted to death. Those who had survived thus far were reminded of their likely fate when the Japanese guards appeared one day with a couple of machine guns, which they pointed in the direction of the camp air raid shelters. The POWs looked on, bemused by the exercise, which ended as quickly as it had begun. It was only afterwards that the penny dropped and the men began to realise that this was a dress rehearsal for a mass execution, come Japan's inevitable capitulation.

Ed Weiss and his mates vowed to make themselves scarce if there was any indication of the Allies attacking Ambon and devised a plan whereby they would conceal themselves within stacks of split wood which they would have previously hollowed out. They would hide there until dark and then make good their escape, running down to the beach, swimming out to sea and coming ashore again well clear of the camp. It might seem a crazy idea in retrospect but the alternative had even less appeal. The prospect of death by machine gun fire only served to reinforce their survival instincts.

———

As the prisoners of war on Ambon contemplated an uncertain future in the first week of August 1945, the war in the Pacific was about to take a dramatic turn.

Some thousand kilometres away on the island of Tinian, the pre-dawn was alive with activity as the crew of the *Enola Gay* prepared for take-off. It was still dark as the B-29 Superfortress, piloted by Captain Paul Tibbets, taxied down the runway with a cargo more deadly than anything known before. It would take six hours to reach his target at the very south-east of Honshu, at a cruising altitude of 7924 metres. The weather conditions were near perfect as Tibbets and his crew lined up their sights on a T-shaped bridge where the rivers Honkawa and Motoyasu join.

The *Enola Gay* had already been detected by Japanese radar, but few of the civilians who were about to be incinerated took much notice of the air raid warnings. They had grown accustomed to the threat of Allied air attacks and assumed this one was no different.

Tibbets noted that it was precisely 8.15 a.m. when he let loose the equivalent of between 12 000 and 15 000 tonnes of TNT from the belly of his Superfortress. He had just dropped the world's first atomic bomb, which would herald the final chapter of the Second World War. It exploded nearly 600 metres above the city of Hiroshima, killing an estimated 140 000 people. The *Enola Gay*'s co-pilot, Captain Richard Lewis, looked down upon the destruction and muttered to the rest of the crew, 'My God, what have we done?'[2]

The full extent of the atomic obliteration was slow to emerge in Japan because communications were down, but it would not be long before the rest of the world heard about the arrival of the nuclear age. In Ambon the news would take even longer to be confirmed, though the rumour mill was working overtime, largely thanks to the language skills of two men.

Walter Hicks, who had spent much of his incarceration as a houseboy cleaning and tidying for the officers at camp HQ, had become an unofficial and quite accomplished translator of Japanese news over the years. Whenever the Japanese chatted among themselves about the progress of the war, he could understand them. When they left newspapers and documents on tables he would take a sly peek and digest the latest developments from overseas. Hicksu, as he was nicknamed by the Japanese, had to be careful whom he told. If word leaked out there was a spy in the HQ leaking sensitive intelligence to the POWs, he might be identified as the source, with all the risks that posed.

As it was, he had the perfect cover. Walter, who was good at household chores, had been taught sewing by his mother, a skill which the officers found particularly useful when they wanted their uniforms repaired. 'I was competent to deal with the work around me in Japanese headquarters and gradually I did more. I got to be doing the cooking and I learned to read, write and speak the language.'[3]

One day he was introduced to the American Mike Maslak, who had also developed a limited command of Japanese, and they agreed to teach each other what they knew and share what they learned. Their linguistic partnership was further strengthened when Hicks managed to engineer a transfer to the American hut, where he remained until the end of the war. Ed Weiss, who built a strong friendship with Walter Hicks in later life, said Hicks and Maslak were able to increase their level of Japanese, and also Malayan, to the level where they had a good idea of events in the outside world.

> Wal and Mike, not wishing to place themselves at risk should the Japanese become aware of their activities, did not circulate what news intelligence they had managed to glean. However this information did surface, sometimes days or weeks later, as rumours which could not be traced directly back to Wal or Mike. So many rumours had come or gone during the period of our activity that scant attention was paid to them. I myself believed that these rumours started somewhere as fact, but of course I had no way of knowing their authenticity and gave them little credence. Mike and Hicks were often the source of these rumours.[4]

Walter's courage in acting as an unofficial intelligence source while under the ever-watchful eye of the officers up at Japanese HQ was to produce the ultimate revelation on 21 August, when he saw a transcript of Emperor Hirohito's surrender speech. Until then, the POWs in Ambon had no knowledge of Japan's defeat, although subtle changes in the guards' behaviour and a small increase in rations had suggested a softening in the enemy's policy towards its prisoners.

Still worried about his safety, Walter was forced to keep the news to himself for the time being. It wasn't until two days later that the surrender became public knowledge, and even then the inmates couldn't believe it.

A new camp interpreter appeared as the men assembled for roll-call on 23 August. His message was short and to the point. 'The war is over. Soon a ship will come and take you away,' he declared. Strangely, the announcement made little difference to the camp's morale. Years of hard physical labour, starvation and disease had left the men incapable of showing emotion. Their hopes had been raised so many times before that no one could believe they were free. It was only when Walter Hicks confirmed what he had read two days earlier that the men of Gull Force and their American counterparts began to savour the luxury of liberation.

From that point on there was a marked improvement in food and medical supplies. Each man was given 680 grams of rice a day, as well as meat, fish and fresh vegetables. Eddie Gilbert's hunger pangs were replaced by 'the excruciating pain of acute indigestion as our shrunken stomachs attempted to handle this sudden increase in food'.[5] Japanese electricians arrived, fitting a power cable and light bulb to every hut. Radio sets also appeared, allowing the men to listen to a world they had had no sight or sound of for three-and-a-half years. It was only then that they heard about the atom bombs dropped on Hiroshima and Nagasaki.

Sadly, the war's end came too late to save the life of Stuart Swanton, who died of beri-beri on 14 August 1945. Leonie, his fiancée, would hear of his death from a telegram addressed to Stuart's father a few days after the surrender on Ambon. The family's only consolation was that Stuart was made a sergeant in the latter part of his imprisonment, but frustratingly, there was no reference to it in official records, which were not regarded as a high priority at the time.

Nearly three weeks had elapsed since the *Enola Gay* delivered its momentous death blow, effectively signalling the end of the Pacific war. Yet still the men of Gull Force remained prisoners.

Inexplicably, Ikeuchi, who was still in charge of the camp, had warned that no POW should venture beyond the guard posts without a Japanese escort. Of even greater concern was a claim that the army commander on Ambon had refused to acknowledge the surrender order and was committed to continuing the war.

When would the misery end? Would they ever be rescued? Where was the Allied invasion force? Crucially, did the Australian or American authorities actually know they were there? Clearly, they needed to send a message to the outside world – and fast.

Ian Macrae and his escape party, now under the protection of nationalist guerillas at their isolated headquarters in the remote interior of Hainan, were beginning to enjoy their new home. The Chinese were under orders to treat the Australians well and both sides were keen to foster cordial relations. As Ron Leech admitted in a magazine interview soon after his return to Australia, there was a lot of drinking. 'The boys hit up the rice wine for a day or two. They drank it in half pint glasses instead of thimble-sized cups. It put them under the table. After that they developed great respect for the drink.'[6]

There was one occasion when Ron and his mate Stuart Campbell become so incapable after a heavy drinking session with their Chinese comrades that they had to be dragged away by Macrae.

What a good friend he was. He threatened, cajoled,
heaved and tugged until we were again on our feet,
swaying and practically without sight. He managed to
get us mobile enough to reach the river bank. Here we
walked, fell in, fell down, then stood up and were pointed
in the direction of our hut.[7]

The following day they were invited to a ceremonial dinner
as guests of General Lee, who was the nationalist guerillas'
commander. Despite the ravages of war and the shortage of food
supplies, there were still more than twenty dishes and fifteen
different sauces, again washed down by copious quantities of rice
wine. The Chinese approached each of their guests with a large
spoonful of liquor and expected them to swallow the contents
in one. Everyone stood up, took a slurp and cried out, 'Bye,
spoon!' The spoon was then passed around each table and the
tradition repeated endlessly. Even Macrae worried about falling
foul of the local grog. 'It was a very delicate operation because
if you had anything more than very small sips you were under
the table very quickly.'[8]

The escapees were clearly revelling in their new-found freedom.
Life with the nationalist army was quite a party, though there
were frequent reminders of the Chinese fighting spirit and capacity
for revenge. Any captured Japanese knew what to expect. One
day the Australians saw an enemy soldier tied to a tree, his eyes
staring like those of a trapped wild animal. Desperate for water,
he was, instead, forced to drink urine by his Chinese captors. Ron
Leech walked away, not wanting to know the Japanese soldier's
fate. 'I felt sickened enough,' he admitted.

Other enemy soldiers who found themselves in the camp
were swiftly disposed of by poison, with which their food was
liberally laced. Four Japanese who met such an end were buried
while they still showed signs of life.

The Australians spent about four months with the guerillas, but
they were not allowed to fight, which was a blessing given their

poor physical state. They were still recovering from the disease and starvation suffered during their three years in captivity, as well as the arduous journey to the guerilla camp. However, they were permitted to roam around their mountain hideaway, a crater set in a terrain of lush forests and gushing waterways. With the northern summer on its way, the surroundings resembled a subtropical nirvana. It wasn't exactly luxury, but compared with what they'd left behind the nationalist HQ was a five-star resort. Said Macrae:

> We were right in the mountains, there was a beautiful stream there and we did move around quite freely, although our health wasn't that brilliant. There was never enough quinine to keep the malaria at bay. You'd go down and have a swim and almost immediately you'd feel the first symptoms of malaria, so we were a bit restricted health-wise.[9]

The escape party was also better informed about the advance of Allied forces in the Pacific than the POWs still being held at the Hashio camp in Bakli Bay. The guerillas had a wireless set powered by a pedal-generator which allowed them to communicate with the outside world. On several occasions they heard that an Allied invasion of Hainan was imminent and that the Japanese had capitulated, but the reports were premature. 'Then one day,' said Ron Leech, 'it came over the Chinese radio that an atom bomb had knocked a hole in Japan six miles deep and ten miles across and the war was over.'[10]

Ron Leech's slight exaggeration of the bomb's capacity for drilling holes in the ground could be forgiven, given the sense of elation the news inspired. But liberation was still weeks away, which meant Macrae and his men would have to be patient.

––––––

Back at the Hainan prison camp the issue of food reached its lowest ebb from 6 May 1945, when each man received approximately

170 grams of rice per day. It was perhaps no wonder that between 17 March and 10 June fifteen Australians died from starvation or malnutrition.[11] But in June, after pressure from Lieutenant Colonel Scott, the rice ration was increased, although, as the CO pointed out, 'Unfortunately there were a number of men too far advanced in actual starvation to save their lives on rice alone.' A month later Scott thanked the Japanese camp commandant for the 'greatly improved food position' but revealed that they were 'still far short of the necessary number of calories per man per day to prevent a heavy death rate'.[12]

The death toll between 1 June and 12 July stood at 23.

The prisoners were so hungry that it was a matter of eat or die. The most readily available source of food was the ever-expanding rat population, which was overrunning the camp. When turned into a stew they were not unpalatable – a mixture of chicken and rabbit, as Tom Pledger described them. 'You wouldn't know they were rats. You'd skin them, cook them and eat them. They were okay. If you're hungry you'll eat anything.'[13]

After the rat population was exhausted, the Aussies turned to snails, lizards and snakes for nourishment. It was a measure of the desperation caused by severe hunger.

Tom Pledger, who was tending to the sick, had an intimate knowledge of the gravity of the situation. On 20 June he noted that the number of surviving Australians and Dutch was down to 197, compared with 263 when they arrived on Hainan two-and-a-half years previously. 'Everybody is hungry from one day to another. It would be lovely to fill your belly with any rubbish so long as it is full,' he observed in his diary. The small ration of rice they were getting was now accompanied by tiny amounts of meat, beans and sweet potatoes. 'Everyone watches the next to see that he gets his rations right. Tempers are frayed but we still exist,' he writes. Tom's weight had dropped to just over eight stone, but he was determined to struggle on. 'These blighters can't last, it only stands to reason they can't fight the world,' he told his mum in a letter home he hoped to post.

Come the third week of July there was even more reason to be optimistic when a group of Allied planes flew over the camp. There were about a dozen of them, including several Hurricanes, which suggested there was an aircraft carrier or land base relatively close by. It couldn't be long before the invasion forces arrived to liberate them, but still their patience would be tested.

Even by the middle of August they'd received no confirmation of the Hiroshima and Nagasaki bombings, which had happened earlier in the month, although they were aware of Germany's defeat. As Tom said in his letter home:

It's three months since they beat Germany. We have a pretty consistent rumour that Russia is in against Japan, so we hope that will hurry it up. No one at home can ever realise what we've been through. I hope you never have to. All we worry about is to get a full belly. Two chaps next to me sat down to a feed of roasted wood grubs and believe me they were good, as I had one to taste. Cheerio. God help us.[14]

14

'YOU CAN KEEP YOUR BLOODY ISLAND – WE'LL BE BACK FOR IT'

I T WAS ON 25 August that the surviving POWs on Hainan learned that the war was over after Lieutenant Green, the adjutant, was called to the guardhouse and given the news. As final confirmation the letters P.W. were painted in giant letters on the roof of one of the huts. After three years of brutal and barbaric behaviour the Japanese wanted to be seen to be doing the right thing, if only to impress the war crimes trials that would inevitably follow.

Tom Pledger was working in the hospital when he heard the news. 'Clive Newnham, one of the officers, came running across from the guardhouse shouting, "The war's over, it's all finished." The whole camp just went mad – we were slapping each other on the back.'[1]

That same afternoon a Japanese Zero swooped low over the camp to drop leaflets announcing that the Americans were on their way and would arrive by parachute shortly. In fact, it took another two days for the nine-man squad to land outside the camp but, frustratingly for the POWs, they were prevented from entering.

The parachute party's senior officer, Major J. Singlaub, demanded to be taken to the Japanese general in charge of

213

the area. Ian Macrae was told later that the general claimed to have 'no knowledge of any armistice and the nine were locked up overnight'.[2] No one was sure what was going on. The tense stand-off led to confusion and the Americans were anxious not to inflame the situation, so decided to bide their time until daybreak.

Major Singlaub assembled the camp and ordered the men to quell their excitement for the moment. 'Don't make a noise. Don't go crazy because there are only nine of us and there are thousands of these Jap blokes here and we don't want to start a blue now. Carry on as usual, we'll get you off,' he reassured them.[3] As John Devenish recalled it, they were desperate to release years of pent-up anger, 'but we couldn't do a thing'.

By the following morning Singlaub and his team had had enough. The senior US officer was not a man to mess with. He'd only recently returned from behind German lines in France, where he'd worked with the French Resistance and played a key role in the D-Day invasion. He would go on to head CIA operations in post-war Manchuria, lead US troops in Korea, manage a secret war along the Ho Chi Minh Trail in Vietnam and later work alongside the Contras in Nicaragua. If anybody could broker a deal with the Japanese, Singlaub was the man.[4]

A hastily convened conference of the Dutch, Australian and Japanese commanders was held in the Bakli Bay hospital and, not unnaturally, the US liberation party insisted on joining them. On entering the room Singlaub found the Japanese standing with their backs to the window, a well-known trick designed to intimidate others. Singlaub was having none of it and quickly rearranged the room so that the Japanese faced the light and the Americans stood with their backs against the glass.[5]

Major Singlaub was losing his patience and made a unilateral decision to take control of the camp. The move required little effort as an electric fence which surrounded the compound was already being dismantled by the Japanese guards.

The Americans had brought a cornucopia of food and little luxuries with them. Jimmy Morrison made himself sick from eating too much chocolate, while the smokers lit up on free packets of Camels. The generosity almost overwhelmed the POWs, who had waited so long for this moment. 'They almost killed us,' said Jimmy, only half-jokingly.[6]

The visitors were also bombarded with questions, the Australians listening agog to the Americans' account of the final weeks of the war. As Private Courtney Harrison described it:

> They showed the element of wonder as they listened to
> the story as told by the American party about the atomic
> bomb being developed and how the war had come to an
> end after the Japanese government refused to surrender,
> although having been well informed about the devastating
> consequences that would ensue.[7]

The Americans moved fast, scouring the district for enemy soldiers who might be hiding and inspecting the stores, which held 250 tonnes of rice and a huge amount of drugs, all so desperately needed by the men over the past few months. The discovery came too late for at least three of the POWs, who were now close to death.

Down at the hospital, mates and medics debated whether to tell Sapper Owen Glynn of the 2/11th Field Company and Sydney-born Sergeant Patrick Byrne, who was just a month short of his thirty-seventh birthday, that the war was over. Better for them to die in the knowledge they were free men, it was agreed. Barely conscious, Owen and Patrick responded with a token nod as the news sank in. An hour later they were dead. Two days afterwards another man, Private Percy Buckland, from Royal Park in Melbourne, died from cerebral malaria at the tragically young age of 22.

It was 30 August and preparations were underway to evacuate all ranks, apart from the seriously ill, to the hospital at Bakli Bay. Lieutenant Colonel Scott made the announcement he'd been waiting to deliver for the past three-and-a-half years: all men were free!

But where were Macrae and the rest of his party? Thankfully, a leaflet drop by a US plane, high up in the mountains where the escapees were waiting, found its target. The message told them to head for Samah, on the coast in the far south of the island. Understandably, Major Macrae, who had just celebrated his fortieth birthday, was in no mood to hang around and immediately made contact with the Americans, possibly via the pedal-powered radio at nationalist headquarters. Singlaub, the epitome of the all-American action hero, requisitioned some transport and headed for the hills. When they eventually met up the Australians were accompanied by seven Dutchmen and fourteen Sikhs who were also keen to be repatriated.

The Americans received a heroes' welcome from the Chinese guerillas, who, according to Macrae, 'really turned it on' for Singlaub. 'He was a magnificent chap.'[8]

There was one more sombre act of remembrance to conduct before Messrs Macrae, Leech, Campbell, Lockwood and Perrin left their jungle hideout. Myles Higgins's uniform was draped across his grave and a few Australian coins planted at the base of four trees to mark his final resting place. The impromptu ceremony complete, the five surviving members of the escape party lowered their heads and said goodbye.

Soon the naval destroyer HMS *Queensborough* arrived off the coast of Hainan, under orders to locate Scott and ferry him to Hong Kong, along with some of the POWs. The captain was surprised to learn that he'd been beaten to the island by the Americans, who had already set up their own headquarters and appeared to have everything under control. If he was miffed by the lack of communication between the British, Australian and American forces, the skipper didn't show it and was generous enough to go ahead with the original plan, inviting the colonel and some 30 Australians, Dutch and Indians to accompany him back to Hong Kong.

The rest of Gull Force would also be repatriated in a style which would offer a greater degree of comfort than their voyage on the *Taiki Maru* nearly three years previously. The plan was to transport the men more than 160 kilometres by train to Samah, where the living conditions would be an improvement on their present accommodation and they would be well positioned for a ship to take them home. It promised to be an easy ride, offering the POWs, who had been cooped up for so long, an opportunity to see what the rest of the island looked like.

The first hint of trouble came about 50 kilometres into the journey, when they noticed a village burning and telegraph poles chopped down. 'We thought, "Oh, Christ, what's going on?" We didn't have to wait long,' Roy Harris explained. 'There were four of us in the first trucks and two guards were sitting on the cow catcher at the front of the engine with rifles.' Suddenly the front carriages lurched uncontrollably off the line and ended up on their side. The train had been deliberately derailed. Someone didn't know the war was over, or if they did, they were ignoring it.

This was bandit country and the renegade Chinese were up to their old tricks. Fearing that it was another ambush, some of the passengers made a run for it, given what had happened to them before. The guerillas were coming at them from every direction and Harris reckoned 'we're gone this time'.[9]

The guards at the front were already dead and the Chinese seemed keen to spill more blood. Then, just as suddenly as they had appeared, the bandits melted away and posed no further threat. The passengers climbed out of the derailed rolling stock and wandered around in a daze. It was a salutary moment for the men of Gull Force, who, despite being so close to safety, were still exposed to danger.

Another locomotive was sent from Bakli Bay to pull the derailed coaches back to camp and another long wait ensued while the sleeper pins were replaced and the line reopened. The men eventually made their second departure and this time the rail journey was without incident. The train steamed into Samah on 5 September 1945.

Two hundred and sixty-three Australians had been sent to Hainan as POWs, but only 191 survived. Out of the 72 who died, 67 passed away between March and August 1945, mainly the result of malnutrition and starvation. If all the food and drugs stored away and later discovered by the Americans had been made available during that period, who knows how many Australians would have been spared?[10]

––––––––

In truth, the death toll on Hainan, while high, was not so bad as that on the island of Ambon, where conditions had arguably been much tougher over the past three-and-a-half years. To make matters worse, the Allied prisoners still remained incommunicado some four weeks after the bombing of Hiroshima and a fortnight after Hirohito's surrender, which was broadcast on 15 August.

Gull Force and their American counterparts wondered whether they'd been forgotten in the chaos and confusion of the past few weeks. The new camp interpreter's promise of a ship – at roll-call on 23 August, when he had confirmed that the war was over – had not materialised and the men had yet to send a radio message revealing their plight.

By 3 September everyone was so restless that the men decided to send a delegation to the Japanese, asking for access to a two-way radio. Ed Weiss, Captain George Lindahl, 'Red' Carson, Clyde Rearick and the Australian, Lieutenant John Van Nooten, climbed the hill to Japanese HQ and demanded to know what was going on. Had the American or Australian authorities been notified of their whereabouts? And where was all the extra food they'd been assured was on its way?

Ikeuchi, rendered speechless by the group's demands, turned his back on them and went inside his office to make a phone call. When he eventually returned, his response was more cordial. He said another officer was on his way and that there was even a large bottle of beer for the men to share – their first taste of alcohol since they were captured.

It took an hour for Colonel Katsura and Captain Wadami, who'd taken over from 'Handlebars' Ando as the officer in charge of the POW camp, to arrive. They drove up in a US Army–issued Plymouth sedan, most probably 'liberated' from some other occupied territory, possibly the Philippines.

After years of being treated as little more than animals, the delegation was in no mood for niceties. Carson was the first to let off steam by accusing the two Japanese of lying when they insisted there was no more food in the camp. Ed looked on nervously, fully aware that the Japanese effectively remained in control and, if necessary, still had the power to inflict life-threatening injury. But the outburst seemed to do the trick, with Katsura guaranteeing that new supplies would be delivered the following morning.

Unfortunately, the group still hadn't managed to send a radio message, although Katsura insisted that one would shortly be on its way to Japanese headquarters in Singapore, who would pass it on to the American military in Tokyo. Knowing how slow communications were in the aftermath of war, Clyde said that wasn't good enough and asked for access to a field radio, which was made available to him. Frustratingly, it didn't work and the men's collective spirits were low. To add to their concerns, fellow American 'Nels' Nelson was critically ill with beri-beri. He put on a brave face to all who visited him, but died the next day.

Tellingly, his grave was dug by some of the Japanese guards, and Bob Grainger was there to perform the funeral rights. Captain Nelson had the dubious honour of being the last POW to die in Tan Tui.

It wasn't until 8 September that the Japanese finally granted access to their own radio transmitter, hidden in a tunnel in the nearby village of Galala. Ed Weiss, who was familiar with morse code, tapped out a simple message: 'SOS FROM POW AMBON.' Seconds later came the reply from the nearby island of Morotai:

'Who are you?' At last the prisoners of Ambon were in contact with the outside world.

Initially the radio signaller on the other end was suspicious and required proof of the POW claim and, more importantly, that the message came from an Australian prison camp. According to Eddie Gilbert, the Morotai radio officer posed a series of questions only a dinky-di Aussie could answer. Fortunately there were some Melbournians in the Japanese radio room, including John Van Nooten, and he was only too happy to oblige.

> The operator quizzed me and said what's your name?
> I said Van Nooten, which didn't sound Australian, so he asked where I was from. I said Sandringham, Melbourne.
> To which he replied: 'How would you like to see Chloe again?'
> I said 'Lead me to her,' and he asked, 'Where is she?'
> I said, 'Young and Jacksons' and he replied, 'You're a bloody Australian.'[11]

Eddie Gilbert recalls it slightly differently, but the drift is much the same. He said the radio officer asked, 'What's the pub on the corner of Flinders Street and Swanston Street?' 'If you know anything about Melbourne, you instantly say it has to be Young and Jacksons,' said Eddie. 'Yeah,' said the radio officer, 'and what's it really noted for?' 'Oh, it's noted for Chloe, a large-scale painting of a female nude.' This famous portrait had graced the walls of the pub since 1909.

The exchange in all its various reported forms has long since become part of battalion history. Certainly, Radio Morotai needed no more convincing. 'That satisfied them they were talking to some genuine Aussies,' said Eddie.[12]

Further radio communication followed over the next few days, during which they were assured that the navy was on its way to evacuate them. Then on 10 September came the final confirmation that rescue vessels were about to enter Ambon Bay.

Ed Weiss realised he was actually in contact with one of those ships, a Royal Australian Navy corvette. The skipper told him to get the POWs assembled on the dockside by mid-morning. They were on their way.

Ed made the journey back to camp by car to spread the news, sitting alongside his arch enemy Ikeuchi, whose face was etched with worry. There was an uncomfortable silence between the two as they entered the compound and climbed out of the vehicle. Ikeuchi was the first to speak: 'War is over. Now you go home.' Momentarily bereft of words but anxious to offer a suitable response, Ed Weiss paused for a few seconds before turning to his nemesis and replying, 'Yes, war is a terrible thing, but you have made it more so by your contribution.'

Ikeuchi knew he was in serious trouble, but privately hoped for an honourable exit. It was not to be. His departure from Ambon later that day would provide the ultimate humiliation.

————

The men of Gull Force presented a pitiful picture as the sick and starving waited to be transported by trucks and ambulances down to the wharf. They were the lucky ones. Of the 528 Australians who had been left on Ambon in October 1942 when the rest were sent to Hainan, only 121 remained alive, and most of them were too ill to walk.

Those who were sufficiently able-bodied mingled with the incapacitated, who lay on stretchers on the cobblestone road leading out of the camp, awaiting the final leg of their journey towards freedom. There was no denying the sense of relief as they smiled and joked with one another.

John Van Nooten orchestrated the transport which would take them to the wharf and as they made their way into town, lines of Japanese soldiers appeared at the side of the road in full battle dress. Was this a belated mark of respect for those who'd been held captive for so long, or was it an effort to save face? The latter might explain why the Japanese were standing with their backs to the departing POWs. The question was never resolved and, to be honest, the Australians didn't care. By now they were assembling on the dockside, their eyes scanning the horizon for a sign of the navy.

It was Private Jack Panaotie who first spotted the *Glenelg*, a mere dot in the distance. 'We couldn't see anything and suddenly I saw this tiny little ship coming in and then another and another.'[13]

The *Glenelg* was followed by the *Junee*, the *Cootamundra* and the *Latrobe*. As the crews sailed up to the wharf they were vaguely aware of some matchstick-like figures standing to welcome them. On board the *Latrobe* Lieutenant Commander Windas Smith did not immediately berth alongside. 'Our task was to keep an eye on the other ships in case of treachery. But when we did berth there were twenty to thirty skeletons on the jetty, as if they were standing in front of Buckingham Palace, and there wasn't a dry eye on the ship.'[14]

How these 38-kilogram men managed to stand to attention on thighs which looked as thin as 'matchsticks and knees like oversized cricket balls' would shock and haunt the *Latrobe* skipper for the rest of his life.

On shore there were a total of 42 men on stretchers who needed to be evacuated without delay. Some quietly sobbed as they were plied with sweet tea and Vegemite sandwiches before being loaded aboard. Most were suffering from severe malnutrition, as well as malaria, dysentery and tropical ulcers.

Back at camp a last-minute crisis had erupted over the fate of the Americans. They were also expecting to be welcomed aboard the corvettes but Captain George Lindahl, effectively the most senior officer among the Americans, announced a change of plan. They had to stay behind and await evacuation by the United States. Simmering tensions between the American and Australian officers were said to be behind the decision, which was blamed on the relationship between the Americans and Major Westley. Ever since the Americans had arrived on Ambon they had felt let down by the Australians' commanding officer. They accused him of poor leadership and a failure to represent the POWs' interests in negotiations with the Japanese.

Whether Westley was getting his own back on the Americans for their whingeing or Lindahl wanted to make a point was unclear, but the news infuriated Ed Weiss, who had been oblivious to the festering animosity. 'I protested strongly, telling him it was stupid and not the way to go, but he was adamant. He ordered that we remain behind and await our own people to evacuate us.'[15]

The nine remaining Americans returned disconsolately to their quarters, alone in the camp, and resigned to an even longer wait before being evacuated. Then, abruptly, a truck pulled up outside and an Australian voice shouted, 'Get ready, mate – you're going with us.' What had prompted the change of heart was unknown, but nobody was disputing the order. The so-called convict gang and the rest of the Americans, including Lindahl, were dressed, packed and ready to go within minutes, and were driven down to the wharf.

On the dockside they were met by a few dozen shirtless Australian sailors bearing sub-machine guns, in case of trouble from the Japanese, who were standing in full uniform to the side. The Japanese admiral was among them, waiting to present a formal surrender to the leader of the Australian fleet.

John Van Nooten, who was standing behind the Japanese entourage with his own men, saw the Australian naval commander step ashore and the senior Japanese officer unroll a scroll detailing the surrender terms. He moved to hand it to the naval officer, who brushed him aside. 'The commander put out a dirty big fist, pushed him in the chest and said, "You can keep your bloody island. We'll be back for it when we're ready." It made me feel ten feet tall.'[16]

What none of the POWs realised at the time was that the Australian flotilla could have come to their rescue a week earlier, had it not been for the intransigence of the Japanese. The four corvettes had been close to the island for the previous seven days, but the Japanese had signalled their intention to resist, with gunfire, if the ships didn't leave the immediate area. Not wishing to make life even more difficult for the prisoners, the RAN had aborted its initial plans and stood some kilometres offshore until it was given the official all-clear to land.

This was of little comfort for those men who were in urgent need of medical treatment during that period, and explained why the Australian naval commander treated the Japanese admiral with such disdain on the quayside that day.

With most of the Australians and Americans now safely on board the corvettes there was one more mission to address. As Van Nooten told it, they received an instruction from Morotai just before embarking, asking Van Nooten to apprehend any war criminals on the island. He sought further guidance on what constituted a war criminal and was told: 'Any bastard who's mistreated you.' One man in particular had no trouble meeting the parameters. He was the Japanese officer largely responsible for much of the suffering at Tan Tui over the past three-and-a-half years: Ikeuchi Masakiyo.

Van Nooten did not need any further encouragement and assembled a group of unarmed Australians, who drove off in a jeep in search of the camp commandant. On finding Ikeuchi they decided to have a little fun with the man who'd made their lives a misery by suggesting he might like to help them keep the POWs on the ship under control. The men were proving a little difficult to handle after years of captivity, Ikeuchi was told; freedom had gone to their heads and they might need a little Japanese-style discipline.

Ikeuchi took the bait, asked for time to pack his bags and was driven down to the dock, where he was piped aboard the *Cootamundra* with full naval honours. Once on board he was taken up to the bridge to meet the captain. Ikeuchi hardly gave the island a backward glance as the ship weighed anchor and moved out into the glistening waters of Ambon Bay.

'Oh and by the way, perhaps you could direct me to my cabin,' he said.

The navy personnel who escorted him downstairs were only too willing to oblige. 'This way,' they said as they thrust him into the ship's vegetable store and slammed the door on him. Ikeuchi Masakiyo was now a prisoner of the Australians.

Outside on the decks of the four corvettes the men of Gull Force leant over the railings, finding it hard to believe their ordeal was over. There were tears too for those they were leaving behind as the 121 Australian survivors observed a minute of silent prayer.

They were heading for the island of Morotai, where they arrived two days later. There they were greeted by a military band and a fleet of ambulances ready to whisk them away to the medical care many of them so desperately needed.

Eddie Gilbert noted that the time was 8 a.m. 'We were immediately transported and put to bed. The sight of Australian army sisters was wonderful. It's hard to express one's feelings at seeing civilization, white men's food and sleeping between sheets,' he wrote in his diary.

Sadly, two more members of Gull Force died while hospitalised on Morotai, but within a few weeks most were sufficiently recovered to set sail for home aboard the hospital ship *Wanganella*. For some, Morotai would continue to dominate their lives as they became involved in the war crimes investigations and subsequent inquiries which were held on the island.

Among those awaiting interrogation were several natives accused of collaboration with the Japanese. One morning Ed Weiss and his mates Bob Grainger and Clyde Rearick were invited by the Dutch military police to visit the prison compound. Much to their amazement they recognised one of the inmates from three years previously. It was White Suit, the traitorous Dutch harbourmaster who had blown their cover on their voyage south from the Philippines on the *Pilar* in August 1942 and betrayed them to the Japanese.

They signed a form verifying his complicity in their capture and Ed admitted that if he'd had a gun with him at the time he would have happily shot him. Instead, just as they prepared to return to their camp, White Suit's jailor told the Americans that if they had not put temptation in White Suit's way, he would not be in custody. 'It was difficult to control my anger at this man,' Ed recalls. 'Had Bob not restrained me I would have punched the hell out of him, not for myself, but for Mac, Swede and Nels. I had a better understanding why the Australians were not fond of the Dutch.'[17]

It was not the only matter to concern the Americans on Morotai. There was one investigation in particular which demanded more immediate attention because of the serious nature of the allegations made against certain members of the Australian military by a few disgruntled Americans. Defending his honour would be Major George de Verdon Westley, whose conduct while commanding officer on Ambon had so angered American personnel.

But how watertight was their case? Westley had survived the war. Would the same apply to his reputation?

15

WESTLEY'S HONOUR RESTORED

IF THERE WAS ever any doubt about the animosity that existed between the American and Australian officers imprisoned in Tan Tui, Major George de Verdon Westley was to put the record straight in his official post-war report into conditions on Ambon between 26 October 1942 and 19 September 1945.

> The Americans, particularly the officers, were a source of nuisance and annoyance. They made things very difficult at times and refused to co-operate. Before the cessation of hostilities they continually complained to me of their treatment but would not themselves approach the Japs. Afterwards, however, they ignored me altogether and made their own demands to the Japs on their own behalf and to the prejudice of the remainder of the camp.[1]

Whatever the truth, there was clearly no love lost between Westley and the two US officers, who made a formal complaint against him and several other Australians while being debriefed by US naval interrogators. Ensign John ('Red') Carson, a career naval officer and Chief Quartermaster Earl ('Pappy') Hunter, who had both been part of Ed Weiss's daring escape party from the Philippines during the early days of the war, accused Westley

227

of not standing up to the Japanese on behalf of the POWs and being more concerned with looking after himself.

There were several other serious charges against him, which also involved some of his close associates, including Lieutenant John Van Nooten, Warrant Officer John Billing, Warrant Officer Milton Ryan, Warrant Officer K. R. Adamson, Staff Sergeant E. Kelly, Sergeant Lyle Gray, Staff Sergeant E. J. Nugent and Sergeant John McMahon. All were named at an official inquiry that assembled on Morotai on the afternoon of 17 September 1945 and continued for nine days. This was serious business, with tarnished reputations threatening to end their military careers.

The charges against the Australians, and more especially Westley, addressed many of the complaints that emerged in later years about the way the camp was operated and went to the root of the perceived injustices which cast a cloud over the battalion in the immediate post-war period.

One of the more serious allegations was that camp staff operated like a 'closed corporation whose primary purpose was their own welfare and saving their own skins'. They were accused of selecting people for work parties 'irrespective of the physical condition of the men'. Frequently, sick and weakened POWs who were clearly too ill for physical labour were pulled from their beds and compelled to go on work parties, using 'violence where necessary to achieve this purpose'.

There was the allocation of food: the two Americans claimed that camp staff 'did not give the men their full share of the rations'. And there was the question of discipline. The court heard that on two occasions Australian POWs who had committed offences were severely beaten by way of punishment by other Australian prisoners. (This appeared to be a reference to the vigilantes who had imposed their own form of discipline on those who stole food.)

As for Westley, the most damning allegations were contained in the last two charges. 'The camp staff, and Major Westley in particular, would never make complaints to the Japanese on behalf of the prisoners for fear of "making them angry" and only under the greatest pressure would Major Westley file requisitions for food and medical supplies.' And finally, 'on occasions Major Westley threatened to hand offenders, when caught, over to the Japanese for punishment, and on one occasion this was done'.[2] (Most probably a reference to Private George Roy's treatment, detailed in Chapter 10.)

As the Morotai inquiry got underway the allegations hung like a dark shadow over Westley and his officers. After all they'd been through during the past three-and-a-half years, now they had to endure this further indignity: an official military investigation into the way they'd behaved behind barbed wire while living in the most appalling conditions. It was almost as though they were being branded traitors or collaborators by their accusers.

When Colonel James McKinley, Lieutenant Colonel Victor Schofield and Lieutenant Colonel Jack Byrne took their seats at 2 p.m. on the first day of the inquiry, their role was to examine the essence of allegations which appeared to be 'substantially supported by the US Army prisoners who were in the camp and by those Australian prisoners of war who were questioned on the matter'.

Westley and the other accused men were all present at the court of inquiry and informed of their rights. The two Americans, Carson and Hunter, were there as well, ready to provide further evidence if asked to do so. There was no mistaking the hatred they felt towards the Australians during the inquiry, where they 'entertained feelings of considerable bitterness towards Major Westley and to a lesser extent against his staff'.[3] 'Their hostility undoubtedly flowed from the fact that they were given no voice or status in the management of the camp.'[4]

Their lack of involvement in camp management was a key issue in the Americans' complaints. Neither US or Dutch participation was permitted in the administration of Tan Tui because Gull Force regarded them as guests of the Australians and not as prisoners of war of the Japanese.[5] Why this was so was unclear, but it obviously rankled the Americans.

However, as the inquiry progressed Carson's hard-line attitude showed signs of softening. When questioned under oath about the distribution of food and his use of the term 'closed corporation', he backtracked, pointing out that the term was not his, though he nevertheless agreed with it because 'we were not permitted to come in and investigate the goings on'. He also denied ever saying that the primary purpose of Army HQ on Ambon 'was its own welfare'.

More crucially, he refuted the statement attributed to him under interrogation that 'Major Westley would never make any complaints on behalf of the prisoners for fear of making the Japanese angry.' Carson's surprise climb-down clearly weakened the prosecution's case against the Australians. And that was just the beginning. When questioned about disciplinary procedures in the camp, Carson denied ever hearing Westley threaten to hand over a POW to the Japanese for stealing a pig; also that two men, Alfred Higgs and Archibald Buchanan, were 'beaten into insensibility'.[6]

The evidence against the Australians was further eroded when Earl D. 'Pappy' Hunter took the stand. He might have been an expert navigator, but he had trouble finding his way out of some of the earlier claims he'd made, particularly an allegation that Private Sidney Crowe was 'repeatedly' beaten by Lieutenant Van Nooten and Warrant Officer Adamson in an effort to make him go to work. According to Hunter's original testimony Crowe insisted he was too weak to stand up and sank back down on his bunk, complaining about having to 'put up with cruel treatment from both the Japs and his own people'. 'Whereupon Adamson pulled him to his feet and knocked him down, pulled him up again and then both Van Nooten and Adamson knocked him down once more, then forced him out and on the work detail.'

In court, however, Hunter admitted that his claims were largely based on circumstantial evidence and that he personally did not see any blows struck. The same mistaken assumptions applied to the alleged 'unfair or discriminatory distribution of food [which] was based on camp rumour and the fact that some men looked fitter than others'.

The court of inquiry went on to hear other damning evidence which was to further undermine the testimony of the American complainants. Ensign Carson and Captain George Lindahl were accused of ignoring a ban on private cooking imposed by the camp medical officer to minimise the danger of an outbreak of dysentery. As a result they were relieved of their cookhouse duties. Despite an arrangement between all the officers that they pool their resources for the mess, Carson and Linhdal were also discovered to be secretly trading food for cigarettes with Australian Corporal Fred Dihood, who was known as the camp 'middleman'.[7]

On one occasion they were also 'publicly rebuked' by Westley for their anti-British sentiments, which, according to the court of inquiry, might explain why the Americans were not given 'official status' while POWs.

As the inquiry continued, the case against Westley and his close group of officers became ever more flimsy, culminating in the two Americans' sudden withdrawal of the charges on oath and their rapid departure for Manila. What had happened to make them change their stories? Had they been leant on by authorities further up the chain of command who were reluctant to place Australian–US relations under such strain? Or were Carson and Lindahl merely badmouthing Westley and his crew to get their own back for not being treated in the manner they believed their officer status should have ensured? Certainly, Ed Weiss, who had forged several close friendships with the Australians, was unaware of the bad feeling, but then so much that went on at Ambon was hard to explain.

Yet the court of inquiry on Morotai was not without its merits, if only because it addressed some of the many controversies that were to arise in later years, including Westley's attitude to work parties, food, discipline and, more especially, the cage.

On the question of work parties the court found that the actions of Westley and his staff were mostly in the interest of the POWs. The officers and NCOs met every night to discuss the Japanese labour requirements and divided the men into six medical categories. After consulting with Dr Ehlhart, now the camp medical officer, they ensured that the manpower available was used in such a way that only the fittest men were allocated to the hardest tasks, while the lighter duties were reserved for the weaker men. If it had been left up to the Japanese, the Australians would almost certainly have been selected irrespective of their fitness level.

Sometimes sick soldiers were forced to take their place in the labour lines because it allowed the release of men who were in an even worse condition. On other occasions a judgement had to be made on whether a man was feigning ill-health in order to avoid hard labour. As the report put it: 'Medical arbitrament was necessary to police the occasional "bludger" who endeavoured to place a greater burden on his mates by his efforts to dodge work.'

As in any environment where men were thrown together and forced to live under gruelling conditions, human nature and personal responsibility did not always live up to the standards of civilised society. Rules and tough decisions were clearly necessary to impose order on the Australians, but there were always the few who had little concern for the greater good of the camp. That particularly applied to the growing of vegetables, which helped to complement the dwindling rations served up by the Japanese every day.

For much of their incarceration the POWs were encouraged to establish and maintain a private garden on land especially allotted for this purpose. As an inducement they were allowed to eat everything they grew. The officers also had their own garden, the produce of which was pooled by them for consumption in their mess. These many and varied vegetable plots had the capacity to produce regular and bountiful harvests, but there was one problem. Often the men were too tired to work them or just couldn't be bothered. 'Generally it appears that a substantial majority of the prisoners, individually or in syndicates, maintained gardens. [But] a proportion of the prisoners did no private gardening through laziness or lack of interest,' the court of inquiry observed.

Westley did his best to encourage the men to work together for the common good, at one stage establishing a communal company garden in which all POWs were required to work. But once again the 'bludgers' refused to co-operate and, even if coerced, did no useful or productive work. It was a poor reflection on the state of morale within the camp when even the commanding officer couldn't inspire the malingerers to action. The simple truth was that the 2/21st Battalion had lost its esprit de corps. Or, as the court's damning assessment put it: 'Corporate spirit does not appear to have ever reached a high standard at any time of the battalion's existence.'

Far more sensible, the court suggested, would have been a long-range policy whereby all gardening was conducted on a communal basis and the produce pooled.

> This would have enabled those whose duties about the camp gave them more time for gardening to have worked to the general benefit of the camp as a whole, particularly for the men whose daily heavy manual labour left them with little incentive for additional work. It was felt that more intensive propaganda by Major Westley could have made a greater success of a communal garden.

This swipe at Westley's unsuccessful attempts to sell the gardening policy to his men provided further evidence of his inability to galvanise Gull Force at a time when the theft of food had become a serious and life-threatening development. 'When a camp was filled with starving men, stealing became rife – either of articles exchangeable for food or for food itself – the most prevalent offence being "bandicooting" or the nocturnal pilfering of another man's garden,' the inquiry went on. Even attempts to raise chickens in the camp proved futile. 'The wholesale stealing of fowls put an end to what might have been a useful addition to the diet scale, particularly of hospital patients.'

Was it lack of conscience or self-preservation that drove some of the men to such wilful acts of disobedience? Where was the mateship, the consideration for the good of the whole? Or was this self-destructive tendency just another symptom of a group of men pushed to the extremes? Could this also explain why Westley had been forced to countenance the erection of the cage, the prison within a prison which caused so much controversy both during and after the war?

The court of inquiry's investigation into the so-called boob provided a valuable insight into the events leading up to and surrounding its construction.

Westley had rightly refrained from handing prisoners to the Japanese guards for punishment, the report of the inquiry made clear, and asked the Japanese for a guard room to be made available to the Australian camp staff for disciplinary purposes. 'This request was refused and the Australians were directed to erect a small place of detention to a specification as to size and material supplied by the Japanese. This building, approximately two metres square and unroofed, was accordingly built out of native material.'

While the description differed slightly from the memories of others who witnessed the boob, the court's account of how it was used seemed accurate enough. 'A number of Australians were committed by Major Westley for various offences, mostly thieving, but no one was committed by Major Westley to day-time detention. Sentences were served at night – as a form of solitary confinement and to prevent repeated acts of "bandicooting".'

Captain Ehlhart, told the inquiry how he examined every man who was held there daily and was certain that no one suffered any harm. Whenever he ordered a man to be freed, he was never returned to the boob. And none of the occupants went without food. Indeed, Lieutenant Van Nooten even 'took risks under the cover of darkness to give detainees their daily ration'.

Most of the petty thieves assigned to the cage only spent a few nights inside but one man was held there for ten days on the personal instruction of Ikeuchi. Alfred Higgs, who was in his mid-twenties and came from Sydney, was a gunner in the 18th Anti-Tank Battery and had been accused of stealing a pig. The porker belonged to Ikeuchi, which might explain the length of the sentence. Higgs was a frequent offender whose behaviour had threatened a reduction in camp rations had he not confessed to his misdeeds, but even ten nights in the cage was not sufficient retribution in Ikeuchi's eyes.

After Higgs' release, the man in charge of the camp's swine, Private Williamson, was ordered by Ikeuchi to thrash him with a length of rope. Williamson had a better idea, preferring to lay into the offender with his fists. Higgs didn't learn his lesson. A few weeks later he was caught stealing fowls with Private Archie Buchanan. Once again, Williamson was ordered to employ his own brand of physical punishment, knocking both men down with his fists.

Lieutenant Van Nooten, who later reproved Williamson for taking the law into his own hands, decided the two chicken stealers deserved further punishment and administered several blows to their buttocks with a light stick. Sufficient allowance in the circumstances was made by the court for 'the unusual punishment' as the inquiry described it.

On the question of the equal distribution of food the inquiry confirmed it was satisfied this was carried out fairly. Each man received the exact share of rations he was entitled to, largely thanks to the exceptional efforts of Warrant Officer Milton Ryan, who went to the trouble of introducing flat cooking trays which enabled meals to be produced in a form easily divisible into portions. 'Each man could see that he got the same quantity as his mates. Anything served otherwise was by ladle and again the men could compare the individual portions received on the mess parades,' the inquiry concluded.

Ryan was a rare breed in Tan Tui, a man who made sure each prisoner was treated equally and someone who was not afraid to stand up for the interests of the battalion in his dealings with the Japanese. He didn't care what he did as long as it produced results. Such was his tenacity that he 'left no means of approach to the Japanese unexplored . . . until he was ordered by the Japanese to desist in bringing daily samples of inadequate and inedible food'.

Ryan, in his mid-thirties, was born in Adelaide but grew up in Melbourne. He was a constant source of irritation to the Japanese, but somehow kept them on side. 'His persistence and imperturbability were sometimes rewarded by slight improvements and he appears to have maintained "face" with the Japanese to an amazing extent,' the inquiry revealed.

Ryan, who had been named by the two American complainants in the charges laid against Westley and his 'closed corporation', was singled out by the court of inquiry for his 'unswerving devotion to duty'. 'To his fearlessness in his dealing with the Japanese, and to his pertinacity and refusal to be side-tracked, and his probity in the distribution of the available food, many men owe their lives.'

Lieutenant Van Nooten's efforts to 'save sick and weakened men' were also recognised. His intervention on behalf of other prisoners may have earned him beatings and abuse, but he was untiring in his efforts towards better conditions for the prisoners and was at all times a loyal executive officer to his commanding officer, the court found. It was recommended that both Van Nooten and Ryan be recognised for their 'marked courage and devotion to duty'. Adamson, Billing and the rest of Westley's administrative staff were also praised.

But a question remained over the man himself. The court concluded that the major 'might have acted with more vigour in his relations with the Japanese and made more use of his rank and seniority'. It also alluded to his lack of contact with his men, given that he was their commanding officer, and his inability to discuss his difficulties with those under his command. 'To this extent there was a lack of leadership displayed by Major Westley,' the court decided.

For all the charges laid at Westley's feet, this was the most serious accusation to stick but it had little bearing on the court's overall findings. The inquiry vindicated Westley and threw out the charges against him. His honour was restored but, rightly or wrongly, his reputation would always be tarnished, not least by the ongoing resentment the men felt about the cage. For his part, Westley praised his officers and resolutely defended his own role. In his report as commanding officer on Ambon he denounced the Japanese for allowing the 'most appalling conditions under circumstances without precedent'.[8]

'The Japanese care nothing for international law. Protests were frequently made both in writing and verbally and I never received any satisfaction. Even when men were dying daily the Japs could not be moved. They certainly permitted us to bury our dead, but beyond that they did nothing,' he wrote. Those Japanese responsible for the inhuman treatment and deliberate violation of the rules should get their just deserts, he urged. 'There can be no justification, in my opinion, for 405 men dying out of 528.'

It would take months and in some cases years for those just deserts to be meted out.

16

VENGEANCE

THE YEAR 1946 began inauspiciously for the people of Japan. On 1 January Emperor Hirohito admitted that he was not a living god after all, and that claims he was descended from the Shinto Sun goddess Amaterasu Omikami were somewhat exaggerated. Further, he announced that the Japanese would have to 'proceed unflinchingly toward elimination of the misguided practices of the past'.[1]

The news did not bode well for the 93 Japanese officers and naval guards who were due to appear before the War Crimes Court on Ambon the next day. If the man who had led them through nearly four years of wanton savagery in a vain bid to conquer Asia was now exposed as a mere mortal, what hope was there for the rest of them?

As the wheels of military justice cranked into life there was a sense of foreboding in the courtroom on the morning of Tuesday, 2 January. Some of the prisoners looked drawn and haggard, fearful of their fate, while others acknowledged each other with a faint smile. Most were held within a wire cage just to the left of the four-man tribunal. The surroundings were familiar to them. It was the building the Japanese had used as their naval headquarters on Ambon during the war. Now, in a bittersweet irony, the same location played host to one of Australia's biggest single trials of alleged Japanese war criminals. Outside, hundreds of natives who had witnessed the subjugation of the island for themselves crowded around doors and windows, anxious to catch a glimpse of the humiliation of their former tormentors.

It was the beginning of several tumultuous weeks which would see the Japanese charged collectively with the inhuman treatment of Australian and Allied prisoners.

Opening the case for the prosecution was Captain John Williams, a Sydney lawyer who had served in signals and intelligence during the war. He had enlisted in 1941 as a private, was later made a lieutenant and was eventually transferred to the Australian Army Legal Corp, where he was given the task of prosecuting at Ambon and Morotai.

Williams said the defendants were all accused of the brutal treatment of prisoners and of forcing the ill and exhausted to engage in heavy manual labour. He alleged that they beat the men into submission and cared little for their health, which was aggravated by the gross medical neglect of the sick and dying.

The figures spoke for themselves. Out of the 528 Australians, seven Dutch and 14 Americans who had been left on Ambon following the departure of the rest of Gull Force for Hainan, only 139 were alive when the Japanese surrendered. Out of this number, seventeen had been executed and 386 had died as a result of 'consistent calculated cruelty and deprivation,' Captain Williams went on.[2]

The prosecution had a vast catalogue of evidence on which to base their case against the defendants, who included Shirozu Wadami, head of the 20th Garrison Unit from November 1943, camp commandant Lieutenant Miyazaki Yoshio, Sub-Lieutenant Shimakawa Masaichi, who commanded the prison guards, and Captain Masakiyo Ikeuchi.

A notable absentee was Ikeuchi's predecessor, Captain Ando 'Handlebars' Noburo, the cruel and vindictive garrison commander who had served from June 1942 and had overseen the vicious beating of prisoners during the so-called Dutch

Garden Party. Noburo had taken his own life as the war drew to a close. Realising the hopelessness of his situation, he had consumed a draught of deadly potassium cyanide, leading to a slow and agonising death.

During the trial most eyes were on Ikeuchi, whose fearsome reputation and brutal nature had already marked him out as the star of the proceedings. There was 'a mountainous weight of evidence' against him, the *Argus* correspondent at the trial, Eric Thornton, reported at the time. Most damning of all was the accusation that Ikeuchi was responsible for the deaths of more than 370 men on Ambon from lack of medical care, poor food supplies and overwork.

Ikeuchi distanced himself from the infamous massacre of about 300 Australians at Laha airfield in the early days of the occupation, though there was little doubt he was implicated in the atrocity, which was only made public after the war. Many Ambonese had been privy to what had happened and had led Allied forces to the graves after the Japanese surrendered. One was marked with a cross and identified as containing the remains of Major Mark Newbury, who was in charge of the Gull Force contingent at Laha. The 31 year old officer from Kew had been savagely put to death by sword on 6 February 1942.

Close to Newbury's grave another 67 bodies were located by the Australian War Graves Service, which ordered a Japanese working party to dig them up. By the time the war crimes trial on Ambon commenced, all the Laha bodies had been found, recovered and would soon be transferred to a specially constructed cemetery on the island. Only 40 were ever positively identified.[3]

Many of those who stood accused before the tribunal had already admitted their partial guilt, including Miyazaki Yoshio, the camp commandant. But Ikeuchi, Miyazaki's underling, was not prepared to own up so readily, admitting to only minor offences. On one occasion he confessed to the court: 'I beat the POW only the slight slap on the cheek one or two times.'[4] He said he saw himself more as a hotel manager working for a strict employer than a prison camp boss.

One of the key witnesses was Sergeant Major Frederick Waaldyk, the Dutch soldier who had helped to organise correspondence between civilian menfolk and their wives and nearly lost his life for doing so. In court he identified guards who had beaten men at the Dutch Garden Party, and others who were involved in the bashing of Australians after they tried to escape. He himself had been tied with his hands behind his back to a barbed wire fence and later fastened like a dog to a tree before being knocked down with a length of gas pipe, he told the tribunal.[5]

Waaldyk even demonstrated to the court two of the most painful forms of punishment employed by his captors. In one, known as the Lockheed torture, prisoners had to balance on the ball of one foot while the second leg was raised in the air to the rear and the arms held level with the shoulders for long periods. POWs had also been forced to hold a heavy stone above their heads until they weakened and the stone dropped onto their skulls.[6]

There was no limit to the guards' capacity for cruelty. One, named Masashi Tanaka and described as 'the lowest form of Japanese non-commissioned officer', had a reputation as a 'professional bash artist' who carried out beltings scientifically.

> Tanaka hit one man 100 times with a pick handle but was careful not to break bones. The man was knocked down every five or six strokes. When not strong enough to stand, the remainder of the strokes were administered while the soldier was on the ground and doused with cold water regularly so that he remained conscious to appreciate the belting. The man was kicked on the head, arms and between the legs.[7]

The next day of the trial, an Ambonese witness by the name of Andreas Joseph identified 31 Japanese guards who had bludgeoned

23 Australian soldiers unconscious with rubber piping. The boy described how they were beaten for six hours, until the piping broke. The following day it had begun all over again. To ensure the accuracy of Joseph's identification, the Japanese were paraded before him in court on three separate occasions, each time in different positions and wearing different clothes. He always got it right. The Japanese seemed unconcerned, grinning and nudging each other as they were picked out.[8]

By now, the war crimes trial had moved to the island of Morotai. The four-man panel who sat in judgement saw through the lies, and particularly Ikeuchi's barely believable defence. They had no doubt he was implicated in many of the executions and the slow starvation of his prisoners. The sentence: death by firing squad.

Shirozu, Miyazaki and Shimakawa were similarly punished.

Ikeuchi stood to receive the sentence with the same impassive expression he had worn during the entire trial and maintained his expression out of court, the Melbourne *Argus* reported. The *Age* said he heard the verdict 'with his normal sullen expression'. 'When he sat down he bowed his head, swallowed hard and showed the first signs of nervousness during the trial.'[9] Said the *Argus*, 'The other three Japanese sentenced to death displayed equal resignation . . . Poker faced Captain Shirozu was the only one who exhibited nervousness.'[10]

All told, 36 Japanese were found guilty and 57 acquitted. The convicted were jailed for between one and twenty years. Tanaka, the man who subjected Private Tait to such a terrible beating and whom the POWs nicknamed Frill Neck, received twenty years and Nichio Takeuchi, known as the Black Bastard, got the same.

Tatsuo Yamamoto, dubbed Giggling Gertie by the men, was sentenced to eighteen years, while Charcoal Charlie, whose real name was Tsunayuki Sonada, got ten. Others, variously nicknamed Horse Face, Frog Voice, Gold Tooth, Creeping Jesus, Grey Mare and Muttering Mick, received between two and eighteen years.

It had taken six weeks to convict the men whose campaign of terror had killed and injured so many but it would be at least another year before the four sentenced to death were executed.

Captain Williams, who had worked so tirelessly on the case for the prosecution said afterwards, 'I am happy it is finished. It has taken a long time but I am satisfied justice has been done. The trial has been conducted strictly and fairly throughout.'[11]

––––––––

The trial of the 93 Japanese eclipsed another hearing on Morotai involving Hideo Katayama, who had been present at the execution of the four Australian airmen on Ambon in August 1944. Now aged 25, the sub-lieutenant was back in Tokyo with his wife, Yuri, when he read his name in a Japanese newspaper. It appeared on a list of men wanted for war crimes. Katayama ignored the advice of friends who suggested he lie low, instead seeking guidance from his English-born aunt, who had a strong faith in British justice and believed he should turn himself in.

He surrendered and on 9 February was incarcerated in Tokyo's Sugamo prison, awaiting transfer to Morotai. He arrived there on 13 February 1946 and was immediately handed a three-page document detailing his part in the execution of the RAAF crew. Fellow executioners Toyoji Takahashi and Kiyosato Yoshizaki claimed the instruction to kill the airmen had come from Katayama, and they confirmed that he had beheaded Squadron Leader John Scott. A third statement from Shigeo Uemura, who had escorted the Australians to their place of execution, also detailed Katayama's role in carrying out the death sentence.

The statements shocked Katayama, who, while admitting he beheaded Scott, maintained that the order to execute the Australians was made higher up the chain of command. He insisted the instruction to execute the men had come from Captain Matuhei Kawasaki, his immediate superior, who had himself been acting on the orders of Lieutenant Commander Baron Masimitsu Takasaki, and that the original sentence had been confirmed by

Vice Admiral Seigo Yamagata, then Commander-in-Chief of the Fourth South Seas Fleet.

Was this just Katayama desperately trying to save his skin? Whatever the truth, his explanation was clearly at odds with the testimony of his two fellow executioners.

None of the senior Japanese officers, including Baron Takasaki, now released after his earlier acquittal by the War Crimes Tribunal, was called to confirm or deny Katayama's story and later he undermined his case by claiming his earlier confession that he killed Scott had simply been a lie designed to protect his superiors.[12] It took the War Crimes Tribunal a mere four days to listen to the evidence and convict Katayama, Takahashi and Uemura of murder. They were sentenced to death by shooting.

Uemura, who many felt was unjustly treated since he hadn't executed any of the Australians, was despatched by firing squad on the island of Rabaul at 8.30 a.m. on 4 May 1946. The other two's sentences were not carried out for another 18 months, pending their participation in the trial of other Japanese in a separate case. During that period Katayama continued to protest his innocence and impressed some of his jailors in the Japanese compound in Rabaul where condemned men were held pending their execution.

Among them was 21-year-old Don Ball, a military policeman who forged a close friendship with Katayama. Ball was convinced of Katayama's innocence and expected him to be reprieved. But on 22 October 1947, Katayama's and Takahashi's sentences were promulgated and they were ordered to be shot the following morning. Tragically for Ball, he was the man assigned to lead the men to the place of execution and tie blindfolds around their heads.

Sergeant Ball was accustomed to attending executions on Rabaul and usually felt no emotion about his role in the punishments because he was convinced the men had been given a fair trial and were guilty. But this was different. Now he was being forced to escort a close friend to his death, a man whom he firmly believed was innocent.

There was a last-ditch attempt to defer the executions but the order had been made in Melbourne and the senior officer on Rabaul did not have the authority to change it.

The condemned men, who were dressed in clean khaki shirts and trousers, were as neat as a pin when they emerged from their cell on that fateful morning. Katayama climbed into the rear seat of Don Ball's truck for the short journey and Takahashi followed in a jeep. At the execution site the sentence was read out and Katayama was helped by Ball to a stake which had a chair beneath it. There he was strapped to the seat and a white target placed over his heart. At first he declined the blindfold, insisting he was not frightened of death, but Sergeant Ball explained it was part of military regulations, to protect the firing squad from seeing the prisoner's eyes.

As the blindfold was tied Katayama began reciting the Lord's Prayer, and Ball, a devout Baptist, accompanied him. On completion the sergeant gave a comforting squeeze to the condemned man's arm and then, fighting back tears, returned to his position. The firing squad, who had remained out of sight behind some trees, now took their place behind a trestle table and aimed their .303 rifles at their target. Seconds later, nine heavy-calibre bullets were fired, almost cutting Katayama in half.

Takahashi's execution followed 45 minutes later.

The two bodies were rolled up in blankets, lifted onto the back of a truck and dumped in unmarked graves several kilometres away.[13]

For Sergeant Ball it was the worst day of his life. Had he just overseen the execution of an innocent man? The case would resonate for decades, finally culminating in a feature film which would strike at the very heart of Ambon's unhappy wartime past, yet also offer some degree of closure.[14]

———

There was no such uncertainty in some of the parallel trials which were being conducted. With the full extent of the Laha massacres now well documented, investigators were determined to bring all those involved to justice.

In one case two officers from Japanese naval units who had landed at Hitu-lama on Ambon's north coast at the time of the invasion were later charged in connection with the Laha massacres and eventually appeared before a military court on Rabaul in July 1947. Commander Kunio Hatakeyama and Lieutenant Kenichito Nakagawa were arrested after an army investigation lasting 20 months.

Earlier, Nakagawa had made a statement in Tokyo admitting to his role in the executions, but claiming he was merely carrying out the orders of Hatakeyama, his immediate superior. Hatakeyama argued that he was also acting on the instructions of his senior officer, but this could not be confirmed, as the man was dead. In the end, Hatakeyama was sentenced to death by hanging and Nakagawa received twenty years. However, in the end the death sentence was not carried out. Hatakeyama successfully appealed and had his sentence commuted to twenty years' imprisonment.

While the Morotai trials dominated much of the media coverage of the day, a later trial in Tokyo saw the prosecution of seventeen Japanese who controlled the Hainan camp. The *Canberra Times* reported on 15 January 1948 that 81 Australians had died there in 'piteous conditions . . . through starvation and ill-treatment'. The accused were all members of the 4th Yokosuka Special Naval Landing Force. They were charged with the inhumane treatment of Allied prisoners, contributing to the deaths of some, causing bodily injury and damaging their mental and physical health. One was acquitted but the rest received prison terms ranging from one to twenty years.

It was not until 24 September 1947 that Shirozu Wadami, head of the 20th Garrison Unit on Ambon, came to terms with his fate. In a letter to his daughter, he wrote calmly:

The time has come for your father's execution. I will receive my sentence bravely, as if dying on the battlefield.

I trust that you know I committed no crime to shame
my conscience and feel sure that this will become evident
with the passage of time. Nevertheless I feel no bitterness
towards the Australians. Just as we did our duty for
Japan, the Australians were doing their duty for Australia.
There was no personal enmity involved whatsoever. I hope
that my death will serve rather as a pledge of friendship
between Japan and Australia.[15]

By the 1950s the appetite for revenge had diminished and many
of those who had been jailed for long terms were released after
serving ten years or a third of their original sentence, whichever
was less. In 1957 even those sentenced to life imprisonment
were freed.

17

ARE THE MISSING STILL ALIVE?

IT WAS THE Melbourne *Sun* of 8 February 1946 that revealed plans for an official search party to visit Hainan, after rumours that some Australian and British POWs had been sighted on the island.

Could they include some of the men who had disappeared with Chinese guerillas after the bandit attack on their work party on 8 April 1944? More than two years had elapsed since that devastating shoot-out in which Australians and Japanese had been ambushed while driving from Hoban to a village 8 kilometres up the road. Two days later, one of those who'd been taken by the Chinese, Corporal John Nelson, had turned up unscathed, having found his way back to Hoban. Two of his injured comrades, Arthur Chenoweth and Freddie Stokes, were still with the Chinese, apparently being well treated, he had reported. But there was a question mark over the fate of the other eight, who had become separated from the trio in the village, though Nelson had suggested they had been invited to join the guerillas.

It didn't take long for the mystery to fuel still more speculation, in which fact and fiction combined to create rumours which, though fanciful, offered hope to those whose loved ones were unaccounted for. Naturally, relatives of the missing men wanted action and pressed the authorities to investigate the sightings, if only to bring closure to the conjecture. The military made it clear there was no reason to believe any Australian servicemen would be found alive by the search party but that they hoped to establish the fate of the missing men who were listed as presumed dead.[1]

The officer tasked with putting the rumours to rest was Major Harry Jackson, who, as a member of the Australian War Graves Service, had heard through 'the bamboo wireless' that escaped Australians were still fighting with guerilla bands in 1945. Like so many others, he was curious to find out more and as he was used to dealing with enquiries about missing men he was the ideal candidate for the job.

Renowned for his determination and energy, he soon set out for Hainan via a roundabout route that took in Balikpapan and Labuan in Borneo, Vietnam and Hong Kong. The mission very nearly ended in disaster when Jackson's transport plane ran out of fuel and crash-landed in Canton in southern China. The crew of four were killed but Jackson and his two Australian assistants escaped relatively unscathed.

The Chinese apprehended the survivors and held them for landing without the necessary paperwork. It delayed the mission for several days, but after much negotiation they were allowed to continue on their way.[2]

By now the Australian party had enlisted the support of the US military, offering to search for missing American airmen in Hainan as well as their own. Backed by the might of US forces, Major Jackson was offered a passage on a US destroyer which would take the search party to Hainan, along with several other Australian and British personnel who hoped to recover the remains of Allied servicemen buried on the island during the war.

They were eventually dropped off on 9 March 1946, but their arrival was fraught with danger. Communist and nationalist guerilla forces were still engaged in armed combat and the last thing Jackson wanted was to be caught up in factional fighting. He had a hastily arranged meeting with the commander of the 4th Kwangsi Army, which was in control of much of northern Hainan, and soon the party was on its way.

There was a lucky break when they met up with a Malaysian–Chinese who had been in contact with some of the Australian POWs during the war, including Major Ian Macrae, who'd escaped from the Hashio camp a year earlier and gone bush with the Chinese guerillas. He was a fount of local knowledge. Thanks to him they were soon in touch with some of the island's other refugees, who told them of white men fighting under the command of a communist general known as Fung Pak Kai. It was a fascinating tip, but was it true?[3]

The information gave Jackson and his men fresh impetus. Could it be that the eight Australian POWs captured in April 1944 were still alive? If the story proved correct it would be an incredible discovery. Clearly they needed to reach Fung for further clarification, but continuing clashes between communist and nationalist rebel fighters forced them to take a long and circuitous route to the general's HQ. It took six weeks behind communist lines to get a message through to HQ via a communist spy, and by then Fung Pak Kai had moved on.

Having received no definitive response to his enquiry about the missing Australians, Major Jackson retreated to the nationalist-held area and eventually to the southern port of Samah. From there he made his way to the site of the former prison camp at Hashio in Bakli Bay, where members of the 2/21st Battalion had spent nearly three years of the war.

There the remains of 76 Australians and several Americans were exhumed and taken by ship to Hong Kong. The Australian bodies were eventually laid to rest at the Yokohama War Cemetery in Japan. The recovery of those members of Gull Force who had died from disease or sheer brutality on Hainan closed a chapter in the battalion's history but did not address the issue which had brought Jackson to the island in the first place. Where were the other ten?

While their fate was unclear, the search party could not remain on the island indefinitely. Now that 76 bodies had been exhumed from the prison camp cemetery Major Jackson's mission was terminated, forcing him to come to a number of conclusions.

Though there was no categorical proof, he reasoned that Chenoweth and Stokes had most likely died from their wounds in the village of Lao-ou, where they had been taken after the ambush. Of the other eight, three had died after trying to make their way back to Hashio. Suffering from severe malnutrition, they were captured by a Japanese patrol and later shot dead.

As for the other five, Jackson received various reports of their fate but they almost certainly died in action while fighting alongside the Chinese. Intelligence provided by a Dutchman who had earlier escaped from Hashio identified one of them as a man who was blind in one eye. This was believed to be Private Leslie Shiells, from Camperdown in Victoria, but like the rest of the men, the names of the five could not be substantiated.[4] A report by Major Jackson concluded that they were almost certainly buried in unmarked graves, along with some 80 000 Chinese coolies, in which case it would be impossible to locate them.

On 5 August 1946, the *Age* reported that the officer had returned to Melbourne believing that all the prisoners had died. 'An Australian War Graves Service officer will continue the quest, but as the unmarked graves of coolie labourers were everywhere in Hainan, the possibility of finding the graves of the Australians, who apparently fought to the last against the Japanese, was remote.' The *Age* also reported that the British consul in Hong Kong had contacted the Chinese commander on the island, who had been told by the captured deputy commander of the communist guerillas that the Australians were dead.[5]

Australian researcher Brendan Worrell, who had lived on Hainan, believed the missing were either killed by the Japanese during sweeping operations, or even by the Chinese, who were partial to shooting or bayoneting men in cold blood, as demonstrated by the ambush.[6]

Yet rumours about the Australians surviving their ordeal refused to go away. One source suggested that some of them might have escaped from the island by boat and sailed to Vietnam, some 500 kilometres to the west of Hainan. Others speculated that they were still alive and fighting alongside the guerillas as late as 1946. Could it be that news of the Japanese defeat had failed to reach the men in their remote camps, hidden away in the island's mountainous interior? Was it possible they didn't know the war was over?

Such a scenario was not implausible, given the tale of Lieutenant Hiroo Onoda, the Japanese soldier who emerged from the jungle on the Philippines island of Lubang in 1974, after believing, until then, that reports of a Japanese surrender were trickery.[7]

It was unlikely, of course, but there was the intriguing testimony of an American missionary who had been told that at least some of the Australians had survived. Nathanial Berkowitz, who had been a Presbyterian missionary on Hainan before the war, returned to the island in the early 1950s, when he received feedback that the missing men were still alive in 1946, and possibly even later.[8]

It would be another three decades before at least some of the mystery was resolved but, even then, other unanswered questions would continue to feed the rumour mill.

In 1981 an Australian aid worker based on the island heard tales of 'tall blond foreigners' living in a Hainan village. The exact year of the sighting was unclear but it was enough to inspire Gull Force survivors back in Melbourne to return to Hainan in 1985 in search of their fallen mates. Locals talked to them about the two blue-eyed men with ginger beards who were looked after by peasants. 'Ragged and with swollen beri-beri limbs, which also meant swollen hearts, their will to fight on was a wonderful and inspiring thing to see,' the Chinese folk told the men from Gull Force.

Sadly, it was also revealed that the two soldiers had eventually died and were buried near Bakli Bay at Lao-ou, where villagers looked after their graves.[9]

While the heartbreaking news was to be expected, it offered final confirmation of the escapees' fate. It also spurred the Gull Force veterans into putting further pressure on the Australian authorities to exhume the graves, remove the bones and give the victims a proper burial. It took another five years for the leaden foot of bureaucracy to complete the necessary steps to expedite the exhumation, which eventually took place on 29 March 1990, largely thanks to the support of the Chinese Red Cross, who made the necessary arrangements.

Six representatives of the 2/21st Battalion travelled to Hainan, including retired Lieutenant Ron Green and Captain Rod Gabriel. There they were joined by Australia's defence attaché to Beijing, Captain Ian Pfennigwerth, and an embassy colleague, Grant Thompson, who oversaw the delicate operation of sifting the soil for bone fragments. The formal ceremony, with Australian and Chinese flags flying, was a big event in the life of the local people, who were desperately poor but whose elderly had a vivid recollection of life under the Japanese yoke.

One spoke of the mass executions that had taken place on an area of land nearby known as the field of death. He told Ian Pfennigwerth how the Japanese would round up a couple of hundred Chinese and chop their heads off after an attack by Chinese nationalists. 'They'd leave the bodies on the ground as an example. People I spoke to in the village told the most horrific of stories. Some estimate 10000 people were killed, which was staggering.'[10]

Pfennigwerth remembered Lao-ou as 'like something out of a spaghetti western. The road was a dusty track and the fields were barren. People scrubbed up for the occasion but it was quite clear the place was impoverished.' The site of the graves, about 50 metres from a dozen mud huts and a school, was sheltered by a grove of trees. Village leaders formed a line beside the graves, which were basically mounds of earth with flowers on top, and bowed three times as the digging began. To ward off evil spirits, the Chinese set off fire-crackers as the soil was placed beneath a Chinese epitaph.

Also standing nearby was 72-year-old Qing Yousheng, who had tended the spot where the POWs were believed to have been buried for the previous 46 years. He had never forgotten the promise he had made to his guerilla comrades in 1944, to honour the memory of the 'tall men with big noses'.[11]

Another veteran guerilla, Qing Jaying, 85, revealed how he used to communicate with the two men by gestures, as he didn't understand their language. Supported by a bamboo walking stick, he wiped the tears from his eyes as he recalled providing the Australians with eggs and chickens while they lay seriously ill in the village. 'They played with the children and seemed comfortable here,' he told *Age* correspondent Peter Ellingsen. Indeed, he believed they brought good fortune to the community after they had died and been buried beneath the sandy soil. Qing Jaying was sorry to see their remains taken away, but understood the reasoning after being told they'd be interred in a proper war cemetery.

For the retired Gull Force officers Green and Gabriel, it was an emotional but strangely comforting experience. At last they were sure they'd found two of the missing men who had disappeared after the ambush, even though they could not be certain of their identities. 'For the present they were two unknown Australian soldiers who were befriended by the villagers of Lao-ou and who left their remains as a memorial to Australian–Chinese friendship,' Rod Gabriel remarked.[12]

Close by, Captain Pfennigwerth monitored the exhumations and reminded the gathering how the Australians were forced into slave labour and kept in the 'most cruel conditions'. 'Although they died, they died as free men among friends and have stayed here among you for many years,' he observed.

But there was a problem. Ian Pfennigwerth had not attended an exhumation before and was unsure what to expect when the ground was excavated. Before leaving Beijing he'd been advised that only major bones such as the skull or ribcage were likely to be in one piece after 45 years, depending on the acidity of the soil, but to everyone's embarrassment there was nothing. 'We went into a huddle and decided we were either in the wrong place or the remains had simply disintegrated in the soil.'[13]

The two embassy officials had brought two beautiful wooden caskets in which to place the remains. In the absence of any bones they thought the best thing to do was to fill them with a shovelful of earth, in the hope that subsequent forensic analysis would confirm the presence of human bone fragments. 'It was a bit of an anticlimax,' admitted Pfennigwerth. 'I irreverently christened these guys Bluey and Curly, because we didn't know who they were, and took them back to Beijing, where they stayed in my office.'

Later, tiny fragments in the boxes were identified as 'probably bones', but whether they were animal or human in origin was impossible to confirm. 'Could you establish that these were in fact Caucasian remains? No,' Pfennigwerth declared more than two decades later. 'It was all very unsatisfactory for everybody.'

Yet there was one positive outcome. The remains were subsequently buried at the Commonwealth War Cemetery in Yokohama, Japan. They were not named and there was no indication as to where they had died, but at least they were in consecrated soil.

While the exhumation had left many questions unanswered, the burial would comfort relatives who would privately hope that their son or brother was one of the two. Like the tomb of the unknown warrior, the bodies' identities would remain a mystery but at least their final resting place would provide a closure rich in symbolism and help to heal old wounds. For families back in Australia it would soften the gnawing agony of never knowing.

18

THE LOST BATTALION'S SEARCH FOR ANSWERS

A s the sacrifice of Gull Force and the full scale of the tragedies on Ambon and Hainan emerged in the immediate post-war years, it was inevitable that questions continued to be asked. Families wanted to know why their loved ones' lives had been lost, and official inquiries were sought.

The search for answers began within days of the 2/21st Battalion's official return to Melbourne, an event which dominated local newspaper coverage, with front page photographs of cheering crowds. The Melbourne *Sun* reported how:

> most of Melbourne from Spencer Street to Heidelberg
> turned out into the streets early today to give the survivors
> of the lost battalion one of the greatest welcome homes
> the city and suburbs have seen.
>
> In every suburb along the route – even in lonely
> streets – there were cheering parties every fifty yards, old
> men with gardening tools, housewives, schoolchildren in
> orderly ranks, toddlers and babes in arms.
>
> A ripple of cheering and whistling, rising to a
> deafening roar, broke out from strongpoints along the

pavement and from office windows and parapets where office and factory girls showered the veterans with a snowstorm of paper.[1]

Above the roar could be heard the strains of 'Hearts of Oak' and 'Waltzing Matilda' as the convoy snaked along a colourful avenue of pennants, flags and banners.

At the head of the victory parade was Lieutenant Colonel William Scott, described by the *Sun* as 'thin but bronzed'.

But while the 2/21st's commander and his men were clearly enjoying the welcome home, there were mixed emotions among the ranks. 'Life at present is bewildering and a little beyond our understanding,' one of them admitted. 'Much has gone under the bridge – a very wide bridge. Some of these men have memories they would rather forget and they don't want to talk.'

Amid the revelry, much was left unspoken, though the *Sun* alluded to the central issue, quoting some survivors as saying 'the defence of Ambon was futile'. Some demanded a parliamentary inquiry into the matter, while an unnamed corporal told the *Sun*'s reporter that the fight on Ambon was virtually over before it began. 'Admittedly ten battalions may not have held it – but that makes the case stronger against sending only one unit there. With the forces opposed to us by land, sea and air, we weren't in the race from the start,' he said.

It was a blunt but accurate assessment of the events leading up to the fall of Ambon and it would gain traction in the months and years ahead as an avalanche of letters questioning the failed military strategy appeared in the press.

The *Argus* carried a letter from Mr P. L. McDonald, who signed himself as a member of the Fathers' Association. It read, in part:

Members of Gull Force have been widely acclaimed as heroes, and unquestionably they did everything humanly possible, as it was expected they would, in the face of overwhelming odds and in a situation which, according to reliable sources, was hopeless from the start. But these facts do nothing to remove grave doubts about the wisdom of placing this superb force in a precarious, isolated position, in which they were cut off by sea and air, and of placing other units of the brigade in similar hopeless positions.[2]

Others took the same line, accusing the military of pursuing a 'hush, hush' policy from the day Gull Force left Darwin, as Ruby Strachan of South Yarra put it. J. Weston, who lost an only son on Ambon, insisted 'there is no doubt a shocking blunder was made. If those in charge were innocent of a mistake, why were they afraid to face an inquiry, which they have been asked to do on many occasions?'

Smith's Weekly reported a call from Senator George McLeay, then opposition leader in the Senate, for a full investigation.[3] He wanted to know why the battalion wasn't withdrawn from Ambon when it 'became evident that they would be annihilated if left at their posts. And why no notice was taken of Commander Roach's expressed misgivings at the time. There was the strongest reason to believe that the first commander of the Ambon force did in fact make an emergency trip to Australia to give the Government the facts and that he was relieved of his command as a result.'[4]

There was one name that could not be avoided in the correspondence pages: that of the officer who subsequently took over from Roach, Lieutenant Colonel Scott. Many of the letters were in response to the commander's fierce defence of the mission entrusted to Gull Force, which most had branded 'ill-fated'. Scott was infuriated by the term, which suggested 'those gallant men who lost their lives in action and subsequently as prisoners of war . . . failed in their objective or suffered some grave injustice at the hands of those responsible for the task of which the force was entrusted'. Their task was to defend Ambon to delay as long as possible the southward advance of the enemy, he explained.

Had Gull Force been withdrawn from Ambon before the Japanese attack, the Japanese division of 20,000 men, together with its navy and its airforce could, and almost certainly would, have by-passed Ambon and proceeded straight to Darwin. Is there anyone who will suggest that this enemy force would have been destroyed on arrival at Darwin in January or February 1942?[5]

Scott might have a valid point but it did not wash with his critics, who bombarded the papers with their own denunciation of the military's wartime strategy. As Mr P. L. McDonald wrote:

My information suggests there was dilatoriness in arrangements dating back months before the Japanese assault. If a force of 1100 men, of whom only 316 returned, was not 'ill-fated' when it was able to fight for about four days and was in enemy captivity for nearly four years, what was it? Honourable and brave certainly, but this has never been disputed.

Another, Mrs K. M. Fiddian, who had lost her husband in the Laha massacre, also wanted answers. 'What is the true story I am to tell my son, who, although never having known his father, was conscious of irreparable loss? Has he not the right to know the facts, considering his father's sacrifice?'[6]

No wonder the survivors and the next of kin were so ropeable. The more they heard about Gull Force and the way the 2/21st Battalion had been abandoned, the more they wanted those responsible to answer for their poor judgement.

But Scott was standing firm and distanced himself from the events leading up to his taking command of the battalion. His official report to his superiors, which was dated 8 May 1946, set the tone.

It is regrettable that I can only report on the history of Gull Force from the date of my assuming command.

The history prior to that time would, to a large extent, be no more than hearsay. It will be admitted, however, that no history can be regarded as complete which lacks beginnings, and there is no observation proclaiming a more profound truth than that which might, with benefit, be more widely known and understood in these difficult times, 'As ye sow, so also shall ye reap.'[7]

What was he suggesting? Was he pointing the finger at the Australian government who had agreed to support the Dutch in the event of a Japanese offensive? Or was he getting at the military establishment which had planned and orchestrated the Ambon mission?

Scott's thinking remains unclear, but he was happy to unload on those he was forced to fight alongside, the Royal Netherlands East Indies Army.

It has not been possible to ignore the Dutch troops or their commanding officer. It was unfortunate that there was nothing to be said which could be regarded as bringing credit either to the one or the other. My unhappy experience with these people both at Ambon and Hainan leave me convinced that there was no one characteristic which an Australian or a Dutchman could find in common.[8]

Scott's damning assessment of his Dutch counterparts was accompanied by his 'unutterable conviction' that he did what his superiors had demanded, viz: 'You will assist the Dutch forces to defend the island of Ambon with the object of delaying for as long as possible the southward advance of the enemy with the available troops and equipment under your command.' Moreover, he wanted to place on record that he believed the mission was 'entirely justified'.[9]

If the commander was trying to deflect attention away from his own inadequacies, he would not succeed. Dr Bill Aitken's detailed account of life under Scott's authority would provide devastating testimony when it was made public after the war. A letter written in August 1945 from him to Captain Newnham, the battalion's second in command on Hainan, provided a foretaste of what was to follow. In it, Aitken said he believed Scott was of 'unsound mind, incapable in so far as certain of his duties were concerned of making sane decisions, unable to carry out these duties efficiently or bear the responsibilities of his position.' He went on: 'I recommend to you that he be suspended from all such duties as require sane thought and decision, for the health and even the lives of many men depend on these decisions.'[10]

Later, Aitken's full and unexpurgated character assessment of his senior officer made for even more damning reading.

> Our daily lives were hampered and made more difficult
> by many minor, unnecessary restrictions imposed by him
> frequently for no other reason than to satisfy his personal
> whims and fancies. His general policy was selfish, weak
> and near-sighted, his attitude to the Japanese conciliatory
> and generally marked by a readiness to temporize and
> to accept and pursue any course that would obviate his
> personal conflict with them, even in matters of the upmost
> importance.[11]

Aitken went on to claim that Scott had shown scant interest in the hospital and taken little notice of his advice about the preparation and distribution of food.

> His continual desire to keep out of personal trouble with
> the Japanese was most obvious in his failure to seize the
> opportunities presented to him to lodge complaints and
> ask for improvements in conditions when Japanese officers
> visited the camp. Almost invariably he had to be requested
> to make approaches to the Japanese by the quarter-
> master, Dutch or myself, and practically never requested

improvements of his own accord, but always had to be driven to it.[12]

Aitken's brutal assessment of Scott's failure, as a leader who did not look after the interests of his men, was in sharp contrast to the commanding officer's sentiments as expressed in his own official post-war report. In it he refers to the medical reports which described the insufficient food and medical supplies meted out by the Japanese, which he hoped would not be easily forgotten by the Australian people. 'Certain it was that those Australians fortunate enough to survive the long period of horror never can forget,' he stated.

He also referred to the 'terrible fate' of those who had died in the Laha massacres. 'As prisoners of war these officers and men were murdered in the manner and under circumstances which were so cold blooded and incredible as to make them comparable only to the horrors of the Spanish inquisition during the 16th and 17th centuries.'[13]

While Scott's post-war reflections may have been sincere, Aitken and others believed he was merely trying to salvage his reputation. Whatever the truth, the damage was done. It was too late to reinvent himself. Though, curiously, his character would be immortalised for generations to come, thanks to a quirk of literary fate.

19

LAYING THE GHOSTS TO REST

MORE THAN THREE decades had passed but the execution of Hideo Katayama on Rabaul for his part in the beheading of four Australian airmen on Ambon in 1944 continued to haunt Don Ball, who had tied the blindfold around the Japanese soldier's head. 'For years there was hardly a night when I would not jerk awake thinking of Katayama,' he told *The Australian*'s Phil Cornford. 'Without my Christian faith I would not have pulled through. I would have been in the nut house long ago.'[1]

Then, in 1980, a chance meeting with a group of Japanese Christians who were on a visit to Lismore in northern New South Wales provided an opportunity to exorcise Katayama's ghost. The group, led by an Australian-born Marist priest, Father John Glynn, was on a pilgrimage for 'the healing of memories'. He had lived in Japan for more than twenty years and felt the only way to resolve the bitterness among the Japanese about the Second World War was to share the grief.

Ex-Sergeant Ball, who worked as an ambulance officer in the quiet rural community of Bonalbo near Lismore, told Father Glynn about Katayama's fate and his long-held concerns about the soldier's innocence. Clearly moved by the story, the priest returned to Japan in the hope of contacting Katayama's widow, Yuri Honjo, a former ballet dancer. It took some time to trace her but finally, in early July 1981, Ball received a letter containing documents which 'establish beyond reasonable doubt' that Katayama, 'acting under orders he could not refuse, beheaded an Australian airman'.[2]

The news comforted Don Ball, who was now certain that the man whose death he had mourned for so long was guilty. It alleviated his own sense of guilt. 'A huge load has been lifted from my conscience,' he admitted.[3] Whether Katayama should have been executed – given that he appeared to have been acting under orders – was another matter. The truth was further complicated by the discovery of a letter to war crimes prosecutor John Williams from Lieutenant Commander Akira Kobayashi claiming that the Japanese had carried out no courts martial between 30 November 1943 and 10 September 1945.

These were issues that would continue to trouble ex-Lieutenant Williams in later life. He had returned to Australia before hearing about the final confirmation of Katayama's death sentence and did not learn of his execution until he read about it in *The Australian* some 34 years later.

That report would also trigger a chain of events culminating in the production of a successful feature film, a semi-fictionalised interpretation of the events on Ambon and the execution of Katayama. The film would be produced by Williams's son, Brian, who had first stumbled across his father's post-war involvement in the War Crimes Tribunal after opening an old black steamer trunk in the garage of his Sydney home. Inside were yellowed documents and black and white photographs of the exhumation of bodies at Laha 'tied together with rope and laid out beside the graves'.[4]

Brian became obsessed by what he read of the POW experience on Ambon and eventually persuaded his father, by now a judge, to give him permission 'to pursue my own story of these events'. It would inspire the much-acclaimed Australian movie *Blood Oath*. John Williams agreed to allow his son to use the material he had amassed after the war, on the understanding that he himself would offer no opinion on the dramatisation and would only provide guidance on factual issues.

Brian spent the next three years poring over a mountain of transcripts and evidence to find a way into the story with fellow writer and producer Denis Whitburn. 'By 1987 after much debate and occasional raging arguments about how we could transform such complex material into a satisfactory drama, we had a treatment ready and then rapidly our first screenplay.'[5]

Like most films, the gestation period was slow and laborious but soon they had a director on board – Stephen Wallace – and an impressive cast was also signed up including Bryan Brown, Russell Crowe, George Takei, Terry O'Quinn, John Polson, Nicholas Eadie, Deborah Unger, Ray Barrett and Jason Donovan.

Meanwhile, Brian's father, by now 73, was writing an MA history thesis about the war crimes trials. The entire Williams family, including John's wife Dorothy, also a keen supporter of the project, were determined to make the movie happen. With backing from the Australian Film Finance Corporation the production was finally unveiled on 15 July 1990. After the Sydney premiere, at which John Williams was guest of honour, the movie opened in Tokyo. It was a highly charged night; no one was sure how the movie would be received.

The producers need not have worried. Over the next four weeks 25 000 people would sit in the small 225-seat cinema to witness how their fellow countrymen had behaved. It was a story that few of them would have known about, given the Japanese government's reluctance to include mention of wartime atrocities in the country's history books.

After the Tokyo premiere, Yoshiro (Peter) Ninomiya, a former Japanese navy sub-lieutenant assigned to Tan Tui, admitted the film made him feel 'very dark inside'. Ninomiya was general secretary of the Ambon Remembrance Society, an organisation of navy veterans who had served as guards at the camp. 'After I watched this film the first time I felt as though I had swallowed lead,' he admitted.[6]

Significantly, the navy veteran stepped forward to deliver a speech recognising the solemn nature of the occasion and echoing John Williams's own sentiments about the need for reconciliation. 'We should not repeat the same mistake and hope that the relationship between our two countries will become closer,' he said. Perhaps more pertinently, he added: 'I wish to apologise for the mistake Japan had caused in the past.'[7] So far as anybody could remember, it was the first unqualified apology about the war by a former member of the Japanese military and was reported extensively in the country's media.

Later at the Sydney premiere Don Ball was introduced to Brian's father for the first time. They had much in common, given their shared interest in the events at the War Crimes Tribunal on Morotai and the judicial conclusion on Rabaul some eighteen months later.

Brian Williams believed that his father did attempt to have the court grant leniency to Katayama but that the tribunal was heavily biased towards handing out the maximum sentence to what they saw as the ringleaders of the 'unjustified' execution of the four airmen. 'The great irony of Katayama, as my father put it, was that he [Katayama] had survived the Hiroshima bombing only to surrender himself to "British justice", on the advice of his English aunt, to then find himself on trial for executing four airmen who were accused of bombing civilians.'[8]

———

On Anzac Day 1991, John and Brian Williams made a long overdue pilgrimage to Ambon itself. It was the first time John had been there since 1946 and it was an unforgettable experience. Said Brian, 'At the conclusion of the ceremony I never forget my father turning to me with his glistening eyes and saying in a cracking voice, "Son, I'm glad you came with me."'

There was to be one more reminder of John's wartime links with the Japanese and, poignantly, it happened just before he slipped away following a stroke on Australia Day 1994. A card from Ninomiya arrived in the letterbox, revealing that Vice-Admiral Shinichi Ichise had just died at the age of 101. He was the Japanese Commander-in-Chief of the Fourth South Seas Fleet, who had taken over Ambon's command just months before the end of the war and who had been persuaded by John Williams to exert his authority on his subordinates to break down the wall of silence which had shrouded the Laha massacre. Ichise had been acquitted by the War Crimes Tribunal.

Brian Williams conveyed the news of the death of Ichise to his father just before he lost consciousness. It was a desperately emotional moment, as Brian leant down and added in a whisper, 'Thank you for our journey together and all you have given me.'

Later he would tell the congregation at his father's funeral at St John's College, Sydney University, 'We salute you, we honour you, my extraordinary father.'

The release of *Blood Oath* in 1991 and the publicity surrounding it had unexpected consequences over the next few years.

Ed Weiss's daughter, Nancy, who lived in Chicago, saw a report by Ronald E. Yates in the *Chicago Tribune* about Japanese reaction to the film that contained the quotes from Peter Ninomiya. She sent the cutting to her father, who read with interest about the Ambon Remembrance Society formed by Japanese navy veterans who had served as guards on the island. By coincidence, Ed also received a letter from Ronald Suleski, who had stumbled across Weiss's self-published memoir, *Under the Rising Sun*, while on a visit to Weiss's home town of Erie in Pennsylvania. Dr Suleski just happened to be President of the Asiatic Society of Japan, an association of like-minded individuals whose aim was to disseminate information about Japanese society, history and literature.

In his reply, Ed asked for help in obtaining a name and address for the remembrance group. He had no interest in exchanging pleasantries with his former captors but merely wanted to trace one of the Tan Tui guards with whom he'd traded a ring in late July 1945 in a desperate bid to obtain food.

Amazingly, the enquiry bore fruit after Dr Suleski managed to contact Peter Ninomiya, who in turn passed on a message to Tanaka Shoichi (not to be confused with Tanaka Masahi, who received twenty years). This guard was a 21-year-old petty officer who would later be sentenced to two years' imprisonment. Unfortunately, he no longer had the ring, having traded it with the Ambonese in exchange for food.

While the search for the missing ring went nowhere, Ninomiya became a valuable source of information as Weiss was planning to update his personal recollections for a second edition of his book. Intriguingly, Ninomiya revealed that he had had several casual meetings with the POWs' nemesis at Tan Tui, Ikeuchi Masakiyo, while the two served on Ambon. His own view was that he wasn't half as bad as the War Crimes Tribunal had painted him, describing him as a good person who was caught between the demands of the Japanese officers and the POWs. He claimed many of the camp guards and officers regarded Ikeuchi with suspicion because he spoke out on behalf of the prisoners' needs for additional food and medical supplies.

While Ninomiya's post-war loyalty to his senior officer was easy to mock, his view was shared by other naval veterans who served on Ambon. This emerged after Ikeuchi's widow and daughter came forward, following the renewed interest in Ambon after the release of *Blood Oath*.

Harumi, Ikeuchi's only daughter, talked to some of the Japanese veterans who knew him and wrote a letter to Ed Weiss to put the record straight. She told him how she learned of her father's attempts to obtain additional food and medicine for the POWs and how he even took it upon himself to get medicine outside the chain of command, passing it on to Dr Ehlhart, who ran the camp hospital. Harumi cited the case of Jack O'Brien, who had his ulcerated leg amputated with a butcher's knife and lived to tell the tale. Her father, she insisted, visited a sympathetic pharmacist to cadge some ether to help alleviate the POW's suffering.

Was this merely propaganda aimed at saving her father's reputation from being further tarnished? Or did it show another side to the man who had made the POWs' lives such a misery?

Ed Weiss stood by what he saw and heard at the time, but admitted he was disturbed by what he'd learned about Ikeuchi since. 'It's becoming more apparent he was a scapegoat,' he concluded.[9]

Ed's investigation into the events on Ambon during the war had consumed him for nearly 70 years. He was still looking for answers, especially as to why the Americans had attacked the bomb dump at Tan Tui in February 1943, leading to such heavy loss of life. The more he discovered, the harder the questions became. He was a man who would not rest until he knew, but time was running out. Now in his early nineties, he combed the internet for old files and wrote to anyone who might be able to shed further light on the many mysteries of Tan Tui.

Sometimes there was a small sense of closure. The American airmen who were brought to Ambon after crash-landing in their plane the *Paper Doll* in January 1944, and who had become known as the strangers in the night, were not dead, as had been feared. When they had disappeared it was assumed they'd been executed, as was so often the Japanese custom with downed aviators. In fact, all six had been taken to Japan for further interrogation and had remained in prison until they were recovered by US forces in August 1945. On 28 November 1993, Ed was reunited with the plane's navigator, Lieutenant Charles R. Shaver – the man who had reached into the bucket of tea to find an old lipstick tube containing a message. It was this ingenious method that had allowed the two men to secretly correspond about the latest state of the war. Almost half a century had elapsed since they last met.

———

As the final decade of the millennium unfolded, the island of Ambon hit the headlines once again as growing unrest between the majority Muslim and the minority Christian populations turned to violence.

Ambon's 400-year history of commercial, political and religious rivalry was about to manifest itself again in the form of angry clashes. More than 200 people were reported killed in the subsequent sectarian conflict. Among the non-human casualties was a tall cross, a central feature of the war cemetery which contained the remains of more than 2000 Australian, British and Dutch defence personnel who died on Ambon and in the surrounding area during the Japanese occupation.

The trouble threatened what had become an annual pilgrimage to Ambon by veterans of the 2/21st Battalion and their families, who had been honouring their lost menfolk since 1967. The Gull Force Association had raised nearly a million dollars for the Ambonese during that period, providing food, books and medical aid for the poor and underprivileged. The veterans had not forgotten the vital role of the Ambonese, who had passed on messages, left food and cigarettes for work parties and provided boats and safe houses for escapees during the war.[10]

The annual pilgrimage was a tradition that showed no sign of waning, despite the passage of time. In September 2013, the association's secretary, Sue Head, whose father, Eric Kelly, had survived his time as a POW on Ambon, took a party of 24 to the island. This time, there was an even more significant reason for going. For nearly three years Sue and fellow members had been raising money for a more permanent memorial to those who had served on Ambon but were fortunate enough to return home. It had finally been completed, thanks to a $15 000 grant from the Commonwealth War Graves Commission.

The site of the 2.5-metre-long Honour Wall, as it was known, was at Kudamati, which had been the scene of a fierce battle with the Japanese shortly before the Allies capitulated. It was tiled, with a bevelled top containing seven plaques bearing the survivors' names. 'The ceremony for the new memorial exceeded our expectations,' said Sue.

There were local people who had grown used to welcoming the Gull Force Association every year, though there were few Ambonese alive who actually remembered the war. An exception was an old lady by the name of Van Capele who lived opposite the war cemetery at Galala, who remembered how she had left food for the Australians near the fence that surrounded the prison camp. Another was an elderly man who had lived in a displaced persons camp at Paso since the sectarian violence. He recalled the day when, as a six-year-old boy, the Australians taught him to sing 'My Bonny Lies Over the Ocean'.

There were other, more tangible examples of the historic link between Australians and the Ambonese. John Gaspersz, whose father used to look after the war cemetery on the island, had since taken over as the official curator and visited Ambon several times a year from his home in Melbourne.

But it was the donation of much-needed clothing and other goods which had cemented the bond between the two peoples. In 2013 the association took more than 240 kilograms of clothing with them on the annual pilgrimage, as well as $2000 worth of bandages for local hospitals. The previous year it had been sheets. In 2014, they would provide cotton blankets. Through such acts of kindness the memory of Gull Force's sacrifice would be immortalised for years and possibly centuries to come.

Their epic struggle, which many felt so pointless at the time, had produced a purpose which few could have imagined during those grim days behind barbed wire. Thanks to the 2/21st's descendants, the so-called Lost Battalion had finally found its much-deserved place in history.

20

REFLECTIONS

AND WHAT OF the characters who played major or supporting roles in this epic wartime struggle, which effectively had its roots in the dying days of the nineteenth century and continues to inspire and intrigue in the early years of the 21st?

Sadly, most would be forgotten over time, but some would continue to make their presence felt in the most unlikely of circumstances.

Occasionally I drive past an old bus shelter on Sydney's northern beaches at Narrabeen, where in 1922 the noted British author D. H. Lawrence alighted from a tram and that same day met up with a man on whom he would base one of his most famous characters. Jack Callcott, who appeared in Lawrence's classic novel *Kangaroo* was a fictionalised version of William Scott, later to become the 2/21st Battalion's controversial CO. They struck up a friendship while Lawrence was writing his book at Thirroul, on the south coast of New South Wales.

Scott, who was treasurer of the fascist King and Empire Alliance and played a key role in building up a secret army aimed at destroying left-wing elements in the event of a socialist uprising, must have been shocked when he discovered how Lawrence had woven him and his secret army into the plot. The author also appeared to have been worried about what he'd written, asking in a letter to his publisher, 'Do you think the Australian Govt. or the Diggers might resent anything?'

Scott's fictional character also pops up in *John Thomas and Lady Jane*, another version of Lawrence's steamy *Lady Chatterley's Lover*.[1]

The *Australian Dictionary of Biography* said Lawrence's observation about Jack Callcott could equally apply to Scott: 'There was a devil in his long, wiry body.' The stern but flamboyant former officer, described as highly attractive to women, married for the third time in 1948 and died childless in Adelaide in 1956.[2]

Ghosts from the past continued to materialise. After a day's research at the Australian War Memorial in Canberra I received a call from the United States while driving back to Sydney. The caller identified himself as Brother Shane from a Carmelite monastery in San Jose, just south of San Francisco. How he had found me or discovered my interest in the island of Ambon I never established, but he had some fascinating news about Bob Grainger, the young lieutenant who joined Ed Weiss on his daring escape from the Philippines in 1942. Grainger, who survived the prison camp and returned to America to become a Catholic priest, was about to be proposed for canonisation.

Robert Grainger, whose mother had owned a chain of department stores in California, had committed the rest of his life to helping the poor. He thought nothing of flying to Mexico to build churches or raising money for the people of the Philippines, who had helped him so much during the war. 'The thing that makes Father Robert interesting is that because he didn't die on the battlefield or in the prison camp he recognised God's role in that and decided to dedicate his life to the service of the Lord and to the church,' said Brother Shane. 'The lives he touched after he came home and the life he led in the service of others make him very special and there were a lot of people who feel this man should be made a saint,' he added.[3]

The possible canonisation of Robert Grainger, who died in 1971, led me to Ed Weiss, and back to Walter Hicks, both of whom had struck up close friendships with 'Saint' Bob during and after the war. Shortly before he died at the age of 93 in 2013, Walter told me how Grainger had helped to keep him going in the camp. 'We had a similar attitude to life and believed in good and religion. We deplored bad language and had a lot in common with each other.' He explained how Robert almost sacrificed his life by giving away his food, ending up as skin and bone.

Walter, too, took time to recover after the war. 'You never forget some of the terrible things that were done,' he said.[4] He returned to the bank, married his wife Margaret and retired in 1984. Soon after the end of the war he wrote his own memoir, which his family was determined to keep private. It contained his very personal recollections of a terrible time. When I asked him if he had ever wondered how he got through it, all he would say was, 'When I read what I wrote in 1946 I can't imagine how I did it . . . I really can't.'[5]

It was a common response among the Gull Force veterans, many of whom took years to recover from the trauma.

Amazingly, many, like Walter Hicks, went on to lead long and productive lives; people like Max 'Eddie' Gilbert, a surprisingly youthful 93-year-old who insisted he had now resolved his 'feelings of antipathy – even hatred – toward my former captors'. In his memoir he admitted he had often reflected on how the Japanese could have been so indoctrinated and dehumanised that they were able to behave in such a barbarous manner. 'I have never come up with an answer. Suffice to say here that I no longer harbour feelings of hostility towards the Japanese.'[6]

Jimmy Morrison, of the 2/12th Field Ambulance, also in his early nineties, was one of those who couldn't settle down. At home he would often wake up screaming from a nightmare – his mum would tell him to stop dreaming – but it didn't happen now. His leg was still scarred from a beating he got from the Japanese and he'd undergone heart bypass surgery, but he continued to enjoy an occasional drink at his RSL.

It seemed a lifetime away from the day he had sailed into Sydney Harbour on board the British aircraft carrier HMS *Striker*. 'It was unbelievable, such a magnificent sight. Of course, I'd never received a letter and didn't know whether my family were alive and then I saw my brother on the wharf shouting, "Everything's okay – Mum and Dad are alright!"'[7]

Fellow medic Tom Pledger, now 97 and still fit enough to take part in the Anzac Day March of 2013, was always certain he'd get out of the camp alive. When he returned, he had his girlfriend Jessie waiting for him on the wharf at Pyrmont, as well as his mum and dad. He married the day after he was discharged and went back to his job on the railways. The war made him a stronger person, he believes. 'It made me more tolerant. Even those people I don't like I tolerate and try to be nice to them.'[8]

Like most of the POWs, John Van Nooten, the young lieutenant who had played such a crucial role in the survival of the men on Ambon, was dead now. After the war his commercial life had taken him to Japan, where he had forged several strong business relationships. 'Some of my greatest pleasures now are going back to Japan, which is a beautiful country,' he said in 1982. 'We should never forget the bastardry that was perpetrated, but I don't think we should let it poison us for ever.'[9]

They were sensible and forgiving sentiments from a man who had every reason to hate his former foe. But, as with so many of the survivors I talked to and read about, there was no longer a desire for vengeance. The war was history and the enemy had been pardoned.

Many of those who played such key roles in the life of Gull Force returned to Australia determined to lead peaceful lives in suburban anonymity. And who could blame them?

After the war crimes trials on Morotai, George de Verdon Westley went back to Melbourne and wed a well-known local singer, Winifred Gardner. It was a marriage that might have been made in heaven. 'I can't remember the time when we didn't know each other,' the mezzo-soprano confided to the *Argus* in April 1946. After all the physical and emotional turmoil – and the bruised reputation – he had endured over the previous few years, it was time to seek sanctuary in a life of domestic bliss.

Another Gull Force veteran, Ron Leech, who had made that perilous escape from the Hainan POW camp with Ian Macrae, found it difficult to settle on his return to Sydney's northern beaches. The former professional cyclist and wrestler hit the bottle and spent much of the money he'd accumulated while a POW on drinking and betting. It wasn't until the 1950s that he got his life together again and set up his own business, growing and selling shrubs and seedlings.

The fun-loving and boisterous Leech told *People Magazine*:

I'm not sorry about the lash I had at it though. If a man had saved his money he might have got a good start in life. On the other hand he might have broken out later on and that wouldn't have been so good. I've got something to look forward to here and I'm making it myself.[10]

Ron became a much respected member of the community at home in the Dee Why area where he lived. He helped to found the Harbord Diggers Club and the Manly Swimming Club.[11] He also formed a close friendship with Francesca Werinussa, who had sailed from Ambon to Australia as a refugee and sought asylum. Sadly, Ron died at the age of 90 in 2009, after suffering a stroke at a veterans' care home on Collaroy Plateau, but Fransina would always be in his debt for the help and support he gave her. Today, she is one of many Ambonese who have settled in Australia, thanks to the backing and encouragement of those brave men who fought for the island's liberty in the dark days of 1942 and forged a link which survives today.

Their memory was immortalised in many different ways. Stuart Swanton, whose coded shorthand diary provided such a detailed account of life in Tan Tui, was now also remembered through music. His nephew, Lloyd, a professional musician and composer, still has the viola Stuart played and soon plans to give the instrument its first workout since the 1930s in a suite of pieces which he has composed, inspired by the Ambon story.[12] The diary itself, formerly held by the Australian War Museum in Canberra, found its way back to Melbourne thanks to the efforts of Les Hohl, who handed it to Stuart's father. Lloyd Swanton understood it was decoded by Stuart's youngest brother, Basil, who also knew shorthand.

As for Colonel Roach, the man who might have saved the 2/21st Battalion had his initial warnings about the folly of defending Ambon been heeded, he was made a reserve officer and seems to have disappeared into relative obscurity. He died in 1979. In an intriguing footnote to Roach's early life, it appeared the 2/21st's original commanding officer had had links with the Victorian branch of the secret militia in which William Scott had played a key organisational role in New South Wales. Indeed, it's claimed that Roach was one of three prominent Melbournians who wrote to John Monash, the celebrated Australian First World War military commander, urging him to establish himself as a dictator in the 1930s. But the man regarded as Australia's most popular soldier had soundly disapproved of the idea.[13]

The fact that Roach and Scott shared similar political beliefs and belonged to the same right-wing organisation raises many questions. Did they know each other before the war? Had they fallen out during the days of the secret army? Was a deep-seated rivalry between the two men at the root of Scott's successful campaign to unseat Roach as head of Gull Force? Were they two old enemies who had taken their grievances with them into the Second World War? It was only a theory, but one which could explain Scott's motivation in the period leading up to the debacle that was Ambon.

Appendix

GULL FORCE NOMINAL ROLL

PRIVATE HAROLD GEORGE ADAMS VX52771
PRIVATE HECTOR HILLARY ADAMS VX20413
PRIVATE JAMES WILLIAM ADAMS VX39777
PRIVATE ROBERT GEORGE ADAMS VX24928
PRIVATE KENNETH RANDALL ADAMSON WX9564
PRIVATE FRANK ALAN AINGER VX46424
PRIVATE WALTER AINSBURY VX54991
CAPTAIN WILLIAM AITKEN VX31470
PRIVATE CECIL WILLIAM ALCOCK VX62375
WARRANT OFFICER CLASS 2 KENNETH CHARLES ALDER NX41769
PRIVATE FRANCIS WILLIAM ALFORD VX21884
PRIVATE MUHABEM ALI VX54223
PRIVATE KENNETH GEORGE ALISON VX31030
PRIVATE HARRY RAYMOND ALLEN VX24799
PRIVATE HUBERT WILLIAM ALLEN VX26850
CORPORAL LESLIE ARTHUR EDWARD ALLEN VX50380
SIGNALMAN ROBERT KIRKWOOD ALLEN NX43711
CORPORAL BENJAMIN CHARLES AMOR VX27319
STAFF SERGEANT FREDERICK ANDERSON VX27063
PRIVATE IAN THOMPSON ANDERSON VX27363
PRIVATE NORMAN THOMAS ANDERSON VX39914
LIEUTENANT SAMUEL FISHER ANDERSON VX24574
SAPPER WILLIAM DANIEL ANDERSON QX8279
PRIVATE ARTHUR JOHN ANDREWS VX25644
LANCE CORPORAL GEORGE ANZAC ANSET VX43804
GUNNER JOHN GEOFFREY ARCHER NX38411
PRIVATE HUGH PERCIVAL ARCHIBALD VX60816
PRIVATE EDGAR SAMUEL JOHN ARGUS VX25556
CAPTAIN GARRY O'DELL ARMSTRONG VX44484
PRIVATE JAMES FREDERICK ARMSTRONG VX47338
PRIVATE EDWARD MICHAEL ARNELL VX61683

PRIVATE WILLIAM CHARLES ARROWSMITH VX25305
WARRANT OFFICER CLASS 2 GEORGE ASHTON VX54217
PRIVATE KEITH ASHTON VX50994
PRIVATE DONALD WRIGHT ASHWORTH VX39778
PRIVATE ALFRED KAYCE ATKINS NX42150
PRIVATE MAURICE WILLIAM ATHERTON NX41368
CORPORAL ALISTER HADLEY AULT VX21558
CORPORAL GORDON WILLIAM AUSTIN VX23351
PRIVATE LEO FRANCIS AYERS VX25004
BOMBARDIER GEORGE FREDERICK BACKHAUS VX48328
PRIVATE ROY WILLIAM BACON NX4409
PRIVATE HAROLD BAILEY VX24955
SERGEANT BASIL EDWARD BAKER NX46586
CORPORAL CHARLES WILLIAM BAKER NX57716
SERGEANT DONALD DOUGLAS BAKER NX46064
PRIVATE FREDERICK EDWARD BAKER VX30890
CORPORAL LIONEL JOHN BAKER VX47837
PRIVATE THOMAS LAWSON BAKER VX31877
SERGEANT NORMAN ERNEST BALCAM VX27160
PRIVATE RODNEY MAURICE BALCOMBE VX31626
PRIVATE AUBREY PATRICK BALL VX20327
PRIVATE NORMAN THOMAS BALL VX24793
DRIVER VERDUN CLIVE BALL NX1677
PRIVATE OLIVER JAMES BALLINGER VX45616
PRIVATE PATRICK BALMER VX44654
GUNNER ROGER JAMES FRANCIS BALMER NX56890
PRIVATE CHARLES REGINALD BANKS VX30371
LANCE CORPORAL DONALD NELSON BANKS VX37151
PRIVATE ROY EDGAR BARBOUR VX29882
PRIVATE REX ARTHUR BARCLAY VX26619
GUNNER COLIN DAVID BARNES NX37545
CORPORAL ROBERT GEORGE BARNES VX30295
PRIVATE WILLIAM HENRY BARNES VX38371
PRIVATE DAVID BARR VX57327
SAPPER STEWART JAMES HAY BATCHELOR QX14554
SERGEANT FREDERICK STANLEY BATES NX46703
PRIVATE MATTHEW BAYFIELD VX53364
PRIVATE HAROLD WILLIAM BEAMSLEY VX28646
CORPORAL ALAN BEATTIE VX36931
CORPORAL RONALD EDGAR BEATTIE VX25019
PRIVATE FREDERICK FRANCIS BEEL VX26813
PRIVATE JAMES ANDREW BEGNONE VX26768
PRIVATE RONALD JAMES BEGNONE VX26767
PRIVATE HENRY BELL VX61155
PRIVATE IAN PALMER BELL VX39920
PRIVATE MERVYN JOHN BEMROSE NX49933
PRIVATE HAROLD WILLIAM BENBOW VX66260
PRIVATE ARNOLD LEONARD BENDLE VX54577
PRIVATE EDWARD THOMAS BENNETT VX22078

PRIVATE RONALD ANDREW BENNETT VX61150
LANCE CORPORAL LAWRENCE DAVID BENVIE VX38728
PRIVATE LEON ALFRED BERLINER VX65015
CORPORAL GEORGE BERRY VX27229
LANCE CORPORAL MAXWELL JERMAN BETHERAS VX65060
PRIVATE THOMAS GEORGE BETTS VX21711
PRIVATE ALFRED WILLIAM BEYNON VX62076
PRIVATE FRANK ALBERT BIDDISCOMBE VX39741
WARRANT OFFICER CLASS 1 JOHN GRAHAM PEMBERTON BILLING VX38726
PRIVATE NORMAN BIRCH VX26617
CORPORAL CLARENCE RUPERT BLACKNEY VX26551
PRIVATE ANDREW BLACKWOOD VX60604
PRIVATE WILLIAM JAMES BLAKE VX30407
LANCE CORPORAL WALTER AUGUSTUS BLANKS VX31646
CORPORAL LEON BLIGHT VX47866
PRIVATE RAYMOND GEORGE BOAK VX31813
CORPORAL SPERRY BODSWORTH VX23435
PRIVATE ALAN CLAUDE BOLDING VX25024
PRIVATE MURRAY ARNOLD BOLDING VX25018
PRIVATE CYRIL ROBERT ASHLEIGH BOLTON VX65678
PRIVATE THOMAS ARTHUR BOLTON VX26315
PRIVATE VERNON BOLWELL VX31547
PRIVATE FRANCIS BOND VX39767
PRIVATE PERCY EDWARD BOREHAM NX7323
CORPORAL DAVID ROY BORRIE VX19295
PRIVATE WILLIAM ARTHUR KEITH BOULTON VX41612
PRIVATE HAROLD JOHN BOWRAN VX61272
CORPORAL CLIFFORD VERNON BOYCE VX23491
PRIVATE WILLIAM FRANCIS BOYCE VX25109
PRIVATE EDWIN BOYLE VX27402
PRIVATE HENRY JOHN BRAETER VX39738
CORPORAL KEVIN ALEXANDER BRAITHWAITE VX38948
PRIVATE ALBERT WARBURTON BRANSON VX25068
PRIVATE REGINALD BRASSEY VX31517
PRIVATE ALEXANDER FRANCIS BREEN VX23014
PRIVATE FRANCIS ALMA BRENNAN VX61692
LANCE CORPORAL DAVID VINCENT GODWIN BREWER QX10484
PRIVATE WALTER HARRY BRIGGS VX39765
PRIVATE DANIEL BRISLANE VX42780
PRIVATE NEIL BLYTHE BROMLEY VX37155
PRIVATE WILLIAM MORRIS BROOKES VX43142
PRIVATE CYRIL OSWALD BROOKSHAW VX31629
PRIVATE ALLAN THOMAS BROWN VX44659
PRIVATE DOUGLAS RICHMOND BROWN NX47729
PRIVATE GEOFFREY WILLIAM BROWN VX61319
PRIVATE GEORGE THOMAS BROWN VX23251
PRIVATE JOSEPH HENRY BROWN VX25072
CORPORAL LESLIE HAYES BROWN VX31288
LANCE CORPORAL NEVILLE WILLIAM BROWN VX50352

PRIVATE RAYMOND CLYDE BROWN VX24803
SERGEANT RAYMOND HENRY BROWN VX15894
PRIVATE TREVOR BROWN VX24480
CORPORAL VICTOR BROWN VX44439
PRIVATE ALLAN LYNTON BROWNLEY NX46670
LANCE CORPORAL HAROLD JOSEPH BRUNSDON VX30720
PRIVATE ROBERT WILLIAMS BRYANS VX53793
SAPPER JAMES STEWART BRYANT QX8038
PRIVATE ALEXANDER JAMES BUCHANAN VX54497
PRIVATE ARCHIBALD DONALD BUCHANAN VX41748
PRIVATE PERCY JAMES BUCKLAND VX55003
PRIVATE ERNEST LESLIE BUCKLEY VX24940
PRIVATE VICTOR ARNOLD BULL VX59610
SIGNALMAN ALAN ARTHUR BURCHER NX48335
PRIVATE ALBERT CHARLES HENRY BURN VX29415
CAPTAIN JACK ROWLAND BURNS NX70405
PRIVATE JOHN BRUCE NX46347
PRIVATE JOHN BURRAGE VX53620
SERGEANT BRENDAN PATRICK BYRNE NX20111
PRIVATE KEVIN BYRNE VX59505
PRIVATE HENRY JAMES CABLE VX27275
LIEUTENANT MAGNUS MAXTON HENRY CALDER VX36750
PRIVATE MELVIN CALDER VX46865
PRIVATE JOHN WILLIAM CALLOW VX26866
SERGEANT ALLEN CAMERON VX42522
PRIVATE RONALD ARTHUR CAMERON VX66583
PRIVATE DOUGLAS GEORGE CAMPBELL NX42202
LIEUTENANT EDWARD PARKYN OSWALD CAMPBELL NX35042
CORPORAL GORDON CHESTERMAN CAMPBELL VX25320
PRIVATE HENRY MICHAEL CAMPBELL VX31038
PRIVATE STUART DALLAS CAMPBELL VX39768
CORPORAL RODERICK JOHN CAMPBELL VX20008
PRIVATE JOHN CANT VX32027
PRIVATE JOHN CANVERT VX27141
PRIVATE JOSEPH ARTHUR CAPON VX31858
PRIVATE BERNARD JOSEPH CARLAND VX61138
PRIVATE FRANK CHARLIE CARLSON VX54900
CORPORAL AUSTIN CARR VX30281
BOMBARDIER MALCOLM LINDSAY HAMILTON CARTER NX45330
PRIVATE NOEL CARTER NX42634
PRIVATE THOMAS CARTER VX26791
PRIVATE WILLIAM KINGSLEY CARTER VX38885
PRIVATE LEONARD HENRY CARTWRIGHT VX39928
CORPORAL JOHN LAWRENCE CASSIDY VX36286
LANCE CORPORAL THOMAS JAMES CASTLES NX37778
PRIVATE MAXWELL HENRY CAUSON VX24953
PRIVATE GUY CAWTHORNE VX54374
PRIVATE JOHN CHAFER VX30820
SERGEANT CECIL ARTHUR CHAFFEY VX23596

LIEUTENANT WILLIAM JOHN CHAPLIN GM VX46446
SAPPER EDWARD BARTHOLEMEW CHAPMAN QX17391
CAPTAIN WILFRID ALEXANDER MANIACHI CHAPMAN VX45199
PRIVATE ROBERT LYNLEY CHARLICK VX24030
PRIVATE JOHN EDWARD CHELL NX28484
PRIVATE ARTHUR HENRY CHENOWETH VX66901
PRIVATE JOHN KELVIE CHESTERS VX67750
WARRANT OFFICER CLASS 1 ALEXANDER CHEW MBE VX45931
PRIVATE WILLIAM BERESFORD CHIBNALL VX39948
PRIVATE LAURIE ALEXANDER CHILD VX39743
CORPORAL JOHN WILLIAM CHUGG VX39748
PRIVATE FRANK GEORGE CLARE VX54650
PRIVATE ARTHUR ETHELBERT CLARK VX34669
SERGEANT HORACE EDWARD CLARK NX42030:N27594
CORPORAL THOMAS WALKER CLARK VX40495
CRAFTSMAN GEOFFREY CLAYBROUGH NX42732
PRIVATE VICTOR GEORGE CLAXTON VX40878
PRIVATE DONALD JOSEPH WILLIAM CLEGG VX30260
PRIVATE HECTOR ROLLAND CLELAND VX24399
CORPORAL ALFRED CHARLES CLERKE VX23112
PRIVATE KENNETH BASIL COATES VX30822
CAPTAIN VINCENT ERNEST COCHRANE VX60727
PRIVATE HENRY WILLIAM COE VX25021
CORPORAL ARTHUR THOMAS COFIELD VX61676
CORPORAL ALFRED GEORGE COLE VX25246
PRIVATE ROBERT WILLIAM COLEE VX39996
PRIVATE ARNOLD JAMES COLLINS NX58046
SAPPER DANIEL JOHN COLLINS QX14731
PRIVATE GEORGE FREDERICK COLLINS VX50037
SAPPER HAROLD SYDNEY COLLINS QX10394
PRIVATE STANLEY CHARLES COLLINS VX62472
SAPPER WALTER HERBERT COLLINS QX10196
PRIVATE ARTHUR NORMAN COMBEN VX26251
PRIVATE CHARLES JOHN COMBER NX43718
PRIVATE THOMAS CONNELLAN VX30410
PRIVATE ROBERT CONNLEY VX27271
PRIVATE ROY CONNORS VX60505
GUNNER THOMAS EDMUND CONNORS NX47290
PRIVATE WILLIAM COOK VX24835
PRIVATE PERCY COOK NX4369
PRIVATE WILLIAM JOHN COOK VX47579
PRIVATE LESLIE WALTER COOKE VX32390
PRIVATE ROBERT THOMAS COOKE VX26300
CORPORAL JEFFERY FRANCIS COOKESLEY VX39910
SAPPER CHARLIE COOMBS QX11042
PRIVATE LESLIE GEORGE CORNELL VX39990
PRIVATE RAYMOND COSTIN VX31882
PRIVATE ERNEST JAMES COUSINS NX46202
PRIVATE ERNEST ARTHUR COWELL VX25082

PRIVATE SYDNEY JOHN COWELL VX25079
PRIVATE WILLIAM COWELL VX44128
PRIVATE ALEXANDER GEORGE COWLING NX46069
PRIVATE HARVEY BLAXLAND COWLING NX46066
SERGEANT FREDERICK LEWIS CRABB VX27172
PRIVATE CHARLES JOSEPH CRABBE VX31044
PRIVATE MURRAY HERBERT CRABBE VX60421
SERGEANT JOHN RAYMOND HENRY CRAIG NX53548
PRIVATE FREDERICK GORDON CRANE VX66408
PRIVATE MERTON LANGLEY CRANE NX38113
SERGEANT GEORGE WILLIAM CRAY VX42530
PRIVATE JACK CRILLY VX38959
LANCE SERGEANT RAYMOND MAXWELL CROFT QX17397
PRIVATE ALBERT CROSHER VX30408
PRIVATE FRANCIS LOUIS CROSS VX25156
LANCE CORPORAL RONALD FREDERICK JAMES CROSS VX26946
PRIVATE EDWARD GEORGE CROSSLEY VX65028
LANCE SERGEANT CHARLES ALBERT CROUCH VX30793
PRIVATE SIDNEY THOMAS CROWE VX54316
CORPORAL ALAN LINTERN CROWTHER QX17389
SAPPER KENNETH JAMES CULLEN NX4407
PRIVATE JOHN ROBERT CULTON VX65540
CRAFTSMAN GEORGE TERRILL CURRAN NX42384
PRIVATE REGINALD CURTIN VX52454
LANCE CORPORAL HERBERT LANCE DAFF VX31477
SERGEANT WILLIAM CHARLES DAHLBERG VX47355
PRIVATE LINDSAY DALTON VX31037
PRIVATE WILLIAM GEORGE DARBY VX39771
PRIVATE ALAN FINDLAY DAVIDSON VX25985
CORPORAL NORMAN ANDREW DAVIDSON VX50344
CAPTAIN PETER MCLEAN DAVIDSON QX6476
LIEUTENANT JOHN LESLIE DAVIS VX44353
PRIVATE LAWRENCE JOHN DAVIS VX45251
PRIVATE ARTHUR THOMAS DEAKIN VX24977
DRIVER RONALD THOMAS DEAN VX27301
PRIVATE NEIL TELFORD DENGATE NX71262
PRIVATE JOSEPH WILLIAM DERBYSHIRE VX27169
PRIVATE ALBERT JAMES DERMODY VX42444
PRIVATE JACK DEVENISH WX10861
PRIVATE LEON LESLIE DEVERE VX27313
PRIVATE HENRY JOSEPH DEVERS VX50334
PRIVATE RONALD JOSEPH DEVLIN NX7377
PRIVATE JOHN ALFRED DEW VX39705
PRIVATE COLIN LLOYD DICKSON NX37767
CORPORAL HARRY DIGNEY VX60812
CORPORAL FREDERIC PATRICK DIHOOD VX32431
PRIVATE SYDNEY GEORGE DOBBYN VX30941
PRIVATE EDWARD WILLIAM DOCKING VX27127
SAPPER WILLIAM DODDS QX22862

PRIVATE GEORGE DOLL VX46656
PRIVATE DOUGLAS JAMES DONALD VX30990
PRIVATE BRIAN DONOVAN VX58655
PRIVATE GERALD FRANCIS DOOLAN VX24064
PRIVATE WILLIAM THOMAS DOOLAN VX35406
PRIVATE JAMES MICHAEL DOOLEY VX31127
PRIVATE TERENCE DORGAN VX25239
PRIVATE JOHN LEWIS DORRINGTON VX26377
PRIVATE ERNEST JOHN DOYLE VX62349
PRIVATE JAMES DANIEL DOYLE VX59981
PRIVATE JAMES FRANCIS DOYLE VX60952
LIEUTENANT HAROLD FREDRICK DRANE VX37080
PRIVATE CECIL HORACE ALFRED DREW NX59797
CORPORAL LAURIE KNIGHT DRUMMOND VX30893
PRIVATE JAMES THOMAS DRUMMY VX31281
PRIVATE JOHN CARL AUGUST DUDDY VX23852
STAFF SERGEANT JAMES FREDERICK DUNCAN VX36074
PRIVATE TERENCE GEORGE DUNCAN VX39757
PRIVATE CHARLES FREDERICK DYER VX60120
PRIVATE JOHN DAVID ECKERT NX41281
LANCE SERGEANT KIERAN RICHARD EDDINGTON VX24981
LANCE CORPORAL JACK ROLAND EDMONDS VX31901
PRIVATE ALFRED WILLIAM EDWARDS VX62389
SIGNALMAN ERIC VERNON EDWARDS VX25404
PRIVATE LESLIE EDWARDS VX67222
PRIVATE NOEL ROSS ELITH NX37751
SERGEANT FRANCIS HERBERT ELLIOTT NX37068
PRIVATE JOHN THOMAS ELLIOTT NX37770
PRIVATE JAMES EDWARD ELLIS VX21573
PRIVATE NOEL ERNEST ELLIS Q132018
PRIVATE NORMAN ARTHUR ELLIS VX32197
PRIVATE NORMAN TREVOR ELLIS VX61195
PRIVATE JAMES FREDERICK ELMORE VX66131
PRIVATE LEONARD ELSEGOOD QX7760
SERGEANT PERCY HENRY FREDERICK ELSUM VX20324
PRIVATE CYRIL ENGLER VX54181
PRIVATE GUSTAV ERIC ERICSON VX32078
CORPORAL GORDON ESCOTT
PRIVATE CHRISTOPHER ALBERT ETHERTON VX42454
PRIVATE DAVID ANDREW EVANS VX51737
CORPORAL JOHN JAMES EVANS VX31857
PRIVATE ROBERT WILLIAM EVERETT VX30543
PRIVATE JOHN THOMAS FAIRBAIRN VX61545
PRIVATE LESLIE JOSEPH FAIRBROTHER VX31121
PRIVATE WILLIAM GEORGE JOHN FALKINGBRIDGE-WHITE VX39754
PRIVATE GARRETT SWANSON FARRELL VX30879
PRIVATE CHARLES HENRY FAULKNER VX46434
PRIVATE CHARLES TREVOR FEATHERSTONE VX46200
GUNNER TERENCE BELLEW FEE NX56729

SAPPER JAMES FEEKINGS QX17547
PRIVATE CHARLES ARTHUR FEENANE VX25309
SIGNALMAN JACK FELUMB NX34517
CORPORAL ARTHUR HARRY FERGUSON VX16156
PRIVATE CYRIL FERNIE NX7345
PRIVATE HUGH REGINALD FERRARI VX30895
STAFF SERGEANT JAMES MOULTON FIDDIAN VX45431
CORPORAL BRUCE ERNEST RICHARD FIELD VX22887
PRIVATE JOHN ROBERT FIELD VX24718
CORPORAL JOHN WILLIAM GERDON FINCHER VX24998
PRIVATE DONALD JOESEPH FINDLAY VX31225
PRIVATE VICTOR JOHN FINDLAY VX31233
SERGEANT NORMAN EDWARD FINN VX20631
PRIVATE CHARLES ARTHUR FISHER VX31769
PRIVATE IVO ROBERT FISHWICK VX20199
PRIVATE THOMAS JOSEPH FLANAGAN NX46547
PRIVATE HEWLETT FLEMING VX39745
GUNNER WILLIAM BIRDWOOD FLEMING NX45364
SAPPER CLIVE BIRDWOOD FLEWELL-SMITH QX10858
PRIVATE WILLIAM FLINTOFT VX32289
GUNNER RAYMOND FLOWER NX53999
PRIVATE ALAN HENRY FLOWERDAY VX61968
LANCE SERGEANT DENIS GREGORY PATRICK FOLEY BEM VX23913
PRIVATE KENNETH FOOTE VX39773
PRIVATE ROBERT HENRY MURDOCH FORD VX39907
SERGEANT JOSEPH THOMAS FORSSMAN VX24943
GUNNER JOSEPH JOHN FORSTER NX56968
CRAFTSMAN KENNETH ERNEST FORWARD WX10869
PRIVATE ERNEST HENRY FOSTER VX25454
PRIVATE PHILLIP NEAL FOULKES VX22511
GUNNER ALAN MALCOLM FOX NX37547
PRIVATE FRANCIS JOHN THOMAS FRAWLEY VX51758
LANCE SERGEANT WILLIAM MONTGOMERY FRICK QX10733
LANCE CORPORAL KENNETH LIONEL FRY VX38953
CORPORAL JAMES CHARLES FURBANK NX52741
ACTING LANCE SERGEANT ROGER CRAWFORD SUTTON FYFE VX43049
CAPTAIN RODNEY CHARLES GABRIEL VX44903
PRIVATE JOHN JOSEPH GALVIN NX42060
PRIVATE GEORGE ERNEST GAMBLING VX19938
PRIVATE BIRDWOOD DOUGLAS GAMBOLD VX23661
SAPPER HAROLD DAVID GANDER QX10747
PRIVATE PATRICK GARVEN VX61189
PRIVATE DESMOND CLIVE GAUNT VX36201
SAPPER JAMES NOEL GEDDES QX17384
LANCE CORPORAL DAVID HECTOR GEE VX26664
PRIVATE GEORGE ALFRED GHERARDIN VX31844
PRIVATE MARIC JEGGO (EDDIE) GILBERT VX31080
SERGEANT KELVIN RAY GILDER VX26511
PRIVATE LEWIS JAMES GILDER VX26504

PRIVATE RONALD GEORGE GILHAM NX42204
SAPPER JAMES FRANK GILL QX9316
SAPPER OWEN GLYNN QX7842
LIEUTENANT RALPH GODFREY VX24681
SERGEANT BARLING GOODALL VX39737
LANCE CORPORAL COLIN CLARENCE WALTER GOODWIN QX10265
PRIVATE FREDERICK WORRAL GOODWIN NX6979
SAPPER HAROLD DONALD GOODWIN QX10266
PRIVATE ROBERT GOODWIN VX27286
PRIVATE WILLIAM CHARLES GOODWIN QX10303
PRIVATE HOUSTON GORDON NX65923
PRIVATE WILLIAM KENNEDY GORDON VX39103
PRIVATE ALBERT THOMAS GOWLAND VX63130
PRIVATE GEORGE STANLEY GOWLAND VX59560
PRIVATE ERNEST STANLEY GOULD VX54939
PRIVATE WILLIAM PLEASS GOVE VX25381
CORPORAL ALBERT JAMES GRADY VX36354
PRIVATE THOMAS GRAHAM VX30928
PRIVATE SYDNEY JAMES GRANT VX54371
PRIVATE ARTHUR ROBERT GRAY VX26339
PRIVATE LEONARD HAROLD GRAY VX54621
SERGEANT LYLE ATKIN GRAY VX52357
LIEUTENANT RONALD JAMES GREEN VX20212
PRIVATE WILLIAM JAMES HOLMES GREEN VX31425
PRIVATE BASIL FRANCIS GREENHAM VX27323
PRIVATE GEORGE THOMAS GREENWOOD VX23066
PRIVATE FRANK LESLIE GREIG VX24336
PRIVATE DALLEY LESLIE GRIFFIN NX67380
CORPORAL JAMES HERBERT GRIFFITHS VX39175
PRIVATE ATHOL RUSSELL MUDIE GRIMISON NX5726
PRIVATE JAMES GROVENOR VX44584
LIEUTENANT ALAN BRAMPTON GROWSE VX45078
PRIVATE DAVID LINDSAY GUEST VX28286
PRIVATE JOHN HENRY GURNEY VX31014
PRIVATE PETER JOSEPH GURRY VX27438
PRIVATE THOMAS GUY VX25396
LIEUTENANT LLOYD FREDERICK HACK QX22449
BOMBARDIER FREDERICK BANNISTER HACKETT NX54061
GUNNER ROBERT MICHAEL HADDON NX26564
PRIVATE KEITH CLEMENT HADDRICK VX26396
LANCE CORPORAL MERVYN JAMES HADLOW VX31437
PRIVATE ALBERT NORMAN HAINES VX44919
PRIVATE BRIAN ALEXANDER EVELYN HALEY VX39736
PRIVATE JOHN CLARENCE HALL NX41321
PRIVATE MORLEY STEPHENSON HALL VX65721
PRIVATE WILLIAM STANLEY HALLIDAY VX27081
CORPORAL STANLEY FRANCIS HALLOWELL VX31253
LANCE SERGEANT JOHN EDWARD HAND VX28945
PRIVATE ROGER FRANCIS HANLON VX39761

PRIVATE ALLAN HANNAH VX53040
SERGEANT EDWARD RAYMOND HANSEN VX46420
PRIVATE JOSEPH HARBINSON VX53909
PRIVATE JAMES ALFRED HARMES VX25136
SERGEANT WILLIAM DAVID HARRIES VX24286
PRIVATE ISAAC WILLIAM ALLAN HARRIS VX39908
PRIVATE JOHN EDWARD HARRIS VX39927
PRIVATE ROY HARRIS VX27312
PRIVATE COURTNEY THOMAS HARRISON VX25325
CORPORAL RAYMOND HECTOR HARRISON VX44574
SERGEANT BRIAN COLEMAN HARRY VX46499
SAPPER MERVYN EDWARD JAMES HART QX22924
LANCE CORPORAL GEORGE NELSON HARVEY VX24935
PRIVATE IAN GEORGE HARVEY VX39951
PRIVATE LESLIE GEORGE HARVEY VX24851
PRIVATE RONALD CHARLES HARVEY VX27234
SERGEANT GEOFFREY THEO HASTIE VX46427
CORPORAL REX HATTERSLEY NX46943
PRIVATE GORDON NEVILLE HAWKES NX42203
PRIVATE ARTHUR ALFRED HAWKING VX40228
LIEUTENANT ALEXANDER STEPHEN HAWKINS VX50008
PRIVATE GERALD AUBREY HAWKINS VX53582
PRIVATE STANLEY ROBERT HAWKSWORTH VX32076
PRIVATE RAYMOND GEORGE CONRAD HAWORTH VX66537
GUNNER WALTER ERNEST HAYDEN NX41297
PRIVATE ALBERT EDWARD HAYES VX22006
PRIVATE JOHN HAYTON VX39739
PRIVATE STANLEY HAZELL VX61335
PRIVATE REGINALD DOUGLAS HAZLEWOOD NX38408
PRIVATE JOHN OAKLEY HEATHCOTE VX57797
PRIVATE BRUCE PITCAIRN HEDDERWICK VX28899
PRIVATE DONALD PATRICK HEENEY VX25002
DRIVER CLARENCE OWEN HEIN VX27320
PRIVATE FREDERICK JOHN HEINTZ VX24926
PRIVATE ROBERT HENDERSON VX66410
PRIVATE JOHN REDMOND HENNESSY VX51133
SAPPER JOHN DOUGLAS HESSION QX9700
PRIVATE DOUGLAS HEWETT VX50064
PRIVATE WALTER DUNSTAN HICKS VX39735
PRIVATE JOHN HIGGINS VX47344
PRIVATE MYLES HIGGINS VX47315
GUNNER ALFRED HIGGS NX37546
PRIVATE JOHN JAMES HILL VX27225
WARRANT OFFICER CLASS 2 SAMUEL HILLIAN NX7305
PRIVATE FREDERICK AUBREY HILLIER VX45436
PRIVATE EDWARD JOHN THOMAS HINCH VX32311
PRIVATE FREDERICK GEORGE HOBBS VX28590
SAPPER JOHN HOBBS QX13885
PRIVATE LESLIE WILLIAM HOCKING VX25441

SAPPER LES PRIVATE WILLIAM ERNEST HODGEN VX31762
PRIVATE EDWARD WILLIAM HOGAN VX32093
SAPPER LESLIE EDWIN HOHL QX5858
PRIVATE EDWARD HOLDSWORTH VX24221
SERGEANT CECIL HOLLIS VX51386
CAPTAIN JOHN EDWIN HOOKE VX44790
PRIVATE THOMAS LAYCOCK HOOKE NX21514
PRIVATE ALBERT SAMSON HOOPER VX54751
PRIVATE LESLIE LYALL HOPKINS VX54980 (ALSO KNOWN AS WILLIAM JOHNSON)
LANCE CORPORAL ERNEST ROY HORKINGS VX31277
LANCE CORPORAL JACK VINCENT HORNER QX16354
PRIVATE ROY EDWIN HOWARD VX27067
PRIVATE ALLAN EDRIC HOWE VX61675
PRIVATE COLIN WILLIAM HOWSE VX39752
PRIVATE REASON ROBERT HUBBARD VX30872
PRIVATE VICTOR FOCH HAIG HUBBARD VX30874
CORPORAL KENNETH ANDREW HUDSON VX25089
CORPORAL ERIC RICHARD HUDSWELL VX24822
PRIVATE WALTER THOMAS HUDSWELL VX24855
PRIVATE CLARENCE IVO HUGHES VS61286
PRIVATE DAVID ARTHUR HUTCHINS VX61202
PRIVATE ERIC EVERARD HUTCHINS VX61201
PRIVATE FRED HUTCHINS VX61203
PRIVATE THOMAS HUTCHINS VX50460
PRIVATE WALTER KEITH HYDE VX28226
PRIVATE ROY SANTILLA HYNES VX47793
DRIVER KENNETH INGRAM NX5494
PRIVATE SYDNEY FREDERICK GEORGE INKSTER VX32393
PRIVATE JOHN HECTOR IRELAND VX50060
CORPORAL DONALD CAMPBELL IRVINE NGX95
SAPPER THOMAS DONAVON ISLES QX14232
COLONEL ALBERT GORDON JACK VX44785
PRIVATE DOUGLAS KENYON JACKSON VX48414
PRIVATE MAXWELL JACKSON VX31357
PRIVATE NOEL JACKSON VX54525
PRIVATE STANLEY ARTHUR JACKSON VX38949
SERGEANT PETER ACLAND JACOBS VX37066
PRIVATE CHARLES PETER JACOBSEN VX24922
LIEUTENANT IAN GORDON JAFFREY VX45190
PRIVATE CHARLES EDMUND JAMES NX7342
PRIVATE HAROLD FRANCIS JAMIESON VX30437
PRIVATE HERBERT ALFRED REGINALD JARVIS VX25834
PRIVATE WILLIAM EDWARD JARVIS VX19962
LANCE CORPORAL ERIC GORDON JAY VX25126
PRIVATE THOMAS BERT JEFFERS VX46513
THOMAS JEFFERY VX31685
SERGEANT THOMAS LEONARD JENKINS VX23587
MAJOR WILLIAM THOMAS JINKINS MBE VX44818

PRIVATE ARTHUR JOHNSON VX26997
WARRANT OFFICER CLASS 2 DONALD JOHNSON VX39936
SAPPER RICHARD WORSTEIN JOHNSON QX14655
PRIVATE SYDNEY GEORGE JOHNSON VX67076
PRIVATE WILLIAM FRANCIS LESLIE JOHNSON VX20839
SIGNALMAN THOMAS STEWART JOHNSTON VX28241
PRIVATE ARTHUR FRANCIS JOLLY VX61730
LANCE CORPORAL ALBERT GEORGE JONES VX44973
PRIVATE FRANCIS RANDOLPH JONES VX30986
PRIVATE GEORGE LAWRENCE JONES VX61857
PRIVATE HERBERT STANLEY JONES VX39918
SAPPER JOHN WILLIAM JONES QX14364
PRIVATE PETER JONES VX31001
PRIVATE FRANCIS HENRY JORDAN VX30836
PRIVATE ROBERT JOHN JOSE VX61162
PRIVATE JOSEPH GEORGE JULIAN NX47715
SERGEANT BRUCE GUSTAVE KAY VX27174
PRIVATE ROBERT JAMES KEATING VX38961
PRIVATE ALEXANDER JAMES KEENAN VX61158
PRIVATE LINDSAY RUSSELL KELLAM VX61271
GUNNER JOHN HENRY KELLETT NX46062
BOMBARDIER THOMAS CURRY KELLETT NX47085
CORPORAL BERNARD MATTHEW KELLY VX42652
STAFF SERGEANT ERIC NORMAN KELLY VX47252
WARRANT OFFICER CLASS 1 FRANCIS JAMES KELLY VX39909
PRIVATE JOHN FRANCIS KELLY VX39953
PRIVATE NICHOLAS TYNONG KELLY VX61703
LANCE CORPORAL ROBERT GEORGE KELLY VX50331
PRIVATE ALAN RICHARD KELSO VX20712
PRIVATE CLYDE JAMES KELTON VX38955
PRIVATE ERIC ARTHUR KENDALL VX38893
SAPPER WILLIAM THOMAS KENDRICK QX22843
SAPPER EDWARD ALBERT GEORGE KENNEDY QX9408
PRIVATE FRANCIS KENNEDY VX53891
PRIVATE FRANCIS EDWARD KENNEDY VX61066
PRIVATE RONALD JAMES KENNEDY VX24915
GUNNER ERNEST WILLIAM HENRY KENNELL NX47242
PRIVATE GORDON KENT VX31876
PRIVATE WALLACE RAY KENT VX37342
PRIVATE ALAN SYDNEY KENWOOD NX47713
PRIVATE LEO JOHN KILMARTIN VX46284
PRIVATE TERENCE JAMES KILMARTIN VX54278
PRIVATE ARTHUR WILLIAM KING VX61762
PRIVATE KEITH LEONARD KING NX42728
PRIVATE JAMES TIMOTHY KINNAIRD VX61755
PRIVATE WILLIAM JOSEPH KIRKMAN VX24846
PRIVATE GEORGE HERBERT KISSICK VX40359
PRIVATE EDWARD THOMAS KITCHENHAM VX30979
PRIVATE HAROLD STRACHAN KITSON VX23324

PRIVATE JACK BLYTH KNIGHT VX28252
PRIVATE ROBERT KEITH KNIPE NX67288
PRIVATE WILLIAM STANLEY KNUCKEY VX30871
PRIVATE RONALD CECIL KOFOED VX30817
PRIVATE CLIFFORD LACEY VX32378
PRIVATE PAUL JOSEPH LAFFERTY VX42265
PRIVATE LESLIE LAMB VX27095
CORPORAL ARTHUR FREDERICK CHARLES LAND VX25317
PRIVATE JOHN JAMES LANGER VX44661
SAPPER ALFRED GEORGE LAPHAM NGX97
PRIVATE ALFRED GEORGE LAPPIN VX42276
PRIVATE BARNET LARKIN VX37430
PRIVATE JOHN DESMOND LARKINS NX38362
PRIVATE RUSSELL JOHN LAVERY VX44985
PRIVATE HARRY LAWRENCE VX25605
CORPORAL WILLIAM LAWS NX41939
PRIVATE KENNETH FRANCIS LAWSON VX43808
PRIVATE FREDERICK JOSEPH LAWTHER VX61298
LIEUTENANT SAMUEL ALEXANDER LAZARUS VX19346
PRIVATE CHARLES JOHN LE MASURIER VX20703
LANCE CORPORAL RICHARD STANLEY LEA QX16410
PRIVATE WILLIAM JAMES LEAHY VX44662
PRIVATE NEIL GILBERT LEARY VX31766
PRIVATE VINCENT ANTHONY LEBEN NX47722
PRIVATE FRANCIS ALAN LEDWIDGE VX44668
SAPPER EDWARD GEORGE LEE QX11385
PRIVATE EDWARD HENRY LEE VX31311
PRIVATE HERBERT FRANCIS LEE VX19761
STAFF SERGEANT ROBERT JOHN LEECH NX65948
PRIVATE GEORGE SYDNEY LEES VX44729
PRIVATE HENRY JAMES LEGG VX27633
SIGNALMAN RICHARD ARTHUR LEISHMAN NX66341
PRIVATE JOHN LESLIE VX30942
PRIVATE MICHAEL LESLIE VX42504
PRIVATE ALLAN JAMES LETCHER VX50425
PRIVATE FRANCIS FREDERICK LEWIN VX31016
DRIVER ALLAN RANKING LEWIS VX26811
LANCE SERGEANT HAROLD THOMAS LEWIS VX31802
PRIVATE JOHN BARTON LEWIS VX26874
PRIVATE ROBERT ERNEST LISTON VX44633
PRIVATE JOHN LITAIZE VX44175
PRIVATE JOHN RONALD LIVY VX30094
LANCE CORPORAL GEORGE GORDON LOCARNINI VX25649
PRIVATE CLARENCE EDWARD LOCK VX30891
LANCE CORPORAL HAROLD REGINALD LOCK VX30885
PRIVATE THOMAS LOCKWOOD VX39919
LANCE CORPORAL FREDERICK CROTTY LONERGAN VX31484
SERGEANT AIDAN HENRY MOUNTJOY LONG VX37077
CORPORAL ROY FREDERICK LONG VX19282

CAPTAIN KENNETH JAMES LOUGHMAN VX45914
PRIVATE GEORGE HOWARD LOUGHNAN VX26965
PRIVATE BENJAMIN LOVE VX24640
LANCE SERGEANT BRUCE LOVE NX53808
PRIVATE BRENDEN JOSEPH LOVERIDGE VX38958
PRIVATE JOHN JOSEPH LOWRIE VX31422
PRIVATE WHITLEY PRESTON LUCAS NX41245
SERGEANT KENNETH EDWARD LUPSON VX37365
PRIVATE WILLIAM STANLEY LYNCH VX27245
PRIVATE COLIN CAMPBELL MACDONALD VX31226
CORPORAL FRANCIS JAMES MACDONALD VX45915
LIEUTENANT MURRAY HAY MACDOWELL VX22291
PRIVATE WILLIAM BERNARD MACK VX53703
SERGEANT EOIN MACKINTOSH MACKECHNIE VX22417
PRIVATE DONALD FRAZER MACKINNON NX47595
LANCE CORPORAL ALEXANDER DOUGLAS MACKIE VX25991
LANCE CORPORAL BREARLEY ROBERT MACKIESON VX26329
PRIVATE EDGAR CHARLES MACKLAN VX29535
LANCE CORPORAL VIVIAN JAMES MACKLAN VX29541
PRIVATE GORDON ALEXANDER MACQUEEN VX40447
PRIVATE HARVEY JOHN BOOTH MACRAE VX41940
MAJOR IAN FARQUHAR MACRAE OBE VX44787
PRIVATE GEROGE CHARLES MAETZE VX23585
PRIVATE WILLIAM ARTHUR MAHER VX24715
PRIVATE HOWARD ERNEST MAILE VX39766
CAPTAIN JAMES FRANK MAJOR VX44506
PRIVATE RONALD WILLIAM MALLETT NX42681
PRIVATE BRIAN MATHEW MANNIX VX58585
PRIVATE WILLIAM VINCENT MARDEN NX39656
CORPORAL JOHN STANLEY MARSH VX26342
CAPTAIN GORDON CARLYLE MARSHALL VX39263
PRIVATE ALLAN JAMES WILLIAM MARTIN VX31202
PRIVATE HAROLD ROBERT MARTIN VX37156
SERGEANT LESLIE EDMUND MARTIN VX28878
PRIVATE MICHAEL MARTIN VX53933
PRIVATE HARRY GIBSON MARWICK VX24723
PRIVATE ALEXANDER JOHN MASON VX44681
PRIVATE ALEXANDER PERCY MASON VX50020
PRIVATE ALFRED JOHN MASON VX26745
PRIVATE IAN KEITH MATHESON VX25398
PRIVATE KENNETH THOMAS MATHESON VX42658
LIEUTENANT ROBERT JOHN MATHEWS VX39058
BOMBARDIER LINDSAY SYDNEY MATTHEWS NX56562
MAJOR IAN HALBERT MCBRIDE MBE VX44612
STAFF SERGEANT ROBERT AUSTIN MCCALLUM VX39666
PRIVATE ALBERT JOHN MCCOOMB VX43298
PRIVATE THOMAS NEIL MCCOOMB VX30770
PRIVATE FRANK MCCORMACK VX44559
PRIVATE ROBERT MCCRACKEN VX39998

PRIVATE CHARLES BERNARD MCCUSKER VX23306
CORPORAL FELIX ARTHUR MCDERMOTT VX2291
PRIVATE DAVID MALCOLM MCDONALD VX44775
CORPORAL ROSS PHILLIP MCDONALD VX48136
SERGEANT CHARLES G. MCDOUGALL NX42265
PRIVATE JAMES EDWARD MCDOUGALL VX27144
PRIVATE JOHN JAMES MCDOUGALL VX25995
CORPORAL HERBERT STANISLAUS MCEVOY NX55934
LIEUTENANT ARTHUR MCGEORGE VX30829
CORPORAL WILLIAM MCGREGOR VX27332
PRIVATE THOMAS ARTHUR JOHN MCGUINNESS VX61745
PRIVATE DAVID STEWART MCILWRAITH VX27240
LANCE CORPORAL ALEXANDER DOUGLAS MCINTOSH VX45054
PRIVATE NEIL DONALD MCINTOSH VX31028
PRIVATE TOM MCINTYRE VX66329
LANCE CORPORAL NEIL MCKELLAR VX35499
PRIVATE CHARLES GEORGE MCKENZIE VX53777
PRIVATE HECTOR MCKENZIE VX54290
PRIVATE RAYMOND CHARLES MCKENZIE VX26680
SAPPER COLIN MCKINLAY QX16564
PRIVATE CLIFTON ALEXANDER MCLACHLAN NX72591
SERGEANT MACK HALLORAN MCLACHLAN NX40097
LANCE CORPORAL BERNARD SAMUEL MCLAUGHLIN VX31898
PRIVATE BERNARD LINDSAY MCLEAVY VX21674
PRIVATE JOSEPH MURPHY MCLEISH VX25452
CORPORAL JAMES MCMILLAN MCLENNAN VX27242
PRIVATE GREGOR DRUMMOND MCLEOD VX25923
PRIVATE JACK RONALD MCLEOD VX45521
PRIVATE FRANK JAMES MCMAHON VX51289
PRIVATE GRAHAM MCMAHON VX26805
SERGEANT JACK LAWRENCE MCMAHON VX50379
SERGEANT JOHN ARTHUR MCMAHON VX25029
PRIVATE JOHN VINCENT MCMAHON VX30945
SAPPER WILLIAM MEIKLE MCMURTRIE QX18497
SIGNALMAN RONALD WILLIAM MCPHERSON VX30670
PRIVATE GEORGE ROBERT MEAGHER VX64017
PRIVATE LESLIE MEAGHER VX53185
PRIVATE THOMAS IVAN MEIKLE VX23599
LIEUTENANT JAMES KEITH MELLOR VX46431
PRIVATE HARRY COLIN MELVIN VX55194
PRIVATE RAYMOND ANDREW MENDOLA VX23591
PRIVATE RONALD ALEXANDER MENZIES VX53604
PRIVATE STEPHEN ARNOLD MERLO VX24673
PRIVATE STEWART ARTHUR MERRY VX27422
PRIVATE RICHARD HEWITT MEYER VX19202
PRIVATE JOHN ROSKELL MILBURN VX39747
PRIVATE ALBERT MARTIN MILES VX44323
PRIVATE HAROLD MILLAR VX39425
PRIVATE GEORGE ERNEST MILLIST VX26510

PRIVATE ARTHUR JAMES MILLS VX62393
PRIVATE CYRIL MAYNARD MILLS VX54997
PRIVATE PERCY OLIVER MILLS VX22055
LIEUTENANT PHILIP PERCY MISKIN VX44795
LIEUTENANT RONALD ELLIS MISKIN VX44804
SAPPER RONALD MILNER QX12156
CORPORAL HARRY WILLIAM MITCHELL VX26263
PRIVATE JACK MOLLOY VX54829
STAFF SERGEANT GILBERT GEORGE MOLONY VX22537
PRIVATE CLAUDE JOHN HERMAN MONK VX26545
PRIVATE REGINALD WADE MONK VX24622
PRIVATE ALEXANDER MORGAN VX42639
PRIVATE JAMES MORGAN VX24245
PRIVATE KEITH THOMAS MOODY VX53614
SAPPER PATRICK JOHN MOONEY QX12429
PRIVATE ALEXANDER THOMAS MOORE VX28690
PRIVATE FRANK EDWARD MOORE VX26514
PRIVATE GERALD WALTER MOORE VX23769
PRIVATE JOHN PATRICK MORAN VX30717
CORPORAL ALLAN MORRIS VX38634
PRIVATE GODFREY MORGAN MORRIS VX31478
PRIVATE WILLIAM SYDNEY MORRIS VX30920
PRIVATE CHARLES WILLIAM MORRISON VX37159
LANCE CORPORAL CLEMENT WILLIAM MORRISON VX40442
PRIVATE JAMES BERTRAM MORRISON NX66149
SAPPER JOHN MORRISON QX10714
PRIVATE JACK MORROW VX31160
PRIVATE RAYMOND ROY MORTON VX22821
LANCE CORPORAL ALLAN ROY MUIR VX43152
PRIVATE CLIVE MULLER VX16539
CORPORAL LINDSAY MUMMERY VX30970
PRIVATE DAVID RICHARD MUNNERLEY VX31184
PRIVATE ALAN THOMAS MURNANE VX43008
PRIVATE DONALD ROSS MURRAY VX45697
CORPORAL WILLIAM JOSEPH NAGLE VX24762
PRIVATE DONALD ROY NEAVE VX27303
CORPORAL JOHN HENRY NELSON VX44200
SAPPER BEAUMONT EDWIN NEVILLE QX10762
MAJOR MARK WILLIAM HORTON NEWBURY VX43876
PRIVATE WILFRED THOMAS NEWELL VX44622
PRIVATE HAROLD NEWMAN VX62557
PRIVATE JOHN EDWARD NEWMAN VX51323
PRIVATE PETER HENRY NEWSOME VX21834
PRIVATE HERBERT NEWTON VX61878
CAPTAIN CLIVE FLORANT NEWNHAM VX44777
PRIVATE MURRAY RAYMOND NICHOLS VX31410
PRIVATE JOSEPH BERNARD NIXON VX55424
LANCE CORPORAL ALFRED MANDEVILLE NOAR VX31176
LANCE CORPORAL CHARLES EDMUND NOAR VX31179

PRIVATE THOMAS RICHARD NOBLE VX31803
PRIVATE DANIEL THOMAS NOONAN VX27000
PRIVATE DANIEL VINCENT NOONAN VX24209
PRIVATE WILLIAM NOONAN VX31287
SAPPER CHARLES ALEC NORMAN QX11324
WARRANT OFFICER CLASS 2 EDWARD CHARLES NORMAN VX38045
SAPPER BERTIE ROBERT NORRIS QX10275
LIEUTENANT ROBERT HARLEY NOWLAND QX19054
STAFF SERGEANT EDWARD JOSEPH NUGENT VX26999
LANCE SERGEANT CLIFFORD HAROLD NYE VX24424
PRIVATE FRANCIS HENRY OAKLEY VX61884
PRIVATE DESMOND LEO O'BRIEN NX44348
SERGEANT JOHN HELLAN O'BRIEN VX31884
PRIVATE LESLIE NORMAN O'BRIEN VX43018
PRIVATE CLARENCE ROY O'BRYAN VX27346
PRIVATE KENNETH ROY KEITH O'BRYAN VX27333
PRIVATE VINCENT RICHARD O'CALLAGHAN VX46561
PRIVATE JOSEPH ALFRED O'CONNOR VX25113
PRIVATE CYRIL GEORGE O'DONNELL VX40002
PRIVATE PATRICK THOMAS O'DONNELL VX27425
PRIVATE PETER JAMES O'DONOGHUE VX39955
CORPORAL ARTHUR THOMAS OGDEN QX9957
PRIVATE FRANK OGILVIE VX43586
PRIVATE CORNELIUS VINCENT O'KEEFE VX61553
PRIVATE JAMES REX O'KEEFE VX27440
SERGEANT KEITH WILLIAM OLIVER VX45438
PRIVATE RONALD ARCHIBALD O'LOUGHLIN VX26843
PRIVATE KEITH KIRKNESS OMOND VX37423
SERGEANT DONALD GERALD O'NEALE VX27187
PRIVATE JOHN ARCHIBALD O'NEILL VX44445
PRIVATE WILLIAM EDWARD ORANGE VX20927
PRIVATE WILLIAM THOMAS ORDISH VX20664
SIGNALMAN DARCY KEITH CLIVE O'REILLY NX21921
PRIVATE ANGUS MCDONALD OSBORN VX27431
CORPORAL MICHAEL FRANCIS OSBORNE VX43727
PRIVATE WILLIAM JOSEPH PAGE VX43215
PRIVATE PERCIVAL HENRY PALMER VX31285
PRIVATE SIDNEY PALMER VX28585
PRIVATE JOHN PANAOTIE VX39981
PRIVATE ARTHUR LEESE PARKER VX23620
PRIVATE ARNOLD KITCHENER PASCOE VX31775
LANCE CORPORAL ROY ALBERT PASCOE VX62562
PRIVATE RAY FRANCIS PATEN VX53701
CHAPLAIN CHARLES HENRY PATMORE VX48124
PRIVATE HUGH HECTOR PATTERSON VX42203
GUNNER ROY ALFRED PAWLEY NX41320
PRIVATE CYRIL NORMAN PAYNTER VX52502
PRIVATE DOUGLAS SAMUEL PAYNTER VX52300
PRIVATE CYRIL RAYMOND PEARCE VX22392

SAPPER ALFRED GEORGE PEARSON QX11190
PRIVATE EDGAR RAYMOND PENNY VX30889
PRIVATE LIONEL JAMES PENNY VX32017
PRIVATE ALFRED GORDON PERRIN VX30870
CAPTAIN DOUGLAS GEORGE PERRY VX44346
PRIVATE EDWARD JOHN PERRY VX39670
PRIVATE RONALD ARTHUR PERRY VX61848
GUNNER EDWARD PETERSON VX67371
PRIVATE WILLIAM ARCHIBALD PETRIE VX41598
GUNNER ABRAHAM CHARLES PETTY NX52875
PRIVATE ALFRED LAWRENCE PETTY VX61595
SAPPER DOUGLAS RICHARD PHILLIPS NGX105
PRIVATE THOMAS PHILLIPS VX25290
PRIVATE WILLIAM JAMES PHILLIPS NX47737
SERGEANT STANLEY CARRINGTON PIGGIN BEM VX24678
PRIVATE WALTER EDWARD PINDER VX21988
PRIVATE DAVID WATSON PINNER VX60325
PRIVATE KEITH ERNEST PITMAN VX31558
GUNNER FREDERICK JOHN PLATT NX46218
CORPORAL ATHOL PLEDGER NX47190
CORPORAL HAROLD LEONARD PLUM VX44694
PRIVATE ERIC LINDSAY PLUMMER VX41858
PRIVATE WILTON ROBERT PLUNKETT VX39903
PRIVATE GEORGE FRANCIS POHLMAN VX39950
LIEUTENANT BARNEY PORTER VX700324
PRIVATE JOHN ALBERT PORTER VX25860
PRIVATE JOHN MELROSE PORTER VX23973
PRIVATE LYELL HENRY PORTHOUSE VX26661
PRIVATE HERBERT FREDERICK POWELL VX60620
PRIVATE FRANCIS EDWARD POWER VX23974
SAPPER GEORGE PRATT QX10876
PRIVATE FREDERICK DENNIS PRETTY VX25364
PRIVATE RONALD STANLEY PRIDEAUX VX53644
PRIVATE FRANCIS JOHN PRINCE VX53664
SAPPER SYDNEY CLARENCE PRINCE QX10323
SAPPER SIDNEY WILLIAM PROUD QX22910
LIEUTENANT GRAHAM RUSSELL PULLIN VX24669
PRIVATE STANLEY FREDERICK PURCHASE VX53272
PRIVATE HENRY ARTHUR PURVIS NX41310
CORPORAL LESLIE OLIVER PYERS NX42145
PRIVATE EDWARD JOHN QUARRELL VX53779
PRIVATE GORDON GEORGE QUIGLEY VX39934
PRIVATE ALBERT JAMES QUINLAN NX973
PRIVATE STANLEY RAINSBURY VX62504
PRIVATE ALLAN JAMES RALPH VX46081
PRIVATE LEONARD WILLIAM RALPH VX39786
PRIVATE ERNEST MALTRAVIS RATCLIFFE VX45863
PRIVATE JOHN LOUDON RAWLING VX38802
PRIVATE ROBERT FRANCIS REDDICK VX31229

LIEUTENANT FRANK ALFRED ERNEST REDHEAD VX51729
PRIVATE RICHARD REDWOOD VX25067
PRIVATE GARNET GEORGE REED VX31274
PRIVATE WILLIAM REDMOND REIDY VX60733
PRIVATE WILLIAM JOHN LANGTREE REILLY VX40295
PRIVATE ALEXANDER RAYMOND REYNOLDS VX54943
PRIVATE JOHN BRUCE RICHARDSON VX27200
PRIVATE LYALL EDGAR RICHARDSON VX28705
PRIVATE SYDNEY JAMES RIDDOCH VX44303
CORPORAL CLEMENT JAMES RIGHETTI VX39753
PRIVATE ALLAN MAURICE RIGNEY VX30894
PRIVATE WILLIAM RIPPER VX24941
PRIVATE CHARLES EDWARD RIVETT VX27338
LIEUTENANT COLONEL LEONARD NAIRN ROACH VX41587
PRIVATE ARCHIBALD FREDERICK ROBERTS VX44381
PRIVATE GEORGE ERNEST ROBERTS VX39906
SAPPER GEORGE HENRY ROBERTS QX15210
PRIVATE ALEXANDER ROBERTSON VX26821
PRIVATE GAVIN JOSEPH ROBERTSON VX27263
PRIVATE JAMES EWEN ROBERTSON VX27262
PRIVATE JOHN ROBERTSON VX26780
PRIVATE HENRY JOSEPH ROBILLIARD VX27409
LANCE SERGEANT CHARLES FREDERICK ROBINSON VX26779
SAPPER HARRY ORDE ROBINSON QX16243
SAPPER HENRY ROBINSON VX39930
PRIVATE THOMAS MAURICE ROBINSON QX19016
PRIVATE HAROLD RAYMOND RODGERS VX20678
PRIVATE ANTHONY JAMES ROGERS VX39978
CORPORAL FRANCIS MICHAEL ROGERS NX42530
SAPPER JACK ROSE QX16485
CAPTAIN SAMUEL ALBERT ROSE NX35057
PRIVATE GORDON MCKIDD ROSS VX25978
CORPORAL ERIC CYRIL FERGUS ROWE NX37747
CORPORAL RICHARD ROWE VX22168
DRIVER JOHN ALBERT VICTOR ROWLAND NX72105
PRIVATE LEWIS HARRISON GEORGE ROY VX30880
CORPORAL CHARLES FRANCIS RUBIE QX10325
CAPTAIN ROLAND OSWALD DYSON RUDDER NX76229
PRIVATE OSCAR JOHN RUNDLE NX42169
LANCE CORPORAL ALBERT OLLEY RUSH QX16277
SAPPER ERNEST ALBERT RUSH DX660
PRIVATE ARTHUR HOLTHAM RUSSELL VX25258
LIEUTENANT GEORGE TOUZEL RUSSELL VX46435
PRIVATE IAN WALTER RUSSELL VX25261
PRIVATE JOHN OWEN CLARKE RUSSELL VX27157
SERGEANT PATRICK KYRAN RUSSELL VX28829
PRIVATE HENRY EDWARD RUSSELL-TALBOT VX25415
GUNNER ALBERT JOHN RUTHERFORD NX47569
PRIVATE JOHN JOSEPH RYAN VX27283

PRIVATE LAURENCE JAMES RYAN VX53328
WARRANT OFFICER CLASS 2 MILTON RYAN VX43614
PRIVATE THOMAS JOHN RYAN VX25437
PRIVATE THOMAS LAWRENCE RYDING VX44377
PRIVATE WILLIAM JAMES SAMSON VX32128
PRIVATE BUILTH HAMILTON SAMUEL VX38636
PRIVATE GEORGE HAMILTON SANDS VX61547
MAJOR DONALD ALEXANDER SANDY VX44354
PRIVATE THOMAS GEORGE SARGENT VX66113
PRIVATE GORDON JOHN SAUNDERS VX26025
PRIVATE VINCENT CHARLES SAUNDERS VX61819
PRIVATE FREDERICK NORMAN SCHAEFER VX19415
PRIVATE AUGUST ERNEST SCHORBACK VX31275
PRIVATE ROBERT GEORGE DENIS SCHWENCKE VX65258
PRIVATE CLARENCE PERCIVAL SCOTT VX25950
STAFF SERGEANT HARRY MCKENNA SCOTT VX37328
PRIVATE NELSON AUSTIN SCOTT VX24863
LIEUTENANT COLONEL WILLIAM JOHN RENDEL SCOTT VX71997
LIEUTENANT EDWARD NEVILLE SEABROOK VX46491
PRIVATE JOHN LESLIE GORDON SEARANT NX40912
PRIVATE HERBERT SEDGEWICK VX20162
PRIVATE EDWARD SHANAHAN VX54854
SAPPER NOEL GEORGE SHARP DX661
PRIVATE PERCIVAL JAMES SHAW VX27329
PRIVATE STANLEY LANG SHAW VX55213
PRIVATE VALLANCE JAMES SHAW VX65632
PRIVATE DALLAS JOHN SHEAHEN VX28986
PRIVATE GEORGE SHEEDY VX27362
PRIVATE ERIC JAMES SHEPHERD VX27352
PRIVATE PETER GEOFFREY SHEPPARD VX50592
PRIVATE LESLIE ANDREW SHIELLS VX27428
SERGEANT CHRISTIAN FIELD SHIMMEN VX29762
PRIVATE EDWARD ARTHUR KENWARD SHOEBRIDGE NX42029
PRIVATE JOHN ROBERT SIDEBOTTOM VX23606
PRIVATE JOHN LINTORN SIMMONS VX24741
PRIVATE JAMES SIMPSON VX65203
DRIVER RONALD ALEX SIMPSON NX7039
PRIVATE ALEXANDER SINCLAIR VX25223
PRIVATE REGINALD H S SINCLAIR VX42320
PRIVATE JOHN HENRY SKEGGS VX34252
PRIVATE WALTER SAMUEL SMALE VX36514
PRIVATE ERNEST WILLIAM SMART VX23434
PRIVATE GORDON CAMPBELL SMART VX30800
PRIVATE HAROLD ERNEST SMETHURST VX24626
WARRANT OFFICER CLASS 2 ALBERT JOSEPH SMITH VX38935
PRIVATE CLIFFORD SMITH VX27256
LIEUTENANT DENIS WASHINGTON SMITH VX34426
PRIVATE EDWARD RICHARD WALTER SMITH VX37154
PRIVATE ERIC SMITH VX27135

PRIVATE ERNEST WILLIAM SMITH VX27198
PRIVATE FREDERICK GEORGE SMITH
BOMBARDIER GEOFFREY MELVILLE SMITH VX46442
LANCE SERGEANT HAROLD LESLIE SMITH VX26133
LIEUTENANT HARRY TEMPLE SMITH VX44500
PRIVATE HENRY ARCHIBALD SMITH VX32124
CORPORAL JACK STUART SMITH NX46498
PRIVATE JOHN SMITH VX31791
PRIVATE JOHN FREDERICK SMITH DX662
PRIVATE JOSEPH ARTHUR SMITH VX61274
PRIVATE LEONARD PERCIVAL SMITH VX61978
PRIVATE REGINALD THOMAS SMITH NX42201
PRIVATE ROBERT SMITH VX27336
PRIVATE ROBERT JOHN SMITH VX39787
PRIVATE ROBERT OSCAR SMITH VX36613
DRIVER VICTOR LESLIE SMITH NX7333
PRIVATE WALLACE LESLIE SMITH VX43745
PRIVATE WILLIAM EDWARD SMITH VX30846
PRIVATE WILLIAM JAMES SMITH VX62135
CORPORAL WILLIAM JOHN STERLING SMITH VX27344
PRIVATE WALTER RAYMOND SNEESBY VX12602
PRIVATE ROBERT SYDNEY SNODGRASS VX30975
PRIVATE JACK SOLOMON NX2116
LANCE CORPORAL ALLAN SAMUEL SPOKES VX27270
PRIVATE FREDERICK SPURGEON VX31790
PRIVATE JAMES THOMAS HENRY STACEY VX39750
PRIVATE EDWARD THOMAS GEORGE STAFFORD VX30303
PRIVATE ERIC JOHN STAGG VX31091
STAFF SERGEANT WILLIAM WALTER GEORGE STANBRIDGE VX37071
CORPORAL LAWRENCE JAMES STEPHENS VX50381
PRIVATE BRAITHWAITE BORROWDALE STEVENS VX36067
CORPORAL HARRY JOHN STEVENS VX44001
PRIVATE ROYSTON CECIL STEVENS NX38716
PRIVATE ALEC JAMES STEWART VX42486
PRIVATE FREDERICK NORMAN PEARSON STEWART NX2137
PRIVATE JOHN GRANT STEWART VX39923
PRIVATE LINDSAY JOHN STEWART VX38950
PRIVATE MALCOLM DOUGLAS STEWART VX31009
LIEUTENANT VERNON LACHLAN STEWART VX46492
GUNNER ERNEST FRANK STIEBEL NX37552
PRIVATE CHARLES ALEXANDER STOCKS VX50058
PRIVATE FREDERICK ALBERT STOKES VX60936
PRIVATE JAMES ALBERT STOKIE VX27259
PRIVATE LEONARD RICHARD STONEY NX5705
STAFF SERGEANT STEPHEN DONALD STORER NX56678
PRIVATE GORDON MURRAY STRACHAN VX50067
PRIVATE DESMOND STRATTON VX30873
PRIVATE FRANCIS LESLIE STRATTON VX27269
PRIVATE LESLIE GEORGE STRATTON VX27435

SIGNALMAN JOSEPH CLIVE STRAUBE NX43706
PRIVATE HOWARD ARTHUR STRUHS VX25118
PRIVATE JOHN SULLIVAN VX30886
PRIVATE WILLIAM WILTON SUMNER VX30391
LIEUTENANT GEOFFREY WESTON SUTCLIFFE VX39163
PRIVATE LEONARD SUTHERLAND VX28325
PRIVATE JOHN WORDEN SWAN VX53487
CORPORAL STUART MILL SWANTON VX25850
PRIVATE HENRY EBENEZER SYMINGTON VX29906
PRIVATE WILLIAM ARTHUR JOHN SYMINGTON VX29892
PRIVATE REGINALD SYMONS VX30513
PRIVATE STANLEY SYMONS VX54988
PRIVATE EDWIN ROBERT ALEXANDER TAIT VX28084
PRIVATE JAMES ALBERT TALBOT VX31823
PRIVATE MALCOLM JAMES TALBOT VX27361
CRAFTSMAN HAROLD WILLIAM TAME NX28422
LIEUTENANT EDGAR STEPHEN TANNER VX67798
PRIVATE ALBERT LAURENCE TAYLOR VX30828
SERGEANT DONALD JAMES TAYLOR VX20686
PRIVATE DOUGLAS TAYLOR VX11348
PRIVATE FREDERICK LEONARD TAYLOR NX50065
PRIVATE FRANCIS OUGHTON TAYLOR VX30242
PRIVATE JACK TAYLOR VX25594
LANCE CORPORAL JOHN TREVOR TAYLOR QX19024
CORPORAL WILLIAM ARTHUR TAYLOR VX24516
PRIVATE WILLIAM READHEAD TAYLOR WX10157
PRIVATE LINDON IRVINE TEPPER VX27353
PRIVATE KEITH JAMES THATCHER VX30892
PRIVATE CLIVE THOMAS VX24949
SERGEANT ROBERT THOMAS NX9748
PRIVATE RONALD BADEN THOMAS VX62736
PRIVATE ARGENT HENRY THOMPSON VX60050
PRIVATE ERIC CHARLES THOMSON VX58463
GUNNER WALTER EDWARD THOMSON NX41265
PRIVATE JAMES THORNBER VX23707
LANCE CORPORAL WILLIAM LESLIE TIBBETT VX28381
SERGEANT ROBERT NORTON TOBIAS VX44555
PRIVATE LEONARD JAMES TORNEY VX61677
PRIVATE GEORGE JOHN LAWSON TRAILL VX54584
PRIVATE GEORGE FORRESTER TRAVERS VX39931
PRIVATE SYDNEY HERBERT TREGENZA VX32135
PRIVATE CLARENCE CLIVE WILLIAM TRELFORD NX4527
PRIVATE GEORGE TREZISE VX31221
GUNNER ALBERT HENRY TOWNING QX1190
CORPORAL THOMAS JOHN EDWARD TOWNSEND VX27293
PRIVATE BERTRIC TUCKER VX42322
PRIVATE CHARLES EDGAR TUCKER VX42333
PRIVATE SYDNEY PHILLIP TUCKER VX25625
PRIVATE WALTER FREDERICK TUDDENHAM VX42291

PRIVATE JOHN NORMAN TULLETT VX27445
LANCE CORPORAL JOHN ALEXANDER TURNER WX10876
CAPTAIN JOHN MORTON TURNER MBE VX45196
PRIVATE NORMAN THOMAS TURNER VX43800
PRIVATE BRIAN BLAKE TYMMS VX39912
PRIVATE OSWALD HENRY UREN VX28803
LIEUTENANT CHARLES EDWARD USHER NX76227
CORPORAL JOHN BAPTIST VALLI VX37300
LIEUTENANT JOHN CHARLES VAN NOOTEN VX36929
PRIVATE EDMUND AUSTIN VAUGHAN VX50281
PRIVATE PETER FRANCIS VAUGHAN VX69024
PRIVATE STANLEY JAMES VAUGHAN VX54960
WARRANT OFFICER CLASS 1 ROY WILLIAM VEREY VX31309
PRIVATE WALTER LEONARD VIANT NX55829
PRIVATE GORDON CHARLES VINCENT VX50400
PRIVATE WILLIAM VERDUN VINCENT VX52561
PRIVATE ALBERT EDWARD VIVASH VX36254
PRIVATE ROY VICTOR WADDLE VX30542
PRIVATE THOMAS FREDERICK JAMES WADHAM VX39756
PRIVATE FRANK WAGHORN VX43155
SAPPER FRIEDRICH WAIBEL QX21854
PRIVATE SYLVESTER WALTON WAKELING VX39764
PRIVATE JOHN KENNETH WALKER VX31616
PRIVATE JOSEPH PHILIP WALKER VX22434
PRIVATE LEO JOHN FORBES WALKER VX23170
PRIVATE SAMUEL EDGAR WALKER VX43820
PRIVATE ROY OLIVER WALLACE VX27398
LANCE CORPORAL RONALD KEITH WALLEY VX44564
PRIVATE FRANK HENRY WALTERS VX62657
PRIVATE OSWALD GUNN WARBURTON VX27407
LANCE CORPORAL GEOFFREY ALEXANDER WARING VX46505
SERGEANT CLIFTON WARN NX678
PRIVATE VIVIAN HENRY WARNE VX28834
PRIVATE ALLAN KEITH WARNER VX30831
PRIVATE EDWARD WARNER VX30838
PRIVATE JOHN RICHARD MAULE WARNER VX39487
STAFF SERGEANT LEO CLEVELAND WARREN VX39687
WARRANT OFFICER CLASS 2 ROY ARMSTRONG WARREN VX38954
PRIVATE STANLEY GORDON WARREN VX50192
CAPTAIN NEIL EDWIN WATCHORN VX45224
PRIVATE DAVID WILLIAM WATKINS NX47237
PRIVATE GEORGE WILLIAM WATKINS VX61320
PRIVATE FRANK WATSON VX46629
PRIVATE ROBERT BOYD WATSON VX30516
PRIVATE ALLAN GERRARD WATT VX32391
PRIVATE JONATHON WILLIAM JAMES WEBB VX50160
LANCE CORPORAL GEORGE VICTOR WEEKES NX36525
ALBERT CHARLES WEGNER VX27317
PRIVATE PERCIVAL WEIGHT VX24897

LANCE CORPORAL BRUCE GEORGE WELLINGS VX46726
PRIVATE ALBERT WILFRED WENZKE VX42264
PRIVATE ERNEST ARTHUR WERNICKE VX31848
CORPORAL BERTIE WERRY VX21843
PRIVATE RAYMOND HAROLD WEST VX24331
MAJOR GEORGE DE VERDON WESTLEY VX44808
STAFF SERGEANT THOMAS MONTAGUE BARCLAY WESTON VX20214
PRIVATE RUFUS SYDNEY WHARTON VX26961
PRIVATE JACK LANCELOT WHEILDON VX48329
PRIVATE RAYMOND THOMAS WHEILDON VX24735
CORPORAL JAMES ROBERT WHELLER VX25891
PRIVATE THOMAS GARDINER WHELLER VX26883
PRIVATE BARCLAY JAMES WHITE VX32070
GUNNER GEORGE FREDERICK WHITE NX53918
CORPORAL JAMES FREDERICK WHITE VX39915
PRIVATE LESLIE MERVYN WHITE VX47685
CAPTAIN STANLEY BOYD MCKELLAR WHITE NX70920
CORPORAL JAMES ROBERT WHITTAKER NX72770
LIEUTENANT JAMES DAWSON WHITTAKERS VX45608
CORPORAL KENNETH JOHN WIDMER VX25435
PRIVATE MITCHELL LINDSAY WIGHTMAN VX29987
PRIVATE LIONEL MUNCKTON WILKINSON VX54728
PRIVATE ALAN GEORGE WILLIAMS VX27408
PRIVATE ERIC DOUGLAS WILLIAMS VX43917
PRIVATE FREDERICK ERNEST WILLIAMS VX61322
PRIVATE GEORGE ALLAN WILLIAMS VX32005
PRIVATE JOSEPH HENRY WILLIAMS VX43389
PRIVATE LEO VINCENT WILLIAMS VX21373
PRIVATE ORMOND LESLIE WILLIAMS VX38278
PRIVATE ROBERT HAROLD WILLIAMS VX36466
PRIVATE ROBERT RAY WILLIAMS VX27427
SERGEANT ROY KEITH WILLIAMS VX38640
PRIVATE WESLEY MURRAY WILLIAMS VX61326
PRIVATE WILFRED JOHN WILLIAMS VX25030
PRIVATE GEORGE FREDERICK WILLIAMSON VX23336
PRIVATE JAMES HENRY WILLIAMSON NX7108
PRIVATE HARRY FRANCIS WILLIS VX53875
PRIVATE WILLIAM WILLOUGHBY VX25183
SAPPER CEDRIC SPENCER WILLS QX11400
PRIVATE CHARLES HERBERT WILSHIRE VX46422
SERGEANT CLIFTON MORGAN MCKIMM WILSON QX7949
PRIVATE AUSTIN GLARE WILSON VX27206
PRIVATE JAMES GEORGE WILSON VX61655
LANCE CORPORAL GEORGE WILSON VX31772
PRIVATE ROBERT ARTHUR WILSON VX39759
PRIVATE WILLIAM LESLIE WILSON VX31373
SERGEANT EDWARD THOMAS WINNELL VX23665
PRIVATE ALLAN FRANK WINSOR NX47187
PRIVATE MAURICE CAMPBELL WINSTANLEY VX39763

CORPORAL WILLIAM JOHN WISEMAN VX25406
LANCE CORPORAL NORMAN PRESTON WOMERSLEY VX62506
PRIVATE KENNETH ROY WOOD VX23773
PRIVATE ERNEST JOHN WOODALL VX61599
PRIVATE REGINALD CORONA WOODMAN VX39749
SAPPER GORDON LEWIS WOODS QX9597
PRIVATE REGINALD THOMAS WOODS VX25875
PRIVATE CHARLES ARTHUR WOODWARD VX37644
PRIVATE DANIEL WOOLFORD VX30993
PRIVATE HERBERT AMOS WORLING NX67382
PRIVATE ALBERT HERBERT WRIGHT VX38930
PRIVATE HERBERT CLIFFORD WRIGHT VX31224
PRIVATE HECTOR GORDON WRIGHT NX47720
PRIVATE HAMILTON JOHN WRIGHT VX31271
PRIVATE KEVIN BRIEN WRIGHT VX60612
PRIVATE ERNEST JAMES YANDLE VX44301
PRIVATE LESLIE NORMAN YATES VX31108
PRIVATE ALLAN YOUNG VX54913
CAPTAIN ARTHUR WELLESLEY YOUNG MBE VX26672
PRIVATE JOSEPH CLEMIS YOUNG VX31987
PRIVATE LEONARD AUGUSTUS YOUNG VX27140
PRIVATE RICHARD CAPSTICK YOUNG VX19210
CORPORAL HENRY CHARLES YOUNGBERRY NX71865

Note: Some individuals mentioned in the text were members of Gull Force but not of the 2/21st Battalion, therefore their names may be omitted from this nominal roll.

ENDNOTES

Prologue

1. Max 'Eddie' Gilbert, interview with author in Melbourne, 8 June 2012.
2. Ambon Court of Inquiry, NAA Series 3856, 146/1/14.

Chapter 1   Preparing for war

1. Interview with Tom Pledger, 19 November 2012.
2. *Argus*, 27 August 1940.
3. *Argus*, 27 August 1940; http://trove.nla.gov.au/ndp/del/article/81972098.
4. http://trove.nla.gov.au/ndp/del/article/11315084.
5. http://trove.nla.gov.au/ndp/del/article/11315084.
6. Sturdee sources: David A. Evans, *Ambon Forward Observation Line Strategy 1941–42: A Lesson in Military Incompetence*, PhD thesis, Murdoch University, 2010; http://adb.anu.edu.au/biography/sturdee-sir-vernon-ashton-hobart-11798.
7. Interview with Max (Eddie) Gilbert by author on 8 June 2012.
8. http://adb.anu.edu.au/biography/scott-william-john-8373; Evans, *Ambon Forward Observation Line Strategy 1941–42*.
9. http://trove.nla.gov.au/ndp/del/article/17029947.
10. http://adb.anu.edu.au/biography/scott-william-john-8373; Evans, *Ambon Forward Observation Line Strategy 1941–42*.

11. Walter Hicks, Australians at War Film Archive, interviewed 24 September 2003.
12. www.awm.gov.au/units/people_1080703.asp?query=roach; Joan Beaumont, *Gull Force, Survival and Leadership in Captivity 1941–1945*, Allen & Unwin, Sydney, 1988, pp. 24–25.
13. Jimmy Morrison, interview with the author, 29 November 2012.

Chapter 2   The doomed grand strategy

1. Lionel Wigmore, *The Japanese Thrust*, Australian War Memorial, Canberra, 1957, Ch. 3, 'Plans and Preparations'.
2. *Australasian*, 28 September 1940.
3. From Lt. Col. William Scott's post-war report: AWM54 573/6/1.
4. Wigmore, *The Japanese Thrust*, Ch. 3, 'Plans and Preparations'.
5. Churchill, *The Second World War*, Vol. II, Cassell, Sydney, 1948–56, p. 440.
6. J. M. Ford, *Allies in a Bind: Australia and the Netherland East Indies in the Second World War*, Australian Netherlands Ex-Servicemen and Women's Association, Loganholme, Qld, 1996.
7. Wigmore, *The Japanese Thrust*, p. 59.
8. *London Gazette*, 22 January 1948; Peter Henning, *Doomed Battalion*, Allen & Unwin, Sydney, 1995.
9. From Scott's report in 1945: AWM54 573/6/1.
10. Joan Beaumont, *Gull Force, Survival and Leadership in Captivity 1941–1945*, Allen & Unwin, Sydney, 1988.
11. Wigmore, *The Japanese Thrust*, Ch. 19, 'The Loss of Ambon'.
12. Letter from Sturdee to Gavin Long, official war historian.
13. David A. Evans, *The Ambon Forward Observation Line Strategy 1941–42: A Lesson in Military Incompetence*, PhD thesis, Murdoch University, 2010; National Archives of Australia, Official History, 1939–45, Records of Gavin Long: AWM67 3/384.
14. Evans, *The Ambon Forward Observation Line Strategy 1941–42*.
15. Roach's letter to Scott: AWM54 573/6/3.

Chapter 3   Destination Ambon

1. Interview with Don Findlay in Beaumont, *Gull Force*.
2. http://en.wikipedia.org/wiki/Amboyna_massacre; http://en.wiki-source.org/wiki/Towerson,_Gabriel_(d.1623)_(DNB00).

3. Eddie Gilbert, interview with the author, 4 May 2012.

4. Letter from Roach to Scott, 1 January 1942: AWM54 573/6/10.

5. Message from Tanner to Sturdee, 13 January 1942: AWM54 573/6/10.

6. National Archives of Australia, Ambon – Japanese Invasion 1942 – Battle for Ambon, B6121/3, 115A.

7. http://en.wikipedia.org/wiki/Japanese_Special_Naval_Landing_Forces.

8. Japanese Monograph No. 16, *Ambon and Timor Invasion Operations*, Military History Section, [US] Army Forces Far East.

9. National Archives of Australia, Ambon – Japanese Invasion 1942 – Battle for Ambon, B6121/3, 115A.

10. National Archives of Australia, *Report on the Japanese Invasion of Ambon*, MP729/7, 35/421/67 and National Archives of Australia, Ambon – Japanese Invasion 1942 – Battle for Ambon, B6121/3, 115A.

11. Wigmore, *The Japanese Thrust*, Ch. 19, 'The Loss of Ambon'.

12. Wigmore, *The Japanese Thrust*, Ch. 19, 'The Loss of Ambon'.

13. Wigmore, *The Japanese Thrust*, Ch. 19, 'The Loss of Ambon', p. 424.

14. http://adb.anu.edu.au/biography/scott-william-john-8373.

15. Wigmore, *The Japanese Thrust*, Ch. 19, 'The Loss of Ambon', p. 426.

16. Ralph Godfrey, telephone interview with the author, November 2012.

17. Walter Hicks, interview with the author, 12 June 2012.

Chapter 4   Surrender

1. *Nippon Times*, 31 January 1943, report by Genichi Yamamoto, writing for the Japanese Navy Press Corp.

2. Wigmore, *The Japanese Thrust*, Ch. 19, 'Loss of Ambon'.

3. Australian War Memorial, diary of W. T. Jinkins, 17 September 1943: AWM67.

4. Dept of Military History, Netherlands Army: Document 9/42.

5. Dept of Military History, Netherlands Army: Document 9/42.

6. Wigmore, *The Japanese Thrust*, Ch. 19, 'Loss of Ambon'.

7. From Eddie Gilbert's diary.

8. Walter Hicks, telephone interview with the author, 22 May 2012.

9. Shaun Mcilraith, 'The Ambon Battle', *People Magazine*, 6 April 1955; 'Gull Force Ambon', *Reveille*, 1 July 1962.

10. Genichi Yamamoto, Navy Press Corp.
11. National Archives of Australia, *Report on the Japanese Invasion of Ambon*, MP729/7, 35/421/67.
12. Takada Haruo, *Laha Battle*: AWM54 573/6/1a.
13. Wigmore, *The Japanese Thrust*.
14. AWM54 576/1A.
15. Eddie Gilbert's memoir, 1993.
16. Australian War Memorial, William Jinkins's diary: AWM67.

Chapter 5   The massacre

1. Statement made during committal proceedings, Japanese Naval Court Martial, 22 December 1945; D. C. S. Sissons, *The Australian War Crimes Trials and Investigations (1942–51)*, National Library of Australia collection no. MS3092.
2. Statements by Takada Haruo and Shiego Hamanishi given to an inquiry at the 33 Infantry Brigade HQ, Ambon, on 6 November 1945.
3. Statement made during committal proceedings, Japanese Naval Court Martial, 22 December 1945; D. C. S. Sissons, *The Australian War Crimes Trials and Investigations (1942–51)*.
4. Statement by Shiego Hamanishi given to an inquiry at the 33 Infantry Brigade HQ, Ambon, on 16 November 1945.
5. James MacKay, *Betrayal in High Places*, Lane Publishers, Stockport, UK, 1996. First published by Tasman Archives, NZ, 1996.
6. Tom Pledger, interview with the author, 19 November 2012.
7. Walter Hicks, interview with the author, 22 May 2012.
8. Eddie Gilbert's memoir.
9. Eddie Gilbert's memoir.
10. Interview with Benjamin Amor, 6 October 2003, Australians at War Film Archive.
11. Ralph Godfrey, interview with the author, 6 April 2013.
12. Leslie Hopkins's memoir.
13. AWM, 54 573/6/1A, Part 2, *Report on Ambon and Hainan*; Drawn from various sources including NAA MP 729/7, 38/421/222.
14. Wigmore, *The Japanese Thrust*, Ch. 19, 'The Loss of Ambon'.

Chapter 6 'I'm gonna get out of this bloody place'

1. Hank Nelson, *P.O.W. Prisoners of War: Australians under Nippon*, ABC, Sydney, 1985; interview with Alec Chew courtesy of Tim Bowden.
2. Patsy Adam-Smith, *Prisoners of War: Gallipoli to Korea*, 'The Fate of the 2/21st', Viking, Ringwood, Vic, 1992, p. 314.
3. AWM 54 573/6/1A. *Report on Ambon and Hainan*, Part 2, p. 5.
4. Joan Beaumont, *Gull Force, Survival and Leadership in Captivity 1941–1945*, Allen & Unwin, Sydney, 1988.
5. Quotes from William Jinkins drawn from interviews by Tim Bowden and published in Nelson, *P.O.W. Prisoners of War* and Adam-Smith, *Prisoners of War*.
6. Quote from Cliff Warn drawn from an interview with Tim Bowden.
7. Quote from William Jinkins drawn from interview with Tim Bowden.
8. http://en.wikipedia.org/wiki/Tanimbar_Islands.
9. Quote from William Jinkins drawn from interview with Tim Bowden.

Chapter 7 'Butchery for a Roman holiday'

1. Wigmore, *The Japanese Thrust*, Ch. 25, p. 605.
2. Much of this chapter has been drawn from the official *Report on Ambon and Hainan* by Lt. Col. W. J. R. Scott (AWM54 573/6/1A); also from the written report by Scott, April 1946: AWM54 573/6/1B.
3. *Report on Ambon and Hainan*: AWM54 573/6/1A.
4. http://en.wikipedia.org/wiki/ American-British-Dutch-Australian_Command.
5. http://adb.anu.edu.au/biography/ sturdee-sir-vernon-ashton-hobart-11798.
6. Interview with Walter Hicks, 24 September 2003, Australians at War Film Archive.
7. Nelson, *P.O.W. Prisoners of War*; interviews with Ian Macrae and John Van Nooten courtesy of Tim Bowden, ABC Radio.
8. Interview with Eddie Gilbert, 5 September 2003, Australians at War Film Archive.
9. Stewart Legge, *Sun* (Melbourne), 7 January 1946.

10. *Sun* (Melbourne), 7 January 1946; *Report on Ambon and Hainan*: AWM54 573/6/1A.
11. Eddie Gilbert's memoir.
12. Nelson, *P.O.W. Prisoners of War*; interviews with John Van Nooten and John Devenish courtesy of Tim Bowden, ABC Radio.
13. Sworn statement by Capt. John Turner to the War Crimes Tribunal: AA B3856 144/14/17.
14. Sworn statement by Albert McCoomb to the War Crimes Tribunal: AA B3856 144/14/17.
15. Sworn statement by Charles Rivett to the War Crimes Tribunal: AA B3856 144/14/17.
16. Sworn statement by Kenneth Lupson to the War Crimes Tribunal: AA B3856 144/14/17.
17. Sworn statement by William Harries to the War Crimes Tribunal: AA B3856 144/14/17.
18. Ailsa Rolley, *Survival on Ambon*, A. Rolley, Beaudesert, Qld, 1994.
19. Appendix 1 to Scott's report, letter dated 29 June 1948.
20. Eddie Gilbert's memoir.
21. Ibid.

Chapter 8 Voyage into the unknown

1. Interview with Frederick Crane, 19 September 2003, Australians at War Film Archive.
2. Ron Leech, *Pacific War Odyssey*, self-published memoir, 1995.
3. http://en.wikipedia.org/wiki/Hainan; Scott's *Report on Hainan and Ambon*.
4. Courtney T. Harrison, *Ambon, Island of Mist: 2/21st Battalion AIF (Gull Force) Prisoners of War 1941–45*, T. W. and C. T. Harrison, North Geelong, Vic., 1988.
5. Report by Capt. John Turner on 28 September 1945, sworn before Lt. Denis Smith on board HMS *Vindex*, Appendix 3 of Scott's *Report on Ambon and Hainan*.
6. AWM 54 5734/6/1A, Appendix 8 to Scott's report.
7. Tom Pledger's diary.
8. Ralph Godfrey, interview with the author, 6 April 2013.
9. Interview with George Williamson by Margaret Evans, ABC, January 1983.
10. Scott's post-war report: AWM 573/6/1.
11. http://en.wikipedia.org/wiki/New_Guinea_campaign.

12. Edward W. Weiss, *Under the Rising Sun*, 2nd ed., E. W. Weiss, 1992, pp. 136–37.
13. Weiss, *Under the Rising Sun* and interview with the author, April 2013.
14. Peter Koop, telephone interview with the author, May 2012 and interview by Fran Kelly on ABC Radio National, 25 April 2012.
15. Walter Hicks, interview with the author, 22 May 2012.
16. Eddie Gilbert, interview with the author, 4 May 2012.
17. Ibid.
18. Interview with Walter Hicks, 24 September 2003, Australians at War Film Archive.
19. Ibid.
20. Peter Koop, interview with the author, May 2012.
21. Ibid.
22. Letter from Don Baker to Mrs Olive Atherton, 19 October 1945.
23. Ibid.
24. Nelson, *P.O.W. Prisoners of War;* interview with Jack Panaotie courtesy of Tim Bowden, ABC Radio.
25. Rolley, *Survival on Ambon;* interview with Les Hohl by Ailsa Rolley.
26. Carson, in *Under the Rising Sun.*
27. Nelson, *P.O.W. Prisoners of War;* interview with John Van Nooten courtesy of Tim Bowden, ABC Radio.
28. Rolley, *Survival on Ambon;* interview with Doug Phillips by Ailsa Rolley.
29. Rolley, *Survival on Ambon;* interview with Charlie Norman by Ailsa Rolley.
30. Ed Weiss, interview with the author, 9 April 2013.
31. Ibid.
32. Weiss, *Under the Rising Sun.*
33. Ibid.

Chapter 9   *Strangers in the night*

1. Interview with Eddie Gilbert, 5 September 2003, Australians at War Film Archive.
2. Stuart Swanton's diary: AWM67 3/387/DPI300.
3. Ibid.
4. Wigmore, *The Japanese Thrust*, Ch. 25, p. 606.
5. Stuart Swanton's diary.

6. http://en.wikipedia.org/wiki/Beriberi.
7. Stuart Swanton's diary.
8. Walter Hicks, interview with the author, 19 December 2012.
9. www.geocities.jp/hhhirofumi/eng02.htm.
10. Eddie Gilbert's memoir, 1993.
11. Ibid.
12. Nelson, *P.O.W. Prisoners of War*; interview with George Williamson courtesy of Margaret Evans, 24 January 1983.
13. Stuart Swanton's diary.
14. John Van Nooten, interview with Tim Bowden, Melbourne, 7 December 1982.
15. Ibid.
16. Weiss, *Under the Rising Sun*.
17. *The Australian*, 19 July 1981, report by Phil Cornford.
18. Record of Military Court, Morotai, 25–28 February 1946.
19. John Van Nooten, interview with Tim Bowden, Melbourne, 7 December 1982.
20. Weiss, *Under the Rising Sun*.
21. Eddie Gilbert's memoir.
22. Ibid.

Chapter 10   'The sick were the fat ladies of the circus'

1. Capt. William Aitken, Medical Report, POW Camp, Hashio, Hainan Island: NAA B3856 144/14/17 Appendix 22.
2. From Scott's post-war report: AWM54 573/6/1.
3. Capt. W. Aitken, Medical Report, Appendix 22.
4. Ibid.
5. Courtney T. Harrison, *Ambon, Island of Mist*.
6. Sworn statement by Lt. Denis Smith, 28 August 1945, NAA B3856 144/14/17.
7. Ibid.
8. Ibid.
9. Letter from Tom Pledger to his mother, Katherine, August 1943.
10. Ibid.
11. Sworn statement by Capt. C. Newnham at Bakli Bay, 28 August 1945.
12. Sworn statement by W/O Edward C. Norman, Hashio POW Camp, 26 August 1945.
13. Scott's post-war report: AWM54 573/6/1.

14. Sworn statement by Lt. R. J. Green, 28 September 1945: NAA B3856 144/14/17.
15. Sworn statement by Private Robert Smith, 27 September 1945: NAA B3856 144/14/17.
16. Sworn statement by J. V. McMahon, 27 September 1945: NAA B3856 144/14/17.
17. Sworn statement by A. Murnane, 27 September 1945: NAA B3856 144/14/17.
18. Sworn statement by J. V. McMahon, 27 September 1945: NAA B3856 144/14/17.
19. Sworn statement by Private F. A. Hillier, 28 September 1945: NAA B3856 144/14/17.
20. Sworn statement by R. J. Green, 28 September 1945: NAA B3856 144/14/17.
21. Signed statement by Corporal J. H. Nelson, 11 April 1944: NAA B3856 144/14/17.
22. Aitken's post-war report on Ambon.
23. Nelson, *P.O.W. Prisoners of War*; interview with Roy Harris courtesy of Hank Nelson, 22 February 1983.
24. Reported by Lt. Smith in his diary notes, which appear in Scott's report entitled 'Administration in Prison Camp – Hainan', AWM54 573/6/1.
25. Ibid.
26. Ibid.
27. Nelson, *P.O.W. Prisoners of War*; interview with Major Ian Macrae. 7 December 1982, courtesy of Hank Nelson.
28. Extracts from diary kept by Lt. Col. Denis Smith from March 1942 to 30 August 1945.

Chapter 11   The cage

1. Walter Hicks, interview with the author, Melbourne, 9 June 2012.
2. Interview with Walter Hicks, Australians at War Film Archive.
3. Hohl quoted in Rolley, *Survival on Ambon*.
4. Stuart Swanton's diary.
5. Eddie Gilbert, interview with the author, 4 May 2012.
6. Ibid.
7. Ibid.
8. http://en.wikipedia.org/wiki/Mateship.
9. Nelson, *P.O.W. Prisoners of War*, p. 95.

10. Ibid.
11. Ibid.
12. Sworn statement by George de Verdon Westley to the War Crimes Commission, 14 October 1945.
13. Interview with Eddie Gilbert, Australians at War Film Archive.
14. Wigmore, *The Japanese Thrust*, Ch. 25, p. 608.
15. Weiss, *Under The Rising Sun*.
16. NAA 3269/B10/A. Series 3856 146/1/14.
17. Ibid.
18. Ibid.
19. NAA 3856 146/1/14.

Chapter 12   Escape from Hainan

1. Tom Pledger's diary.
2. Ibid.
3. Medical report of conditions at Bakli Bay, Hainan, in sworn statement by Capt. W. Aitken, September 1945, Appendix 22.
4. Ibid.
5. www.nhs.uk/chq/pages/1126.aspx?categoryid=51.
6. Medical report of conditions at Bakli Bay, Hainan, in sworn statement by Capt. W. Aitken, September 1945, Appendix 22.
7. Jimmy Morrison, interview with the author, 30 November 2012.
8. Scott's report A, p. 25.
9. Ian Macrae, interviewed by Tim Bowden, Melbourne, 7 December 1982.
10. Ibid.
11. Leech, *Pacific War Odyssey*.
12. Scott's report A, p. 26.
13. Ibid.
14. Roy Harris, interviewed by Hank Nelson, 22 February 1983.
15. Jack Devenish, interviewed by Tim Bowden, Perth, December 1981.
16. Scott's report A, p. 26.
17. Ibid.
18. Leech, *Pacific War Odyssey*, p. 121.
19. Leech, *Pacific War Odyssey*.

Chapter 13   The beginning of the end

1. Weiss, *Under the Rising Sun*.
2. Roger Maynard, *Hell's Heroes*, HarperCollins, Sydney, 2009.
3. Walter Hicks, telephone interview with the author, 22 May 2012.
4. Weiss, *Under the Rising Sun*, p. 222.
5. Eddie Gilbert's memoir.
6. *People Magazine*, 26 April 1950.
7. Leech, *Pacific War Odyssey*.
8. Ian Macrae, interviewed by Tim Bowden, Melbourne, 7 December 1982.
9. Ibid.
10. Ron Leech, interviewed by *People Magazine*, 26 April 1950.
11. NAA B3856, 144/14/77.
12. Letter from Scott to camp commandant, 12 July 1945.
13. Tom Pledger, interview with the author, 19 November 2012.
14. Tom Pledger's letter home, 16 August 1945.

Chapter 14   'You can keep your bloody island – we'll be back for it'

1. Tom Pledger, interview with the author, 19 November 2012.
2. Ian Macrae, interviewed by Tim Bowden, 7 December 1982.
3. John Devenish, recalling Singlaub's words to the camp in an interview by Tim Bowden, Perth, December 1981.
4. www.spartacus.schoolnet.co.uk/JFKsinglaub.htm; http://en.wikipedia.org/wiki/John_K._Singlaub.
5. Ian Macrae, interviewed by Tim Bowden, 7 December 1982.
6. Jimmy Morrison, interview with the author, Sydney, 30 November 2012.
7. Courtney T. Harrison, *Ambon, Island of Mist*, p. 241.
8. Ian Macrae, interviewed by Tim Bowden, 7 December 1982.
9. Roy Harris, interviewed by Hank Nelson, 22 February 1983.
10. D. C. S. Sissons, *The Australian War Crimes Trials and Investigations (1942–51)*.
11. John Van Nooten, interviewed by Tim Bowden, 7 December 1982.
12. Eddie Gilbert, interview with the author, 8 June 2012.
13. Jack Panaotie, interviewed by Margaret Evans, Melbourne, 21 January 1983.

14. Ralph Godfrey's record of an interview with Windas Smith.
15. Weiss, *Under the Rising Sun*, p. 229.
16. John Van Nooten, interviewed by Tim Bowden, 7 December 1982.
17. Weiss, *Under the Rising Sun*, p. 239.

Chapter 15 Westley's honour restored

1. Morotai Court of Inquiry, September 1945: AA Series 3856 146/1/14.
2. Morotai Court of Inquiry, September 1945: AA Series 3856 146/1/14.
3. *Report of Morotai Court of Inquiry*, 2 October 1945.
4. Ibid.
5. Ibid.
6. Ibid.
7. Ibid.
8. G. de V. Westley, *Report on That Portion of Gull Force Remaining on Amboina from Oct 26, 1942 to September 10, 1945*, 23 November 1945.

Chapter 16 Vengeance

1. Newspaper reports published throughout Japan on 1 January 1946.
2. *Sun* (Melbourne), 3 January 1946; report by Stewart Legge.
3. *Argus*, 22 October 1947.
4. Statement by Ikeuchi during proceedings of Military Tribunal, 1 February 1946.
5. *Sun* (Melbourne), 7 January 1946; report by Stewart Legge.
6. 'Report from Ambon', *Age*, 9 January 1946.
7. Ibid.
8. *Sun* (Melbourne), 10 January 1946.
9. *Age*, 15 February 1946.
10. *Argus*, 18 February 1946.
11. *Herald* (Melbourne), 22 July 1947.
12. Professor Hank Nelson, '*Blood Oath* – a "reel" history', *Australian Journal of Historical Studies*, 1991.
13. *The Australian*, 21 July 1981, report by Phil Cornford.
14. Professor Hank Nelson, '*Blood Oath* – a "reel" history'.

15. Letter from ex-Captain Shirozu Wadami, Commander, Ambon POW Camp, to his daughter, 24 September 1947. Translated from the original text by staff of the Japanese Studies Centre, Macquarie University.

Chapter 17   Are the missing still alive?

1. *Sun* (Melbourne), 8 February 1946.
2. From Major H. W. Jackson's report, as told to Courtney T. Harrison, in Harrison's memoir, *Ambon, Island of Mist.*
3. Ibid.
4. Ibid.
5. *Age*, 5 August 1946.
6. Brendan Worrell, interview with the author, 4 January 2013.
7. http://history1900s.about.com/od/worldwarii/a/soldiersurr.htm.
8. Brendan Worrell, interview with the author, 4 January 2013.
9. *Age*, 30 March 1990; report by Peter Ellingsen.
10. Ian Pfennigwerth, interview with the author, 3 December 2013.
11. *Age*, 30 March 1990; report by Peter Ellingsen.
12. Ibid.
13. Ian Pfennigwerth, interview with the author, 3 December 2013.

Chapter 18   The lost battalion's search for answers

1. *Sun* (Melbourne), 25 September 1945.
2. *Argus*, 8 October 1946.
3. http://adb.anu.edu.au/biography/mcleay-george-11012.
4. *Smith's Weekly*, 12 October 1945.
5. Scott's letter to the *Argus*, 28 September 1946.
6. *Argus*, 10 October 1946.
7. Scott's report: AWM54 573/6/1A.
8. Ibid.
9. Ibid.
10. Letter from Dr William Aitken to Capt C. Newnham, 23 August 1945.
11. Official report by William Aitken on Scott's behaviour.
12. Ibid.
13. Scott's report: AWM54 573/6/1A, Part 1.

Chapter 19   Laying the ghosts to rest

1. Phil Cornford, 'The Ghost of Katayama', *The Australian*, 22 July 1981.
2. Ibid.
3. Ibid.
4. Brian A. Williams' personal recollections, published on the *Blood Oath* DVD, 1990.
5. Ibid.
6. *Chicago Tribune*, 12 May 1991, report by Ronald E. Yates.
7. Brian A. Williams's personal recollections, published on the *Blood Oath* DVD, 1990.
8. Email to the author from Brian A. Williams, 9 December 2013.
9. Weiss, *Under The Rising Sun*.
10. *Age*, 28 January 1999.

Chapter 20   Reflections

1. Robert Darroch, *D. H. Lawrence in Australia*, Macmillan, South Melbourne, 1981.
2. http://adb.anu.edu.au/biography/scott-william-john-8373.
3. Brother Shane, interview with the author, October 2012.
4. Interview with Walter Hicks, 24 September 2003, Australians at War Film Archive.
5. Walter Hicks, interview with the author, 21 June 2012.
6. Eddie Gilbert's memoir.
7. Jimmy Morrison, interview with the author, 30 November 2012.
8. Tom Pledger, interview with the author, 19 November 2012.
9. John Van Nooten, interview with Tim Bowden, 7 December 1982.
10. *People Magazine*, 26 April 1950.
11. Julian Larkin (Ron Leech's nephew), interview with the author, 13 December 2013.
12. Email from Lloyd Swanton, 25 January 2014.
13. Michael Cathcart, *Defending the National Tuckshop: Australia's Secret Army Intrigue of 1931*, McPhee Gribble/Penguin, 1988.

BIBLIOGRAPHY

Adam-Smith, Patsy, *Prisoners of War: From Gallipoli to Korea*, Penguin, Melbourne, 1992.

Beaumont, Joan, *Gull Force: Survival and Leadership in Captivity 1941–1945*, Allen & Unwin, Sydney, 1988.

Darroch, Robert, *D.H. Lawrence in Australia*, Macmillan, Melbourne, 1981.

Harrison, Courtney T., *Ambon, Island of Mist: 2/21st Battalion AIF (Gull Force) prisoners of war 1941–45*, self-published, Victoria, 1988.

Lawrence, D.H., *Kangaroo*, W. Heinemann, London, 1923.

Lawrence, D.H., *John Thomas and Lady Jane*, W. Heinemann, London, 1972.

Leech, Ron, *Pacific War Odyssey*, self-published, Sydney, 1995.

MacKay, James, *Betrayal in High Places*, A. Lane Publishing, Stockport, England/Tasman Archives, Auckland, New Zealand, 1996.

Nelson, Hank, *P.O.W. prisoners of war: Australians under Nippon*, ABC Enterprises, Sydney, 1985.

Rolley, Ailsa, *Survival on Ambon*, self-published, Australia, 1994.

Weiss, Ed, *Under the Rising Sun*, self-published, Pennsylvania, US, 1992.

Wigmore, Lionel, *The Japanese Thrust*, Australian War Memorial, Canberra, 1966.

Williams, Brian A., *Blood Oath*, Angus and Robertson, Sydney, 1990.

ACKNOWLEDGEMENTS

To research a subject that happened some 70 years ago and compile a comprehensive picture of it requires the help, generosity and understanding of many people and organisations. To those who have provided their assistance and insight over the past two and a half years, I offer my heartfelt gratitude. In particular my thanks go to Tara Nichols, National Archives of Australia; Sue Head, Secretary of Gull Force Association; Brian W. Williams, Producer, *Blood Oath*; Peter Koop; Phil Cornford; Edward Weiss, *Under the Rising Sun*; Ailsa Rolley, *Survival on Ambon*; Courtney T. Harrison (deceased); Walter Hicks and his family; Max Gilbert; Tom Pledger; Nan Lloyd (Tom Pledger's daughter); Ralph Godfrey; Michael Caulfield; Australians at War Film Archive; Robert Darroch, writer, and founder of the D.H. Lawrence Society of Australia; Judy Wilson, daughter of John Leslie Searant, Gull Force Anzac Day march organiser in Sydney and for providing copies of Japanese war crimes tribunal documents. Ray, Barry and Chris Mallett; Les Edwards; Christine Moore, daughter of Stanley James Vaughan; Noel Jordan, nephew of Francis Henry Jordan; Peter Reeve, nephew of 'Bertie' Tait; Brother Shane, Carmelite Monk, San Jose. Neal Starkey; Jimmy Morrison and his daughters Vicky and Margaret; Brendan Worrell, Hainan expert; David Evans, whose thesis, 'The

Ambon Forward Observation Line Strategy 1941–1942', raised so many pertinent questions about events leading up to the 2/21st Battalion's mission to Ambon; Tim Bowden, who provided copies of the original interviews he, Hank Nelson and Margaret Evans recorded for the making of *Prisoners of War: Australians Under Nippon*; Joan Beaumont, author of *Gull Force: Survival and Leadership in Captivity 1941–1945*; Allen & Unwin publishers, for granting me access to *Gull Force*; Mrs Jan Nelson, widow of Professor Hank Nelson, academic and author of *Australians Under Nippon*; Julian Larkin, Ron Leech's nephew; Fransina Werinussa, friend of Ron Leech; Robert Reid, grandson of Ben Amor; Colin Crane, son of Frederick Crane; Bob Mosse, University of Ambon; Ian Pfennigwerth, for help in researching the exhumation on Hainan; Jeff Thorpe, great-nephew of Harry Digney; Don Baker and his family; Lee Hopkins, whose father was Private William Johnson; Lloyd Swanton, nephew of Stuart Swanton, whose war diary provided such a detailed insight into POW life. Also for drawing my attention to Roach's past link with the Secret Army and providing pictures and background material; Fran Kelly and the ABC National Radio *Breakfast* team for their interviews with Max Gilbert and Peter Koop and putting me in contact with them; Margaret Gee, my agent; Matthew Kelly, my publisher; Karen Ward, my editor; Tricia Dearborn, copyeditor; The Australian War Memorial in Canberra and the National Archives of Australia.

And all the people who have assisted with my research into the events surrounding Gull Force. If I have inadvertently overlooked anybody in the above list, my sincere apologies.

Finally, my thanks go to my family, who have had to put up with me during my own self-imposed, albeit more comfortable, incarceration while investigating the 2/21st Battalion's extraordinary story.

INDEX